Studies in Public Choice

Volume 33

More information about this series at http://www.springer.com/series/6550

Peter Bernholz

Totalitarianism, Terrorism and Supreme Values

History and Theory

Springer

Peter Bernholz
Center for Economics and Business (WWZ)
University of Basel
Basel
Switzerland

ISSN 0924-4700
Studies in Public Choice
ISBN 978-3-319-56906-2 ISBN 978-3-319-56907-9 (eBook)
DOI 10.1007/978-3-319-56907-9

Library of Congress Control Number: 2017937505

Printed on acid-free paper

This Springer imprint is published by Springer Nature
The registered company is Springer International Publishing AG
The registered company address is: Gewerbestrasse 11, 6330 Cham, Switzerland

Preface

Presently each day mass media are filled with news concerning new atrocities of the "Islamic Caliphate" in Iraq and the Levant, of Boko Haram in Nigeria and the Taliban in Afghanistan: murders of Christians, Shiites and Yesidi, abduction of girls and women, suicides by true believers in these Islamic creeds, destruction of cultural monuments in Assyria and Palmyra. It seems that a new type of religiously motivated violence has erupted, beginning with the destruction of the Trade Center in New York and the Pentagon in Washington on 9/11 in 2001 by adherents of Al Qaeda.

But are such events really new? And does no similarity exist with the mass murders committed by Nazi and Bolshevik regimes during the first half of the twentieth century? Or with the Christian Crusaders wading in the blood of Moslems and Jews when they conquered Jerusalem in 1099? Had all these terrible events nothing to do with the fact that either metaphysical ideologies were promising true believers a paradise in after-life or non-metaphysical ideologies at least a paradise on earth? These are the questions which will be discussed and answered in this volume.

The author who grew up during the Nazi regime in Germany first took up these questions in a paper presented at Karl Brunner's famous annual Interlaken Seminar on "Analysis and Ideology" in 1988. At this occasion he first postulated the existence of a lexicographic preference function for supreme values considered typical for totalitarian regimes, according to which the supreme values establishing the ideology had to be preferred to everything else, similar to the fact that the letter "a" is pre-ordered to any other letter like "b" or "u". For an economist this means that no rate of substitution exists with other goods which are not comprised of the supreme values. I still recall that one of the participants in the Interlaken Seminar, Prof. Meckling from Rochester University USA, asked after my presentation: "You really believe that there exists no rate of substitution?" I answered "Yes!" "Then you are dead wrong!" he retorted. "But how do you then explain the existence of martyrs?" And, indeed, presently cases about terrorists who consider themselves to be martyrs are reported about every day. These are empirical facts which like many others are demanding a theoretical explanation in tune with historical experience.

At the Seminar at Interlaken the well-known monetarist Allan Meltzer once asked me how I became a liberal in the European sense. I referred him to my experiences as a boy in the totalitarian Nazi regime, where I hated to be forced once or twice a week to participate in the then obligatory "service" in the Hitler Youth, and often just did not turn up. Because of this un-conformal attitude, I experienced increasing pressure. Finally in either 1944 or 1945, when I was 15 years old, our leader (the "Gefolgschaftsführer") had the police call me whether I were an opponent of National Socialism. Of course, I answered "no!" But I am not sure what had happened to me if the war had not ended the Nazi regime. Only after its end I learned that my paternal uncle Johann Bernholz had been incarcerated for two years in heavy prison in Kassel just for listening to an enemy broadcast by BBC, a fact which had been hidden from us boys by our parents.

In the years after the war I observed what happened in countries suffering from communist regimes. And in the late 1960s as a young professor at the Technische Universitaet in Berlin I witnessed the wall in the divided city and how people tried to flee from East Germany in spite of endangering their lives. Moreover, my own experiences with the East German border guards, too, were not of a pleasant nature. Therefore, it is perhaps not surprising that I became strongly interested in totalitarianism.

My own theory of ideocracies characterized by supreme values, of totalitarianism and of terrorism evolved in several presentations and articles since 1988. In working out my ideas I certainly did not start from scratch, but began by building on the works of people like Hannah Arendt,[1] Carl J. Friedrich and Zbigniew K. Brzezinski.[2] I had even the privilege of meeting the latter in their Seminar when attending Harvard University as a Rockefeller Fellow in 1963. However, the traditional theory of totalitarianism, in spite of its undisputed merits, has mainly remained a static theory and was on the whole limited to non-metaphysical regimes. It was static in the sense that only concepts were developed describing the characteristics of totalitarian systems at given periods in time. I tried to overcome these shortcomings of the theories of totalitarianism in several papers since 1988, and was happy to find out that two other authors, Piekalkiewicz and Penn,[3] tried to move into the same direction.

In this book I abolish the limitations mentioned and present a theory capable of explaining *which factors* may *lead*, under specified conditions, to *Totalitarian Regimes, and which factors* change those regimes in time, and finally *bring about their transformation* into other regimes *or cause their breakdown*. In doing so I am going to generalize the theory in a way that it covers a much broader class of cases

[1]Hannah Arendt, The Origins of Totalitarianism, New York 1968/1951.

[2]Carl J. Friedrich and Zbigniew Brzezinski, Totalitarian Dictatorship and Autocracy, Cambridge 1965/1956.

[3]Piekalkiewicz, Jaroslaw and Penn, Alfred W., Politics of Ideocracy, Albany 1995.

of ideocratic regimes, i.e., regimes based on ideologies with supreme values, and relate them to other political systems. It is obvious that such a theory needs to describe the forces which drive nontotalitarian systems towards totalitarianism and are also capable to change or to abolish these regimes. These forces have also to be able to overcome obstacles in the way of a totalitarian development, and conditions have to be stated under which they are probable to succeed. Moreover, the consequences have to be analyzed for cases in which the relevant driving forces are not successful.

It is shown that the invention and introduction of an ideology with supreme values is a necessary condition for the development of a totalitarian regime. But also that this is not a sufficient condition, since it has to be combined with the secular power of a state to make such a regime possible. And a combination of spiritual and secular power can only occur during a crisis and if a well-organized ideological movement is created with a spiritual leader or leadership, who alone have the right to interpret the ideology. Both conditions are necessary to provide a chance to grasp secular power. Thus, e.g., the absence of a monopoly of interpretation will usually lead to sectarian developments and thus weaken or even split the movement.

I include in Chaps. 8 and 11 mathematical models of the theory of Terrorism, Totalitarianism and Mature Ideocraies based on Supreme Values to provide a logically compelling presentation of my thinking. But the corresponding sections of the book have been characterized by inserting a*, so that they can be skipped by readers not interested in them without losing the thread of the argument.

This book owes much to many people. Among them I would like to mention especially my teacher Hans Möller, next Karl Brunner as the originator of the Interlaken seminars, and the philosopher Gérard Radnitzky who encouraged me to present my ideas at several conferences organized by him. I am also indebted for their valuable support to Hans Jürgen Jaksch, Heide and Winfried Reiss. Christoph Bauer helped with many critical discussions to clarify my thoughts about ideocracies. Unforgotten is our dispute on whether the Empire of Assyria should be considered to have been a totalitarian regime or not, because it based its expansionary wars on the commands of its god Assur.[4] But I should also not conceal that two referees of earlier papers suggested that I should not mention Christian and Islamic regimes as totalitarian and that the editor of one journal told me confidentially that he did not want to publish one of my articles since he was not a very courageous person.

[4]"The Assyrians were convinced that the rule of the world belonged to their God Assur. And that, because of this they had not only the right but even the duty to force other nations with all available means to recognize this fact of world domination. Revolting against it meant a violation of God-set legal order. … Therefore Assyrian warfare was always very harsh, and often cruel and brutal …" (W.v. Soden (1954): Herrscher im alten Orient. Berlin, Heidelberg, New York: Springer, p. 64; my translation).

I am also deeply indebted to my wife, Elisabeth Bernholz and my daughters Irina Siegrist and Juliane Bernholz who patiently endured their husband and father spending too much of his time with an—at least at that time—obscure subject.

Basel, Switzerland Peter Bernholz

Contents

Chapter 1
Introduction

The Western tradition of political thinking has begun and has been dominated by using the political regimes categorized by the ancient Greeks, especially Plato and Aristotle: Monarchies, Oligarchies, Polities, Democracies, and Tyrannies. The Romans added the concept of Dictatorship. It is therefore not surprising that only after the modern emergence of National Socialism in Germany, Fascism in Italy, and Communism in the Soviet Union attention began to turn to regimes dominated by ideologies postulating supreme values. On the other hand, however, already Flavius Josephus tried to explain to the Romans in the first century A.D. the ideological and metaphysical basis of the Jewish State by creating the concept of theocracy.[1] But in spite of his related approach the development of a theory of totalitarianism had to wait until the beginning of the twentieth century, though it had several precursors.[2] Such a theory is faced with an important difficulty, which has been the background for many heated discussions: What are the common characteristics of totalitarian regimes which are usually empirically combined with terror, mass murders, suppression of free discussion, ruthless dominance of the state, but also with martyrdom of true believers and at the same time with very different ends contained in their supreme values? What are the common traits of the Nazi movement striving for the dominance of the Aryan race, Communism working against the suppression of the proletariat by Capitalism and the Islamic State in Syria and Iraq fighting for their interpretation of Allah's commands?

Are these not all regimes which have no real similarities to each other? One of the solutions proposed to solving this problem has been formulated by Andreski with his definition of totalitarianism "to designate a political regime whereby the government controls the totality of social life."[3] This definition of totalitarianism was invented by early critics of Italian fascism and then taken up by the fascist movement itself, and formulated by Benito Mussolini as follows:

---

[1]Flavius Josephus, Contra Apionem.

[2]Uwe Backes, "Ideocracy"—eine begriffsgeschichtliche Skizze, in: Backes, Uwe und Kailitz, Steffen (eds.), Ideokratien im Vergleich, Göttingen: Vandenhoeck und Ruprecht, 2014, 19–45.

[3]Stanislav Andreski, The Uses of Comparative Sociology. Berkeley and Los Angeles 1965, p. 311.

P. Bernholz, *Totalitarianism, Terrorism and Supreme Values*,
Studies in Public Choice 33, DOI 10.1007/978-3-319-56907-9_1

> … for the Fascist everything is within the state and there exists nothing human or spiritual, or even has value, outside the state. In this sense Fascism is totalitarian and the Fascist state interprets, develops and multiplies the whole life of the people as a synthesis and unity of each value (pp. 847–848).[4]

But though it is true that regimes considered to be totalitarian show a tendency to regulate many aspects of life according to their supreme values, this is not necessarily always true. Moreover, such a definition would even turn democratic and autocratic regimes in which most aspects of life would be regulated by a majority (for instance because of “political correctness”) or a despotic ruler into totalitarian regimes. We will thus prefer another definition, following the example of earlier thinkers starting from the empirical evidence. Graf Ballestrem[5] was able to show after the fall of the communist regimes that the theory of totalitarianism as formulated by Friedrich and Brzezinski has been, on the whole, much more successful in explaining events than the alternatives offered by other approaches. He demonstrated this by discussing the five characteristics used by Friedrich and Brzezinski to define totalitarianism: a dominant totalitarian ideology, a monopoly party, a secret police applying terror, a monopoly of information, and a centrally planned economy. But the approach taken by Friedrich and Brzezinski was mainly inspired by the experiences with Nazi and Communist regimes and it is revealing that ideologically inspired regimes like presently the Islamic State in Syria and Iraq show similar characteristics of applying terror and by trying to suppress unwanted information without instituting a planned economy. And there can be no doubt that instead of a monopoly party a similar role can also be played by a monopoly church or by other organizations controlling information. And terror may be applied by ordinary military forces composed out of ardent believers in the supreme values of the respective ideologies. This means that we accept the hypothesis common to several approaches taken in forming a theory of totalitarianism; but believe that the installment of supreme values believed to be absolutely true has been the critical element causing other developments often related with totalitarian regimes. This is also in tune with the fact that regimes based on ideologies, which we call ideocracies, which have reached their aims do not apply terrorism because the respective populations have already accepted the behavior and believes implied. We call these regimes Mature Ideocracies in contrast to totalitarian regimes which have still not completed the ends demanded by their supreme values. This was already true for the theocracy described by Flavius Josephus and has been also true in other historical cases to which we will turn later.

But does not another obstacle exist for a consistent theory of totalitarianism? Namely, that the supreme values of these ideologies are very different and in most cases even contradictory? As will be shown below this obstacle is not decisive because of two facts: (1) All supreme values are at least according to the underlying

---

[4]Benito Mussolini, Fascismo. In: Enciclopedia Italiana, Mailand 1929.

[5]Karl Graf Ballestrem, Aporien der Totalitarismus Theorien. Politisches Denken, Stuttgart, Jahrbuch 1992, pp. 50–67.

creed lexicographically preferred to all other aims; (2) They are all considered to be absolutely true. This has the consequence that the real believers of such ideologies have to try to convert all people to the true creed who are able according to the supreme values to become believers (convertibles); and this aim has to be reached, if necessary, even by force because of the true benefit for those not yet believing. On the other hand, people not convertible according to the supreme values (in-convertibles) have to be suppressed and either put to useful work to reach the ideological tenets, or to be driven out or to be eliminated if they are a danger to reaching them. It further follows from the fact that force may be needed to accomplish these and other aims postulated by the supreme values that the secular power of the state has to be won.

It follows from these deliberations that the following definition of totalitarian regimes is adequate:

> A totalitarian regime is an ideocracy, which has not yet reached the aims implied by its supreme values and which tries to pursue them with the spiritual and secular power available after it has gained domination of a state.

Subsequently, we will develop the theory of totalitarianism and of mature ideocracies by studying the empirical evidence. Here we conclude by presenting in Table 1.1 the historical cases of ideocracies (mature ideocracies and totalitarian regimes) covered by our theory.

Table 1.1 demonstrates the very different contents of the supreme values of the many ideocracies in history and their widely diverging aims. But as will be shown subsequently, all these ideologies have two traits in common. They are believed to be absolutely true and have to be preferred lexicographically to all other aims. The true believers have to be prepared to sacrifice everything, including their own lives and those of others to reach the aims postulated as supreme values.

Since the supreme values of the different ideologies are often or even mostly contradictory, they cannot all be true from a scientific point of view. This is also the case for the subcategory based on religions,[6] at least as far as their prescriptions for a correct life on earth are concerned. And since all these ideologies promise a better life in the future if their aims are followed, if not in this life so at least in the life to come, they are all referring to expectations of human beings concerning future events. The explosion-like development of the human brain has endowed man with the admirable capability to form mental images of the surrounding world and to visualize possible future events. In this way humans can evade dangers and sometimes even change their environment and thus their own future. In a sense man is able to let ideas about the future die instead of himself, or to express it with the words of the philosopher Karl Popper:

[6]We do not doubt the metaphysical truths of religions, but are only concerned with the consequences of their prescriptions for this life.

Table 1.1 The historical cases of ideocracies (mature ideocracies and totalitarian regimes)

Country	Period	Totalitarian regime	Mature ideocracy	Ideology
Mongolian empire	13–15th CT	Yes	No	God granted world dominance
Incas	Until 16th CT	Yes	No	God granted expansion of rule
Aztecs	Until 16th CT	Yes	No	To keep Sun running by human sacrifice
Calvin's Geneva	1542–46	Yes	No	Enforcing true Calvinist creed
Muenster anabaptists	16th CT	Yes	No	Enforcing true anabaptist creed
French revolution (Jacobin terror)	1788–96	Yes	No	Enforcing true revolutionary ideology
Taiping revolution	1851–64	Yes	No	Enforcing aims of Christian revelation
Sudanese Mahdi empire	1885–1897	Yes	No	Enforcing true Islamic creed
NS-Germany	1933–45	Yes	No	Installing dominance of Aryan race
Soviet Union	1917–90	Yes	No	Enforcing Marxist Communist ideas
China	1949–76	Yes	No	Ditto
Vietnam	1954–90	Yes	No	Ditto
Cambodia	1975–79	Yes	No	Ditto
North Korea	1948	Yes	No	Ditto
Ethiopia	1979–91	Yes	No	Ditto
Cuba	1959–96	Yes	No	Ditto
Eastern Europe	1946–89	Yes	No	Ditto
Islamic State in Iraq and the Levant	Since 2013	Yes	No	Enforcing and spreading pure Sunnite Islamism
Puritans Massachusetts	1620–91	No	Yes	Follow true Puritan Christian creed
Tibet of Dalai Lama	1912–50	No	Yes	Follow true Tibetan Lamaism (Buddhism)
Jesuit State in Paraguay	1609–1767	No	Yes	Spread true Catholicism among Indians
Saudi Arabia	Since 1924	No	Yes	Live according to Wahhabite Islam
Iran	Since 1979	Yes, first	Yes	Live according to true Shiite Islam

> Error elimination [during evolution] may proceed either by the elimination of unsuccessful forms (the killing of unsuccessful forms by natural selection) or by the (tentative) evolution of controls which modify or suppress unsuccessful organs, or forms of behavior, or hypotheses [about the future].[7]

But this remarkable capability of man is also fraught with great dangers: Human beings may form terribly wrong perceptions about reality and believe them to be absolutely true. It is well known that science cannot deliver absolute truths. To mention just one example: Newtonian theory of space and time had to be replaced by that of Einstein, since the latter better corresponded to empirical observations. And this has not been the only and last change of scientific theories. In contrast to science, the assertion by ideologies that they are absolutely true is characteristic for them. And exactly their wrong image of reality together with this assertion has led totalitarian regimes based on them to apply repression, torture, and to commit millions of murders. It follows that the development of ideologies has to be considered to be a typical human disease, a disease which cannot be observed for any other living being.

In Chap. 2 we will first discuss some evidence relating to the secular totalitarian regimes of the twentieth century, since their study led to the original development of the theory of totalitarianism. Next we will discuss the evidence that also religious ideologies can serve as a basis for totalitarian movements. In Chap. 3 the first part of a detailed theory of totalitarianism based on this evidence will be presented, whereas in the following chapters other empirical cases of totalitarian regimes will be discussed. The second part of the theory of totalitarianism will be developed in Chap. 6. Next mature ideocracies will be taken up. In Chap. 8 we will turn to terrorism as an effort to establish or to renew totalitarian regimes and develop the corresponding theory. After that the economic and political problems faced by Totalitarianism and also its constitution will be discussed. Next its influence on economic well-being, innovation and development, as well as on science and culture will be studied. The book will end with the presentation of a mathematical model of totalitarianism and a summary of the theory.

---

[7] Karl R. Popper (1966): *Of Clouds and Clocks. An Approach to the Problem of Rationality and the Freedom of Man.* St. Louis (Missouri): Washington University Press, p. 23.

Chapter 2
Ideologies of National Socialism, Communism, Christianity, and Islam

In this chapter, the empirical evidence for supreme values will be discussed for National Socialism, Communism, and Christian and Islamic believes.[1] In doing so, we especially have to show whether these ideologies include aims which are lexicographically preferred to everything else and which are considered to be absolutely true, since these two facts in which all ideocracies agree form the basis of our theory.

2.1 National Socialism

There can be no doubt that National Socialism followed Supreme Values and that it believed that everybody and everything had to be subordinated to their aims. According to Hitler:

> Would humanity be divided into three categories: Into those creating culture, those preserving culture and those destroying it, then only Aryans could be considered to be representatives of the former (1933, p. 318).
>
> Because of this the path the Aryan had to walk was clearly predetermined. As conqueror he subjugated lower human beings and regulated their practical work under his command, according to his will and for his aims … (p. 324).
>
> No, the Jew does not own any strength to create culture, because he does not have, and never had the idealism without which there is no higher development of humanity. It follows that his intellect will never work constructively, but destructively … (p. 332).

This chapter has been partly reproduced from Necessary Conditions for Totalitarianism, in: G. Radnitzky and H. Bouillon (eds.), Government: Servant or Master, Amsterdam and Atlanta, Rodopi 1993.

[1]I stress again that the metaphysical truth of these religions is not doubted at all, but that only the possible consequences of their statements on earth are discussed.

P. Bernholz, *Totalitarianism, Terrorism and Supreme Values*,
Studies in Public Choice 33, DOI 10.1007/978-3-319-56907-9_2

> It [the National Socialist Movement] has thus, without regard to "traditions" and prejudices, to find the courage to gather our people and its strength together to advance on the road leading out of the narrowness of its present living space to new land and soil. i.e., to advance on the road which free them forever from the danger to vanish from this earth or to have to work as an enslaved people in the service of others (p. 732).

Everything and everybody has to be subordinated to these commands of the Supreme Value:

> The greatness of each powerful organization as an embodiment of an idea on this earth, consists in the religious fanaticism in which it succeeds intolerantly and fanatically convinced of its own right against everything (p. 385).
>
> The movement has principally to educate its members in a way that they consider fight as something to strive after by themselves and not as something indolently adopted from education. They have thus not to fear the hostility of foes, but to feel it to be a precondition of their own right to live. They have not to shy away from but to desire the hatred of the enemies of our nation (Volkstum) and of our world view (Weltanschauung) and of its expressions. But to the expressions of this hatred belong also lie and deceit (p. 386).

Each Aryan has, if necessary, to sacrifice his own life for the Supreme Value. Such a trait is even part of his racial inheritance:

> This will to sacrifice the use of personal work and, if necessary, the own life for the sake of others is inbred (ausgebildet) most strongly in the Aryan … The will to self-preservation has reached in him its noblest form by subordinating the own self to the life of the whole and to sacrifice it if demanded by the hour (pp. 325 sq.).

It should be clear from these quotations that not only any potential Aryan has to subordinate himself to the tenets of the creed, but that enemies, pagans, and heretics have to be defeated and to be eliminated:

> The soul of the people can only be won successfully, if besides the leadership of the positive fight for one's own aims the opponent of these aims is destroyed (p. 371).
>
> If the Jews of the international financial system inside and outside Europe should succeed again to plunge the nations into a World War, then the result will not be the bolshevization of the earth and thus the victory of the Jewish race (Judentum), but the annihilation of the Jewish race in Europe! (Hitler's speech on January, 30, 1934 at German Reichstag, Verhandlungen des Reichstags).

But not only the Jews had to be persecuted or to be eliminated as unconvertible people. According to a speech given by a leader of the SS at the Ordensburg Vogelsang in Fall 1937:

> The selection of the new leadership is, positively, reached by the SS on a first level through the National Political Education Institutions (Napola), and by the Ordensburgen as true universities of a coming National Socialist aristocracy … negatively through the elimination of all elements which are inferior from a racial and biological point of view. Moreover, by the radical removal of any un-corrigible political opposition refusing principally to acknowledge the ideological (weltanschauliche) basis of the National Socialist State and of its fundamental institutions (Kogon 1947, pp. 21 sq.).

We have seen that the main implications of the Supreme Value were already fully developed in Hitler's book Mein Kampf, first issued 1925–27. The same is true for other characteristics. War to spread the Supreme Value is an obvious and necessary measure:

> The pacifist and humanist idea is perhaps quite useful at the time when superior man has conquered and subjugated the world in a way which makes him the only lord of this earth. … Consequently, first fight and then pacifism (Hitler 1933, pp. 315 sq.).

Morality has to serve the Supreme Value. Himmler, the leader of the SS, expressed this idea clearly in a speech to a meeting of SS group leaders in Posen on October 4, 1943:

> … One fundamental principle has to be absolutely valid for the SS man: We have only to treat honestly, decently, faithfully, and as a comrade, those related to our own blood, but nobody else. I am totally indifferent as to how the Russians and the Czechs fare. That which is of good blood of our kind in nations we will fetch by taking away their children and educating them. Whether other nations live in prosperity or perish by hunger interests me only so far as we need them as slaves for our culture … (International Military Tribunal 1947, vol. 29, pp. 122 sq.).

Hitler is already concerned in Mein Kampf with the centralization of spiritual leadership. When discussing the advantages of local party organizations he explains:

> Such formation of sub-organizations has, however, only to take place, when the authority of the spiritual founder and of the school established by him has been acknowledged unconditionally. This is necessary to prevent a disruption of the unity of the teaching (Hitler 1933, p. 381).

> The aim of a political reform movement will never be reached through work to enlighten or by influencing the ruling powers, but only by gaining political power. Each world-moving idea not only has the right but the duty to secure those means which allow the accomplishment of its ideas (p. 377).

It is thus not surprising that Hitler established the leader principle (Führerprinzip):

> The movement advocates on the smallest and on the largest scale the principle of unconditional authority of the leader joined with highest responsibility (p. 378).

2.2 Marxism

We show first that the teachings of Marx are considered by communists as Supreme Values which have to be realized on earth and which are absolutely true. Let us quote Lenin (Three Sources and Three Essentials of Marxism, 1913):

> … The teachings of Marx are almighty since they are true. They are complete and harmonious in themselves. His doctrine provides men with a unified world view, which is not consistent with any superstition, any reaction, any defense of bourgeois suppression…

> Only the philosophic materialism of Marx has shown to the proletariat the way out of the spiritual slavery under which all oppressed classes have suffered until now (Lenin 1962, pp. 1293–1299).

Marx himself[2] already basked in the "communist proud of infallibility" (Marx and Engels 1956 sq., vol. 27, p. 324). Engels believed with Marx that the latter had discovered the vital law of humanity:

> Like Darwin who discovered the law of the evolution of organic nature, so Marx found the law of evolution of human history. … But moreover, Marx also discovered the special law of motion of the present capitalist way of production and of the bourgeois society created by it … (Marx and Engels 1956 sq., vol. 19, pp. 335 sq.).

In fact, according to Marx, communism will bring about the solution of all riddles of the world (Marx and Engels 1956 sq., supplementary vol. 1, p. 536), and lead to the end of the division of labor, of exploitation, alienation, and class dominance (compare article "state" in Löw 1988b).

The above quotations prove that the teachings of Marx were considered by himself and by his adherents to embody Supreme Values and that its contents were not only absolutely true but that its final aim would be reached with necessity.

Let us now turn to the question of heretics. Already Marx and Engels disapproved of the competition of other socialists diverging from their own ideas:

> The sects, which were first levers of the movement become an obstacle when they have been outrun by it; then they become reactionary; … (Marx and Engels 1956 sq., vol. 18, pp. 33 sq.).

> The communists, i.e., those who best interpret the hidden meaning of the class struggle going on in front of our eyes, are the last to commit the mistake to approve or to promote sectarianism (vol. 32, p. 671).

Now, these statements by the founders of Marxism do, of course, not imply that heretics should be punished or even be eliminated. But Marx' threat against Bakunin "He should be on his guard, otherwise he will be excommunicated officially" (vol. 32, pp. 349 and 351) sounds already more ominous. And in the statutes of the League of Communists (Bund der Kommunisten) of December 1847 we read:

> Art. 41: The district authority condemns criminal acts against the League and executes the sentence.

> Art. 42: The League has to watch over removed and expelled individuals as well as over suspicious persons. It has to render them harmless (vol. 4, p. 600).

Concerning the removal of enemies opposing the revolution to be brought about by the Supreme Value society, i.e., the pagans, Marx and Engels are not less outspoken. As Marx puts it:

> We are reckless, and we do not ask for your consideration. When it will be our turn we will not palliate terrorism (vol. 6, p. 505).

---

[2]The following presentation of the statements of Marx and Engels rests strongly on Löw (1988a).

And Engels states:

> Did these gentlemen never see a revolution? A revolution is certainly the most authoritarian event which exists; through it one part of the population coerces its will on the other part with the help of rifles, bayonets and guns, i.e., with most authoritarian means; and the victorious party has to make this domination durable by the terror which is infused by its arms into the reactionaries; otherwise it will have fought in vain (vol. 18, p. 308).

Note that the true creed has to be spread by revolutionary force, but that in Marx' and Engels' thinking this will happen with absolute necessity. But in spite of this conviction pagans, i.e., capitalists, bourgeois and landed proprietors have to be terrified not to turn back the wheels of history.

The suppression of un-predestined people belonging to these groups has to take place through the Dictatorship of the Proletariat, which has to be established after the power of the state has been destroyed and grasped in a revolution. In his well-known "State and Revolution" written from August to November 1917, Lenin quotes from Marx' "Critique of the Gotha Program" contained in a letter to Bracke of May 5, 1875 (published 1891 in "Neue Zeit", vol. 9 I):

> Between capitalist and communist society exists the period of revolutionary transformation from the former into the latter. Corresponding to it is a political transition period in which the state can only be the revolutionary Dictatorship of the Proletariat.

Lenin then explains:

> The further evolution, i.e., the evolution to communism, cannot proceed in any other way, since no one besides the proletariat can break the resistance of capitalist exploiters …
>
> … the Dictatorship of the Proletariat brings a number of limitations for the oppressors, the exploiters, the capitalists. They have to be kept down to liberate humanity from wage slavery, their resistance has to be broken by force … (Lenin in Fetscher 1970, p. 72).
>
> On the other hand he (Marx) stated that the "destruction" of the machinery of the state is necessary in the interest of workers and peasants, that it unites them, puts them in front of the common task to liquidate the "parasite" and to substitute something new for him (p. 35).

In 1920, after having been in power for nearly three years, Lenin makes it clear in "The Tasks of Youth Organizations" that communist morality has to serve the Supreme Value to bring about Communism as the highest stage of socialism:

> Class struggle still goes on, and it is our task to subordinate everything to this struggle. We also subordinate our communist morality to this task. We assert: that is moral which serves the destruction of the old exploitative society and the gathering of all workers around the proletariat … (Lenin in Weber 1967, p. 125).

After having grasped power, Lenin did not hesitate to move on with these ideas which had emerged from the implied logic of the Supreme Value. In his essay "How to Organize Competition" of January 7 and 10, 1918 (Lenin 1956 sq., vol. 26, pp. 402–414) he proclaimed the united purpose of "purging the Russian land of all kinds of harmful insects" (vol. 26, 1961, p. 413, compare for this quotation Solzhenitsyn 1973, vol. 1, p. 27). The term insects not only included all class enemies but also "workers malingering at their work". It also included intellectuals, for "In what block of a big city, in what factory, in what village … are there not saboteurs who call themselves intellectuals?" (p. 413).

It is clear that Lenin wanted to use extended terror also against heretic socialists like the Mensheviks and the Socialist Revolutionaries. In a letter written in 1922 to Kursky he writes: "Comrade Kursky! In my opinion we ought to extend the use of execution by shooting (allowing the substitution of exile abroad) to all activities of the Mensheviks, SR's, etc. We ought to find a formulation that would connect these activities with the international bourgeoisie" (quoted from Solzhenitsyn 1973, p. 353). Note that this letter was written to influence the formulation of a new Criminal Code.

We have shown how the development of the implied logic of the Supreme Values led to the demand to persecute and to eliminate heretics and pagans and also to the quest for secular power in the form of the Dictatorship of the Proletariat. Needless to say that this power had to be centralized and to be combined with spiritual leadership. Lenin expressed this in April/May 1920 in his "The "Left Radicalism", the Infantile Disease of Communism": "I repeat: The Experience of the victorious Dictatorship of the Proletariat in Russia … has shown clearly that unconditional centralization and strongest discipline of the Proletariat are one of the most important conditions for a victory against the Bourgeoisie" (Lenin in Fetscher 1970, vol. 2, p. 302).

In "State and Revolution" (August/September 1917) Lenin expressed his view that

> Until the "higher" phase of communism has arrived, socialists ask for the most rigorous control through society and the state concerning the measure of work and consumption (Lenin in Fetscher 1970, vol. 2, p. 79).

Concerning spiritual college and party leadership, it is interesting to look at a draught for the Statutes of the Socialist Democratic Workers Party of Russia written by Lenin in 1903:

> 5. The Central Committee unites and directs the whole practical activity of the party and administers the central party finances and all technical institutions of the party as a whole. It settles all conflicts among the different organizations and institutions of the party as well as within them.
>
> 6. The ideological leadership is in the hands of the Editorial Board of the central newspaper. The Editorial Board edits the central newspaper of the party, the scientific paper and the pamphlets.
>
> 7. The Party Council consists of five members and is elected by the plenary meeting of the party out of the members of the Editorial Board and the Central Committee. The Council decides on all quarrels or disagreements between the Editorial Board and the Central Committee …
>
> 8. New Committees or Federations of Committees have to be confirmed by the Central Committee … (Lenin in Weber 1967, p. 45).

Let us finally look at the holy war to spread the creed. First, there can be no doubt that world domination by communism was derived from the tenets of the

Supreme Value. Read Lenin's short sentence written in 1921 in "On the Importance of Gold now and after the Full Victory of Socialism":

> When we have been victorious on a world scale, then, I believe, we will construct in some of the greatest cities of the world public toilets out of gold (Lenin in Weber 1967, p. 133).

Note that gold symbolized for Lenin the exploitative Capitalist System.

Secondly, Lenin and Sinowjew state in "Socialism and War" in 1915 that "Marxism is not Pacifism. It is necessary to fight for the quickest end of the war. But the demand for 'peace' has only a proletarian meaning if it is connected with a summons to revolutionary fight" (Lenin 1929, vol. 18, p. 284).

2.3 Christianity

The seeds for logical implications of the Supreme Values can already be found in the New Testament. First it is clear that according to the New Testament, Jesus Christ offered a Supreme Value, everlasting life, to the true believers:

> Verily, verily I say unto you, He that believeth on me hath
> Ever-lasting life.
> I am that bread of life.
> Your fathers did eat manna in the wilderness and are dead.
> This is the bread which cometh down from heaven, that a man may
> eat thereof, and not die.
> I am the living bread which came down from heaven; if any man
> eat of this bread, he shall live forever: and the bread that I
> will give is my flesh, which I will give for the life of the
> world (St. John 6, 47–51)

Also, the Supreme Value is seen as an absolute truth:

> Jesus saith unto him, I am the way, the truth and the life: no
> man cometh unto the Father, but by me" (St. John 14, 6).

Everybody is therefore called to follow this Supreme Value:

> … I come not to send peace, but a sword. …
> He that loveth father or mother more than me is not worthy of
> me.
> And he that taketh not his cross, and followeth after me, is
> not worthy of me.
> He that findeth his life shall lose it: and he that loseth his
> life for my sake shall find it (St. Matthew 23, 34–39).

Here we find already the material out of which martyrs are formed. Also the punishment is mentioned, which is threatening if one loses one's belief:

> And fear not them which kill the body, but are not able to
> kill the soul: but rather fear him which is able to destroy
> both soul and body in hell (St. Matthew 10, 28).

It is also well known that Christ charged the Apostles with missionary work already during his lifetime:

> And he called unto him the twelve, and began to send them
> forth by two and two; and gave them power over unclean spirits
> …
> And whosoever shall not receive you, nor hear you, when ye de-
> part thence, shake off the dust under your feet for a testimony
> against them. Verily I say unto you, it shall be more tolerable
> for Sodom and Gomorrha in the day of judgment, then for that
> city (St. Mark 6, 7–11).

It is, of course, true that Christ referred to punishment for pagans and for renegades, who would not listen, only at the day of the last judgment. Otherwise he would scarcely have said.

> But I say unto you which hear, love your enemies, do good to
> them which hate you (St. Luke 6, 27).

However, we have already argued, that a Supreme Value begins to develop its own inherent logic at the hands of subsequent followers. If the salvation of the eternal soul is of supreme importance and if one should "fear not them which kill the body", is it then not necessary to save the soul of pagans and heretics, even if this can only be accomplished by taking their lives? And must pagans and heretics not be hindered, if necessary by force, to poison the souls of believers or to prevent the spreading of the new gospel? True it is not necessary to draw these conclusions, and most Christians, especially today, would consider them to be an aberration. But it is not surprising that St. Augustin holds it to be the duty of the Roman emperor to protect the church, to defend it against heretics and those causing schisms, and to act against them as against criminals (Epistula 133, 3).

In one of his letters to the Donatists, who were North African heretics, St. Augustin explained:

> 5. As you see, you rise with force against the peace of Christ. Thus you are not suffering for Him but for your misdeeds. What a delusion that you claim the glory of martyrdom in spite of your wicked life and your criminal acts, for which you are rightly punished. Consequently, if you coerce people in arbitrary audacity - how much more are we obliged to resist your frenzy with the help of the legal authorities, which God has subordinated to Christ in accordance with his earlier announcement. We are obliged to resist to free pitiable souls from your despotism, to cure them from a very old delusion and to accustom them to

> the light of the most manifest truth. For though you assert that we force people against their free will, it is true that many like to be forced, as they confess before and afterwards, since they escape by this fact from your oppression. …
>
> 12. Take note, that God himself has truly spoken in this law through the heart of the king which rests in his hand. He has spoken in this law of which you assert that it has been enacted against you. Though, if you want to understand it, it has been enacted for your sake. … (Augustinus 1878, vol. 7, pp. 438–439, 444).

St. Ambrose has similar convictions. Concerning religious matters, the church is placed above imperial competence, and not vice versa. The emperor, as son of the church, owes obedience to it. He does not stand above the church, but as a member within its community. He is not allowed to assign churches to heretics (Epistulae 21, 4.9 ff.; 21, 36; 51, 12; 41, 27; 21, 2); for a general discussion, see Schilling (1923).

An episode which took place between St. Ambrose and Roman Emperor Theodosius I is revealing. In Callinicum in Mesopotamia Christians had burned a Synagogue. The emperor ordered to punish the criminals severely and commanded the local bishop to restore the Synagogue. Ambrose heard about this and wrote a lengthy letter to Theodosius asking him to pardon the guilty. A Christian emperor was not allowed to act as an advocate of the Synagogue and to help the Jews to win a triumph against the Church (Ambrose, Epistula 40). When the emperor next went to church, St. Ambrose preached about the necessity of what had been done, the glory of the Church, the abjectness of the Synagogue, and asked for pardon. He only continued the holy service after Theodosius had promised complete amnesty (Lietzmann 1976, p. 120; Jones 1966, p. 69). The attitude of St. Ambrose means, of course, that Christians have the right or even the duty to destroy synagogues.

This interpretation is supported by a letter written some years earlier to emperor Valentinian III in which St. Ambrose tried successfully to prevent the reinstallation of the pagan Victoria altar in the Curia (the Roman Senate):

> Whereas all men … serve you, the emperors and masters of the earth, you yourself serve God and the holy creed. …
>
> Everybody serves this true God. And he who accepts him to honor him with deep love, is not indifferent and tolerant, but zealous in his belief and his piety. If he is like that, he is not allowed to consent that the images of pagan gods are worshipped and that pagan customs are cultivated (Ambrose, Epistula 17 in Klein 1972).

Firmicus Maternus, a writer of about the same period, who had been recently converted, is much more outspoken. In his book on the "Errors of Pagan Religion" he writes:

> XXVIII, 6. Take away, take away without hesitation, most holy emperors, the treasures of the temples. These gods may be molten by the fire of the mint or the flames of the furnaces. Use all presents devoted to them for your own benefit and make them your property. …
>
> XXIX, 1. But you also, most holy emperors, are ordered to punish and to chastise. You are commanded by the Law of the Supreme God that you severely persecute the crime of idolatry with all means …

2. According to God's command neither the son nor the brother shall be saved, and God even permits the execution with the sword of the beloved wife … (Firmicus Maternus 1913, see also Schneider 1978, pp. 605–612).

The logic inherent in the Supreme Value is systematically unfolded in the Middle Ages by St. Thomas of Aquino in his Summa Theologica.

The commands of Christ "Love your enemies, do good to them which hate you" (St. Luke 6, 27) and "My kingdom is not of this world" (St. John 19, 36) may have prevented, on several occasions and for a long time, the prescription to fight paganism and heretics here on earth. But the resistance need not be permanent, for the internal logic of the Supreme Value will, in time, take care of these obstacles. For love of fellow men requires to do them good first of all concerning the salvation of their immortal souls, and only then concerning their well-being on this earth. Thus stubborn heretics not prepared to repent and to forswear have to be left to secular power, i.e., to be eliminated according to St. Thomas Aquinas. For if their lives were saved, they might pervert others by infecting them or by returning to their heretical practices (St. Thomas, Summa Theologica 2, 2 q.11, a.4; Chap. 9 X; De Haereticis 5, 7; see Thomas de Aquino 1933 sq.). Though milder against pagans, St. Thomas speaks out against tolerating the pagan cult (Summa Theologica 2, 2 q.10, a.11).

His attitude concerning heretics St. Thomas formulated as follows:

Heretics deserve not only to be separated from the Church by excommunication, but also to be severed from the world by death. For it is a much graver matter to corrupt the faith which guidens the soul than to forge money, which supports temporal life. Therefore, if forgers of money and other evil-doers are condemned to death at once by the secular authority, much more reason is there for heretics as soon as they are convicted, to be not only excommunicated, but even put to death.

But Thomas Aquinas at least proposes to give them another chance, and to condemn them to death only after a relapse into heresy.

The Fourth Council of the Lateran (1215) codified the theory and practice of persecution of heretics. In its third canon, the council declared: "*Secular authorities, whatever office they may hold, shall be admonished and induced and if necessary compelled by ecclesiastical censure, ... to take an oath that they will strive ... to exterminate in the territories subject to their jurisdiction all heretics pointed out by the Church.*"

In view of the implied logic of supreme values, it is not surprising that the attitude toward pagans has not been always as lenient in the Middle Ages. In his famous speech asking for a crusade at the Council of Clermont in 1095 Pope Urban II asked the potential crusaders.

Let the deeds of your ancestors move you … and of your other kings, who have destroyed the kingdoms of the pagans, and have extended in these lands the territory of the holy church. Let the holy sepulcher of the Lord of our Savior, which is possessed by unclean nations, especially incite you, and the holy places which are now treated with ignominy and irreverently polluted with their filthiness. …

> But if you are hindered by love of children, parents and wives, remember what the Lord says in the Gospel, "He that loveth father or mother more than me, is not worthy of me." … Enter upon the road to the Holy Sepulcher; wrest land from the wicked race, and subject it to yourselves. …
>
> … undertake this journey for the remission of your sins, with the assurance of the imperishable glory of the kingdom of heaven (quoted from Weber 1972, p. 248 sq.).

This is certainly a call for a holy war. Finally, let us turn to the problem of the spiritual college and the executive committee. It is well known that already in the late Roman Empire the Councils of the Church like in Nicaea or Chalcedon, began to act as intermittent spiritual colleges. In that time, the Pope in Rome succeeded in gaining spiritual leadership in the Western part of the crumbling and dissolving empire. In the Middle Ages, Popes like Gregory VII, Innocent III and Boniface tried to subordinate the secular powers to their own authority and thus to combine the executive with the spiritual leadership of Western Christianity. Boniface's famous bull Unam Sanctam defines these papal claims:

> … we learn from the words of the Gospel that in this church and in her power are two swords, the spiritual and the temporal. … Both are in the power of the Church, the spiritual sword and the material. But the latter is to be used for the Church, the former by her; the former by the priest, the latter by kings and captains but at the will and by the permission of the priest. …
>
> Thus, concerning the Church and her power, is the prophecy of Jeremiah fulfilled, "See, I have this day set thee over the nations and over the kingdoms", etc. … Whoever therefore resists this power thus ordained of God, resists the ordinance of God. … Furthermore, we declare, state, define and pronounce that it is altogether necessary to salvation for every human creature to be subject to the Roman pontiff (quoted from Weber 1972, p. 226 sq.).

The strict attitude against heretics is also shared by founders of the Protestant Christian Churches. Though Luther had been rather tolerant concerning them in his younger years, he became rather radical in his older days and stated:

> Heretics are not disputed with, but to be condemned unheard, and whilst they perish by fire, the faithful ought to pursue the evil to its source and bath their hands in the blood of the Catholic bishops, and of the Pope, who is a devil in disguise.

Not surprisingly, the definition of heretics has changed according to the new creed. Luther also takes a strict position against Jews as nonbelievers:

> Burn the synagogues; take away their books, including the Bible. They should be compelled to work, denied food and shelter, preferably banished.

Calvin was more radical than Luther. He explains:

> "Those who would spare heretics and blasphemers are themselves blasphemers." The "implacable severity" of the death penalty is mandatory because "devotion to God's honor should be preferred to all human concerns."

The Catholic Church of the fourteenth and fifteenth centuries especially in Spain was as radical in persecuting heretics. After the conquest of the last Islamic state of Granada 1492 Queen Isabel of Castile and King Ferdinand of Aragon issued on March 31 the Alhambra Decree banning all Jews from Spain, who did not convert to Catholicism. Approximately 200,000 left Spain, but about 50,000 took baptism to be able to remain. But many of these so-called "Conversos" secretly kept their traditions. The same was true for many Muslims who converted to the Catholic church, the "Moriscos".

This could, of course, not be tolerated and the inquisition headed by the Great Inquisitor Tomàs de Torquemada (since 1483 until his death in 1498) began to persecute them. It has been estimated that about 2000 victims of these groups were killed by the inquisition.

2.4 Islam

Let us now look whether and to which degree the logic inherent in supreme values has historically emerged in Islam, which is well known for advocating the use of war against infidels:

> In the Muslim community, the holy war is a religious duty, because of the universalism of the (Muslim) mission and (the obligation to) convert everybody to Islam either by persuasion or by force. Therefore, caliphate and royal authority are united in (Islam), so that the person in charge can devote the available strength to both of them at the same time.
>
> The other religious groups did not have a universal mission, and the holy war was not a religious duty to them, save only for purposes of defenses. It has thus come about that the person in charge of religious affairs in (other religious groups) is not concerned with power politics at all. (Ibn Khaldûn 1967, vol. 1, p. 473).

This is a classical statement by the famous scholar Ibn Khaldûn, who lived around 1400. Accordingly, each Muslim is obliged to spread the Supreme Value by persuasion or force. Pagans have not to be spared. Spiritual and Executive Power have to be combined in the Caliphate to make the missionary task more effective. Specifically referring to Christians, Ibn Khaldhûn explains "We do not think that we should blacken the pages of this book with discussion of their dogmas of unbelief. All of them are unbelievers. This is clearly stated in the noble Qur'an. (To) discuss or argue those things with them is not up to us. It is (for them to choose between) conversion to Islam, payment of the poll tax, or death" (vol. 1, p. 480, 1967).

There can be no doubt that the belief in God (Allah) is considered by Islam to be a Supreme Value:

> It should be known that the Lawgiver (Muhammad) commanded us to believe in the Creator whom he considered as the sole source of all actions, … He informed us that this belief means our salvation if we have it when we die (Ibn Khaldûn 1967, vol. 3, p. 44).

The Qur'an also embodies the absolute truth: "Inimitability is restricted to the Qur'an. The other Prophets received their books in a manner similar to that in which our Prophet received (certain) ideas that he attributed to God, such as are found in many traditions. The fact that he received the Qur'an directly in its literal form, is attested by the following statement of Muhammad..." (vol. 3, p. 193). "The Qur'an is the clearest proof that can be, because it unites in itself both the proof and what is to be proved" (vol. 3, p. 192, 1967).

In the case of Islam, the implied logic of the Supreme Value unfolded itself rapidly. In fact, many of the ideas emerged already during the lifetime of Muhammad and can even be found in the Qur'an. Unbelievers have to burn in hell, whereas true believers will be rewarded:

> And they will say further: "If only we had listened,
>
> We would not be burning." So they confess their sins.
>
> Far from God's mercy are the dwellers in the flames,
>
> But those who fear God without seeing Him,
>
> To them shall come forgiveness and great rewards.
>
> (Qu'ran, Sura 67)

The doctrine of the holy war was also already conceived during the life of the prophet:

> They ask you about making war in the sacred month. Say: Warfare in this month is a great offence, but to obstruct the way of God and to deny Him, to hinder men from the holy temple, and to expel his people thence, that is more grievous to God. For idolatry is worse than killing.
>
> They will not cease from fighting against you until they have made renegades from your faith, if they are able. And whosoever becometh a renegade and dieth an unbeliever, his works shall come to nothing in this world or the world to come. Such are the rightful owners of the Fire, and they shall abide there forever (Qur'an, Sura 2).

It is thus stated, that Holy War is even allowed in the sacred month. For otherwise, the pagans may attempt or force believers to give up the Truth.

During the last years, we have witnessed another restatement of the implications of Shiite Islam as a Supreme Value Society. Let us quote the words of Ayatollah Khomeini.

> Each secular power... is necessarily an atheistic power, the work of Satan. The Islamic government, however, is subject to the law of Islam, which is neither derived from the people nor from its representatives, but directly from Allah and His Divine Will. The law of Qur'an, which is nothing than the Divine law, is the whole of each Islamic government and rules infallibly above all individuals.
>
> If a destined man embodying these highest virtues reveals himself to the public with the intent to form a truly Islamic government, then he has been endowed by the Almighty with the same message as once the prophet: he has to lead the people. In this case it is the absolute duty of the people to obey him. All military and civil power, which has been transferred by the Almighty to the Prophet is also at the disposal of the Islamic government of today (Konzelmann 1980, pp. 43 and 47).

Concerning the Holy War, the Ayatollah from Qum stated:

> The Holy War means a conquering of territories which are not dominated by Islam. Precondition for the declaration of Holy War is the formation of a Holy Islamic government… The final aim of the Holy War is the subjugation of the world under the law of the Qur'an… But the world shall know that the universal predominance of Islam is fundamentally different from the claim for power by ordinary conquerors. Guarantor of the difference is the authority of the Imam, the man of faith. He does not wage an unjust or tyrannical war of conquest (Konzelmann 1980, p. 38).

2.5 Conclusions

1. The four ideologies we have considered in this chapter are empirically characterized by Supreme Values lexicographically preferred to all other aims and believed to be absolutely true.
2. People not willing or unable to be converted to the right creed (Jews, Bourgeois, capitalists, pagans and heretics) have to be suppressed or to be eliminated.
3. Non-Aryans, especially Jews cannot be converted according to National Socialism.
4. The same is true in Communist Societies for capitalists.
5. The enemies of the true creed have to be defeated. Nazism and Communism are outspoken in their aims to conquer the secular power of the state and to spread their creed over the globe. But the Christian church has also been set over the nations according to several Popes and Islam has used the Caliphate to spread its true belief as far as possible across the world.

References

Alighieri D (1904) De Monarchia. Edited with a translation and notes by Aurelia Henry. Cambridge, Boston, New York

Augustinus A (1878) Ausgewählte Schriften des hl. Anrelius Augustinus, edited by Valentin Thalhofer, Köln

de Aquino T (1933 ff.) Die deutsche Thomas Ausgabe, Summa Theologica, Salzburg

Ensslin W (1976) Staat und Kirche von Konstantin dem Grossen bis Theodosius dem Grossen. In: Ruhbach G (ed) Die Kirche angesichts der konstantinischen Wende, Darmstadt, pp 74–99

Fetscher I (1970) Lenin Studienausgabe, 2 vols. Frankfurt und Hamburg

Hitler A (1933) Mein Kampf. München. First edition 1925–1927

Ibn Khaldûn (1967) The Muqaddimah. An introduction to history. Translated from the Arabic by Rosenthal F, 3 vols. Princeton, NJ

International Military Tribunal (1947) Der Prozess gegen die Hauptkriegsverbrecher. Nürnberg

Jones AHM (1966) The Decline of the Ancient World. London and New York

Klein R (1972) Der Streit um den Victoriaaltar. Einführung, Text, Uebersetzung und Erläuterungen. Darmstadt

Kogon E (1947) Der SS-Staat. Stockholm

Konzelmann G (1980) Die islamische Herausforderung. Hamburg
Lenin WI (1913) Drei Quellen und Bestandteile des Marxismus. In: Lenin (1962) (ed) Werke, Bd. 19. Institut für Marxismus-Leninismus beim Zentralkomitee der SED, Berlin (Ost)
Lenin WI (1929) Sämtliche Werke, 2nd edn. Wien and Berlin
Lenin WI (1956 ff.) Gesammelte Werke. Ostberlin
Lietzmann H (1976) Das Problem Staat und Kirche im Weströmischen Reich. In: Ruhbach G (ed) Die Kirche angesichts der konstantinischen Wende. Darmstadt, pp 112–121
Löw K (1988a) Totalitäre Elemente im originären Marxismus. In: Löw K (ed) Totalitarismus. Berlin, pp 166–184
Löw K (1988b) Marxismus-Quellenlexikon. Köln
Maternus F (1913) Schrift vom Irrtum der heidnischen Religionen. Aus dem Lateinischen übersetzt von Dr. Alfons Müller. Bibliothek der Kirchenväter, 2nd vol. Kempten und München
Marx K, Engels F (1956 ff.) Werke. Editor: Institut für Marxismus-Leninismus beim Zentralkomitee. Berlin (East)
Neue Zeit (1891)
Schilling O (1923) Die Staats- und Soziallehre des hl. Thomas von Aquin. Paderborn
Schneider C (1978) Geistesgeschichte der christlichen Antike, München
Solzhenitsyn AI (1973) The Gulag Archipelago, 1918–1956, I–II. New York, Evanston, San Francisco and London
Weber H (1967) Lenin. Aus den Schriften 1895–1923. München
Weber E (1972) The western tradition, 3rd edn. Lexington (Mass.) and Toronto

Chapter 3
The Theory of Totalitarianism and Mature Ideocracy, Part I: Evolution and Development

In this chapter, we develop the theory of political regimes based on ideologically oriented Supreme Values, which are considered to be absolutely true, that is of Ideocracies. Ideocracies can be observed in two different forms, those that have already reached the aims contained in their supreme values and those for which this is not (yet) the case. Empirical evidence for the former will be presented later, whereas we have already done so in four cases for the latter in Chap. 3. Additional historical cases will be discussed in later chapters.

3.1 The Birth of Ideology and the Progress Toward Ideocratic Regimes

We have stated that ideologies with supreme values, which are considered to be absolutely true are a necessary condition for the development of ideocratic regimes. It follows that such ideologies have first to be invented or reinvigorated by charismatic personalities, prophets, or gifted leaders. These men or women must be capable to convince people to become true believers, especially, a group of other strong personalities (apostles, old guard) who are able to effectively propagate the new creed. In this way, a growing supreme value movement of believers is established. To prevent that the movement may split up in time into sects with different interpretations of the ideology, one spiritual leader or at least a small group of such leaders has to maintain a monopoly in interpreting the meaning of the creed. If the founder of the ideology is still alive, he will usually be an obvious candidate for this position. Hitler and Lenin both strongly stressed the necessity of a monopoly of interpretation. But also in Catholic Christianity, the monopoly of a spiritual leadership has been secured by the introduction of the Papacy. In Sunnite Islam, the Caliphate served a similar purpose for a few centuries.

P. Bernholz, *Totalitarianism, Terrorism and Supreme Values*,
Studies in Public Choice 33, DOI 10.1007/978-3-319-56907-9_3

If the aims included by the supreme values are not very limited the ideological movement has to strive to gain the secular power of the state (Compare Fig. 6.1). For since resistance by nonbelievers, in-convertibles (like Jews or capitalists) or adherents of other creeds has to be expected, the power of the government has to be won to be able to break this resistance and to force people to their own well-understood luck, if necessary, as for instance expressed by St. Augustine in his letter to the Donatists (see above).

But how can the secular power of the state be won? This is regularly only possible, if many people are dissatisfied with their present plight. This means that a crisis has to develop, which may be of a political, economic, or a spiritual nature. A lost war, a great depression or hyperinflation, a growing dissatisfaction with the dominating religious ideas are important examples. The Bolsheviks would probably not have had any chance to win secular power without the loss of World War I by Russia; and National Socialists would not have been able to gain secular power in Germany without the lost war and the Great Depression. Moreover, in such crises the offered ideology must be thought by many people to be adequate to solve their present problems.

The means to take over the government depend, moreover, on the political regime in the respective nation. In democracies, a majority has to be won, or at least such a share of votes that a coalition government can be formed. This was the case in Germany, where the National Socialists could form a coalition with right wing partners who could be removed after the government had been grasped. Things are different with autocratic regimes. Here, it is important to win adherents in the military and the police, especially in the officer corps. Even a revolution like in Russia can only succeed, if the military and police are not energetically fighting the revolutionaries.

Let us sum up:

1. Ideologies with convincing supreme values have to be invented and spread by charismatic innovators.
2. A monopoly must be installed for the right to interpret the creed.
3. A well-organized movement has to be established to win enough converts and to strive for secular power.
4. A crisis has to develop convincing many people that the aims contained in the supreme values promise to solve their problems.
5. The means to overtake government powers are depending on the existing political regime.

It is obvious that not all of these conditions may be fulfilled, so that no ideocracy can be established by the ideocratic movement. Moreover, the resistance of the present rulers of a nation may be so strong that the movement does not succeed even if the preconditions mentioned are fulfilled. This is confirmed by much historical evidence. For instance, the Christian movement was unable to conquer the secular power of the state during late antiquity in the Roman Empire or in the states of the Middle Ages. This though several Popes strove energetically to subjugate emperors and princes under their sovereignty. During the sixteenth and seventeenth centuries, the establishment of Caesaropapism, that is of ideocratic regimes, was prevented in Central and Western Europe because neither the princes representing the Catholic Church nor those adhering to the new protestant "sects" could win the religious wars, for instance during the Thirty Years' War (1618–1648). This implied that Christian movements gained only exceptionally secular power in small states for some time, like in Geneva (see below) and the Muenster of the Anabaptists. Apart from these cases a secular and non-ideological outlook developed in the political systems of Western and Central Europe and its offsprings in America, Australia, and New Zealand, which only ended for some decades in Germany and Russia because of the emergence of the National Socialist and Bolshevik totalitarian regimes based on their secular ideologies.

3.2 Further Development after Winning the Secular Power of the State

After gaining the secular power of the state the political system has to be rigorously adapted to the aims stated in the supreme values of the ideology. As a first step secular and spiritual leadership have to be combined. In rare cases, this is not a problem, namely if all inhabitants of the respective country can be won for the creed because they are convinced by the new creed or accept it for opportunistic reasons, since they hope to gain better jobs or a chance to move into positions of political power. In such cases, a Mature Ideocracy develops in which people have not to be forced and suppressed. Some empirical evidence for Mature Ideocracies will be discussed later.

However, in most other historical cases the situation looks quite different. Many people are not prepared to accept the new ideology and offer secret or open resistance. They may even believe in another opposed ideology. This was for instance the case with communists when the Nazi movement tried to gain power in Germany. Moreover, according to the contents of the supreme values of the new rulers there may exist groups of in-convertibles like Jews under the new rule of National Socialists in Germany or Bourgeois under the Bolsheviks in Russia. Finally, the aims of the ideology may be so expansive that they cannot be reached by securing the domination of only one nation. In all these cases Ideocracies emerge which still have to use government power to reach their ends. Such Ideocracies we have defined as Totalitarian Regimes, for they have to use their spiritual power and the secular power of the state to convert people, to drive out nonbelievers or in-convertibles, to eliminate them if necessary and to pursue their aims outside the borders of the nation ruled by them.

Concerning the contents of the supreme values, the following differentiation offers itself:

1. Universal ideologies: These are ideologies demanding that all human beings are converted to the true creed.
2. Ideologies demanding universal domination of the globe: The supreme values of these ideologies are not aiming at the conversion of all people on earth, but postulate their rule by a minority elite determined by the ideology. The world dominance of the Aryan race would be an example.
3. Expansionist ideologies: These ideologies are striving for a limited expansion of their territory or of the number of their believers, or of the resources they need to reach the aims of their supreme values. A nationalist movement striving to comprise all people speaking the same language in one state would be an example.
4. Restrictive ideologies: These ideologies do not ask for any further expansion of their territory or do not aim at winning more converts with the help of power.

These categories allow us to clarify somewhat the differences between totalitarian regimes and mature ideocracies. For as mentioned, totalitarian regimes have not yet reached their aims, whereas this is the case for mature ideocracies. Obviously, the latter will usually be characterized by the fourth and in some exceptions by the third category. For reasons still to be explained the first two categories and often also the third one will be typical for totalitarian regimes.

In the next chapter, we will present empirical evidence for the remaining cases of totalitarian regimes mentioned in Table 1.1 before we turn to the second part of the theory of totalitarian regimes.

Chapter 4
Further Historical Cases of Totalitarian Regimes

Modern totalitarian regimes like Nazi Germany, the Soviet Union under Lenin and Stalin and China under Mao have been widely analyzed. Thus, there is no need to discuss them again (but compare Bernholz 1993). Here,we want to highlight earlier historical cases which, according to our theory, were also totalitarian regimes, namely the Mongolian, Aztec and Inca empires, Geneva under Calvin, Münster, during the Anabaptist regime, the caliphate in the Sudan of the late nineteenth century, the rule of the Taliban in Afghanistan, and the Islamic caliphate in Syria and the Levant (ISIS).

4.1 The Mongols Under Genghis Khan and His Immediate Successors

In his article, *Mongol Orders of Submission to European Powers, 1245–1255*, Voegelin (1941) analyzes several letters mainly addressed by the Mongolian emperors to Popes and French kings. He proves that these letters, in fact, contained orders to submit to Mongolian rule, since the Mongolian emperors believed to be destined by God to establish His order all over the world. Let us quote Voegelin:

> The thesis [in the documents] that Genghis Khan is the only and supreme Lord of the Earth may be considered as part of a dogmatic system explaining the true nature of government in the cosmos … But since … at least the earthly part of it, is a world in the making, the formula proves to be a claim to ruler-ship for Genghis Khan and to submission by all other earthly powers …. Bringing down revealed essence to earth, incorporating essence into

Parts 4.1–4.4 of this chapter are republished with permission from Ferdinand Schöningh Verlag; Paderborn, München, Wien, Zürich. Original Publication: Bernholz, Peter (1997), Ideology, Sects, State and Totalitarianism. A General Theory. In: Maier, Hans and Schaefer, Michael (eds.): 'Totalitarismus und Politische Religionen', Band II, 272–298.

P. Bernholz, *Totalitarianism, Terrorism and Supreme Values*,
Studies in Public Choice 33, DOI 10.1007/978-3-319-56907-9_4

history, is the far-reaching comprehensive intention of the Order. It is brimming with dynamic energy and pregnant with the fanatical acts born of the desire to transform the world of man into a likeness of God's rule in Heaven (p. 405).

In such cases of a regrettable lack of understanding for the perfectly peaceful and law abiding intentions of the Mongol Imperial Government who did nothing but carry out an Order of God, punitive expeditions had to be undertaken - like that of 1241, carried into Eastern and Central Europe, which had been the proximate cause for the Papal mission of 1245 (p. 406).

de Rachewiltz (1973) extends and confirms the analysis by Voegelin by studying earlier sources, and especially the Secret History of the Mongols. He concludes that

Since the crime of turning a deaf ear to the Mongol court's order of submission was not … merely an offence against the emperor, but an overt offence against Heaven's Decree, punishment of the offender, had, of course, to be proportionate. Hence the frightful massacres and destruction, and the complete lack of pity towards the civilian population, which was often annihilated. Here again we find an exact parallel in the practice of the crusading armies (p. 25).

It should be clear from these citations that the Mongols followed a universal dominance ideology. The supreme values contained in it ordered them to extend their Empire and its Order given by God to the whole world. It justified cruelties and massacres against all who did not voluntarily submit to God's and thus to their emperor's demands.

4.2 Aztecs and Incas

Let us turn next to the Aztecs (Mexica) and the Incas. Both rose from unimportant beginnings to become masters of huge empires within a few decades. During the pre-imperial time a "process of centralization of power and incipient social stratification" took place, which

was a successful adaptive response to the environmental-demographic-political pressures made manifest in the threats posed by the larger and stronger societies surrounding the early Mexica and Inca.

The continuing operation of these same pressures eventually triggered the two parallel transformational crises - the Mexica's overthrow of the Tepanecs and the Incas' defeat of the Chanca. In both cases, victory brought power to a small corps of military leaders who set about restructuring their societies by intensifying existing developmental trends. Each transformational crisis was followed by a series of reforms enacted by the new leadership …

However, …, the most critical measures were religious reforms. … (Conrad and Demarest 1984, pp. 179 sq.).

Manipulations of the upper pantheon began in pre-imperial times with the crystallization of patron deities, the Mexica's Huitzilopochtli and the Incas' Inti, out of fluid, manifold sky gods….

Huitzilopochtli and Inti ultimately became imperial patrons, intensifying the 'solarization' of Aztec and Inca religion. This emphasis on solar aspects of the divine complexes is hardly surprising. … (pp. 180 sq.).

4.2.1 *The Empire of the Mexicas*

The elevation of Huitzilopochtli to become dominant god in the Mexica pantheon would not have been sufficient to create expansionary ideologies. But, an imperial cosmology was developed by a handful of men, especially Itzcoatl, Montezuma I, and above all Tlacaelel, a high priest and chief adviser (Conrad and Demarest 1988, Chap. 2). Huitzilopochtli now became identified with the warrior sun and the

> imperial cosmology held that the Mexica must relentlessly take captives in warfare and sacrifice them; the spiritual strength of the sacrificed enemy warriors would strengthen the sun and stave off its inevitable destruction by the forces of darkness. Thus, it was specifically the Mexica's sacred duty to pursue a course of endless warfare, conquest, and sacrifice to preserve the universe from daily threat of annihilation. The new vision of the cosmos accelerated the pace and scale of human sacrifices beyond all previous measure, associating these ancient rites specifically with the Mexica state and the expansion of the Triple Alliance (Conrad and Demarest 1988, p. 38).
>
> The new ideology set the Mexica apart from their neighbors and predecessors and irrevocably altered the course of Aztec history. … Through an accelerated process, mass human sacrifice would reach unimaginable proportions by the late fifteenth century, with single ceremonies sometimes involving the massacre of literally thousands and even ten thousands of captives. These rituals and the cosmology which demanded them would launch the Mexica armies on a divine quest, a quest which would result in the sprawling Aztec Empire (p. 42).

Let us also note that the new dogma was propagated by art, literature and education (pp. 42 sq.) through a comprehensive propaganda program.

4.2.2 *The Empire of the Incas*

The expansionary ideology of the Incas was based on quite different religious beliefs.

> In imperial times Inca state religion assigned special importance to three sub-complexes of the sky
>
> god: a universal creator with a variety of titles, the best known being Viracocha; the sun god Inti; and Illapa, the thunder or weather deity. …
>
> Underlying the upper pantheon, and inextricably linked to it, were two more fundamental religious concepts: ancestor worship and **huaca**. …
>
> The word is a generic term for any person, place or thing with sacred or supernatural associations; it conveys a sense of embodied holiness (Conrad and Demarest 1988, Chap. 3).
>
> Above the level of the family, the fundamental unit of Inca social organization was the **ayllu** …
>
> which was a kin group tracing its descent from a common ancestor, … The **ayllu** was also the basic landholding group" (p. 97) The ancestors defined the **ayllu** and legitimated its land tenure and protected its members. Therefore, it is no surprise that the **ayllu**'s prosperity depended on proper care of its mummies, fetishes, and other **huacas** (p. 105).

In 1438, a major crisis threatened the small Inca state around Cuzco, when the Chanca invaded its territory and besieged the city. The ruling Viracocha Inca fled with his designated heir, Inca Urcon. The defense was left to another son, Cusi Inca Yupanqui, who succeeded with supernatural help of the sky god and of allies secured by offering them rewards, in driving away the Chanca invaders and to rout them in subsequent battles. Thereafter, he replaced his father and brother as ruler and assumed the name Pachakuti, "He who remakes the World." Cusi Inca and his leading followers instituted some important governmental and ideological reforms and embarked upon the remarkable sequence of conquests that established the Inca Empire.

The reforms were built on the existing religion sketched above. According to Inca oral history, Cusi Inca Yupanqui, when awaiting the final Chanca onslaught, beheld in a dream or vision

> a supernatural figure of terrifying aspect. … this apparition identified itself as the Incas' sky god …, calling him 'my son'. It then proceeded to reassure him if he kept to the true religion, he was destined to be a great ruler and to conquer many nations (Conrad and Demarest 1988, p. 111).

It follows that at least from this time the Inca rulers were considered to be direct descendants of the sky god and its aspect as sun god, Inti. Connected with this, the royal ancestor cult was now greatly expanded. When an Inca emperor died, the rule of the empire passed to one of his sons. But the

> deceased emperor's palaces …, servants, chattels, and other possessions continued to be treated as his property and were entrusted to his **panaqa**, a corporate social group containing all of his descendants in the male line except his successor [i.e., a kind of **ayllu**]. These secondary heirs did not actually own the items named above. Instead, ownership remained vested in the dead king. …
>
> The primary purpose of the **panaqa** was to serve as the dead king's court, maintain his mummy, and perpetuate his cult (p. 113).

These innovations had far-reaching consequences, since the new king had to acquire new property and wealth for himself.

> He had two principal means of doing so. First, he could demand additional periods of service from his existing subjects, increasing their tax burden [in form of obligatory labor services]. Second, he could conquer new territories … and impose taxes on their inhabitants.
>
> However, the emperor could not levy taxes at will in his provinces, whether new or old. His own demands, like those of the state as a whole, were regulated by principles of reciprocity. He had to sustain and entertain citizens while they worked for him. Therefore, the emperor's fundamental economic need was for agricultural land whose produce could be used to fulfill his reciprocal obligations to the taxpayers (p. 121)
>
> … the rights of dead rulers placed considerable amounts of land and labor outside a new emperor's control and left him facing the question of how to create his own agricultural states and have them farmed. There was one obvious solution to this problem: he could conquer new territory and exploit their wealth (p. 122).

It follows that the religious reforms created the driving force behind the expansion of the Inca Empire. But to reach this goal, the citizens had also to be convinced of its value. This was reached by an incessant propaganda and, especially at the beginning, by material benefits to be gained. The propaganda reminded people that their king was a god whose interest coincided with their own and that their welfare depended on the prosperity of their past and present rulers.

> Finally, in every stratum of society the brave soldier's rewards continued long after his death. The Inca believed that those who fought with courage and skill would eventually occupy 'the principal place in Heaven' (p. 124).

We conclude that the Incas had created an expansionary ideology that brought them to establish a totalitarian empire, in this case with a state-controlled economy (Baudin 1956). Note also that a formal training program for sons of the nobility and the sons of the native provincial aristocracy was instituted in Cuzco, where the state religion and the official (rewritten) Inca history were taught.

4.3 The Rule of the Anabaptists in Münster

The next case to be mentioned as a totalitarian regime is the rule of the Anabaptists in Münster (Westphalia) in 1534–35. In this city, a kind of stalemate had developed between the mainly Lutheran city council and the Anabaptists, since the Lutherans needed the help of the latter to prevent the Catholic bishop from dominating Münster again and reinforcing the Catholic creed. Thus religious freedom was granted to the Anabaptists in Münster, though they were outlawed and persecuted in the Holy Roman Empire to which the city belonged. Thus more and more Anabaptists moved to Münster, among them the Dutchman, Jan Matthijs, the new leader of the Anabaptists in the Netherlands. On the other hand, the Bishop soon recruited an army to retake the city. Afraid of both the Anabaptists and the Bishop, many Lutherans left Münster. As a consequence, at the regular annual election of the Münster Council on 23 February 1534, only Anabaptists were elected, with the visionary Knipperdolling as leading burgomaster. Soon, however, practical power was no longer exercised by the legitimate city government but by the charismatic apostolic messenger, Jan Matthijs (Stayer 1976, Chap. 11; van Dühlmen 1974; Goertz 1980).

The Münster Anabaptists were a part of the Melchiorites, the sect founded by Melchior Hoffman. "According to Melchiorite teaching, baptism would be resumed in a time of grace at the end of all persecution, and in a particular New Jerusalem. Earlier, this had meant Strassburg, the most tolerant city in the Germanies from the Anabaptist standpoint. Now Münster assumed a parallel role, or was said to have replaced Strassburg as the New Jerusalem" (Stayer 1976, p. 230).

Melchiorite Christianity awaited the temporal reign of the returned Christ in the immediate future and built heavily on the prophesies of Daniel and other prophets. Originally, their doctrine asked for the peaceful endurance of persecution during the time they waited for the coming of Christ. But the events in Münster, and especially the siege by the Bishop, led them to turn to a more aggressive interpretation of the Scriptures. Also, the escape of the Anabaptists from military defeat on February 10, 1534 was soon interpreted as a miraculous event.

Bernhard Rothmann, an Anabaptist preacher in Münster, who had done much to bring them to power "articulated the crusading consciousness of the Kingdom in a number of pamphlets devoted to a sort of propagandistic theology" (Stayer, p. 239). He pointed out that the saints had to take arms to carry out the vengeance on the ungodly as a necessary prelude to Christ's Second Coming:

> it has pleased [the Lord] that we and all true Christians should not now limit ourselves to fending off the power of the godless through the Sword. He also wants to give the Sword into the hands of his people to take revenge on everything that is unjust and bad throughout the whole world … (Rothmann 1970, p. 212).

We conclude that the Münster Anabaptist movement, in spite of their weak secular forces had created a universal dominance ideology, since they believed in God's help. With this, a totalitarian regime was inescapable as soon as they had (quite legally) grasped power. Already four days later the unbaptized population was either forced to accept baptism or driven out of the city. Unlike earlier emigrants, they were not allowed to take their belongings with them.

Prophet Matthijs' de facto rule, however, lasted only for one month. In April 1534, he was killed during a sortie to which he was probably driven by one of his visions. Jan of Leyden, who became his successor as chief prophet, used this occasion to give the holy city of Münster formally a holy constitution, Replacing the city council chosen by men, the prophet as God's representative selected 12 god-fearing men as Elders. Jan of Leyden himself became the official spokesman during the administration of the Twelve Elders who wielded the Sword of Justice from April/May to September 1534. Now the Scripture as law replaced officially the secular law of the city. Spiritual and secular power had been formally combined.

Under the Elders, claims to universal dominion developed. Coins were minted "to claim universal dominion for the Münster Anabaptists." They bore the slogan, "One king established over all," followed by the other Anabaptist universals, "One God, one faith, one baptism" (Stayer, p. 238). This was done although the use of coins as money was forbidden. The expression "king" refers to Jan van Leyden, who was raised to kingship in September 1534. This followed God's command to Jan and a sign from God he had prayed for, namely the proclamation that Jan should be made king by another prophet, John Dusentschar from Warendorf.

Let us complete the description of this Münster episode by describing some of the measures taken by the totalitarian regime. We have already mentioned forced baptism and exile at the beginning of the regime. Later all citizens were forced to surrender their money and to accept polygamy. Persons "blaspheming" against Anabaptist prophets and ministers were executed. A former nunnery served as a jail for the few who had neither accepted expulsion nor rebaptism. In time, the use of terror increased. Those who resisted the confiscation of money and precious metals or the introduction of polygamy were executed. When a group of people rebelled against polygamy under ex-alderman Mollenhecke, 47 of the original conspirators were executed and buried in mass graves. After the fall of Münster, the King himself admitted to having seven or eight people beheaded, whereas his chief administrator and executioner Knipperdolling acknowledged to having decapitated eleven or twelve persons (Stayer, p. 256).

4.4 Calvin's Regime in Geneva

As a further historical case of a totalitarian regime, we discuss Geneva during Calvin's lifetime. Here the citizens assembled in public on May 21, 1536 and decided, by raising their hands that they would live in the future solely according to the Bible and the word of God. This happened after the Protestant revolution had taken place and after the Catholic Church had been suppressed with the help of terror and force. The actual implementation of the supreme values was left to Jean Calvin especially from 1541 on, when he was recalled from a few years' exile by the City Council (Compare the well-written account by Zweig 1936/1983). Calvin had already written earlier:

> The power with which the preachers should be endowed will here be clearly described. Since they are called as administrators and propagators of the word of God, they have to dare everything and to coerce all the great and mighty of this world, to bow to God and to serve him alone. They have to give orders to all, from the lowliest to the most elevated. They have to introduce the statute of God, to destroy the kingdom of Satan, to spare the lambs and to exterminate the wolves. They have to exhort and to instruct the obedient, to accuse the reluctant and opposing. They can bind and absolve, cast lightning and thunder, but all this according to the word of God (Calvin 1887).

In agreement with these ideas, Calvin undertook a comprehensive theocratic restructuring of political and social life. A Consistory was formed consisting of six Preachers and twelve Elders, who had to be proposed by the Preachers and to be confirmed by the congregation. The Consistory had the right to issue laws and to judge people not attending church service, who violated the strict moral code or adhered to or propagated heterodox religious opinions even of a protestant nature. Condemned they were transferred to the worldly authority for punishment. Even the mildest opposition against Calvin's views was suppressed. All actions, words and even expressions were strictly supervised. From 1542 to 1546 alone, 58 persons were executed, some of them burnt at the stake; 76 were banned. Theater and dancing were forbidden; children were only allowed biblical first names when they were baptized. "Luxury" clothing was not permitted and even popular Swiss-German costumes forbidden. Bachelors and spinsters had to live with families, writings not allowed by the Consistory were banned. All these measures led to the resistance of a freedom party, the Libertins, who comprised many of the most reputed citizens of Geneva. Calvin suppressed it with a regime of terror, assisted by the many Calvinist refugees who had been made citizens following his proposal. Several people not able to flee were executed.

In this way, Calvin had by 1555 reached absolute domination of Geneva, which he turned into a "protestant Rome." 1554 the famous Theological Academy was founded to educate Calvinist ministers to propagate the true Christian faith to France, England, Scotland, and the Netherlands. A kind of secret police was formed which even extended its activities to foreign countries.

4.5 The Mahdist State in the Sudan 1881–1898

The later Mahdi Muhammad Ahmed was born on the island Darar in Dongola in 1843 A.D. (1258 Hedjra). His father was a carpenter and after his death the brothers of Muhammad Ahmed took over the business, whereas he began to study the Koran in Khartum. His colleagues admired his god-fearing piety and he became famous because of his ascetic life which he pursued with fanatical zeal. After his studies, he entered the religious order of Saih Muhammad Serif, and after seven years his master allowed him to go where he wanted and to decide himself whether new aspirants could become members of the order. Soon he became well known in the whole country and won a growing following. But, the friendship with his master soured because of his claim to be the Mahdi, the "rightly guided," that is the expected messiah of the Muslim tradition. Moreover, Muhammad Ahmed criticized his former master for not following the precepts of Islamic creed, for instance by allowing women to kiss his hands and to allow his students invited in great numbers to sing and to dance after circumcisions. Because of this critique Muhammad Ahmed was expelled from the order. But, this very event proved to be the beginning of his rise as religious leader.

He withdrew into a cave, which he dug below the earth, and was visited by more and more people because of his reputation as ascetic and his religious zeal. Even travelers on the Nile stopped their ships to obtain his blessings and to make presents to him, which he distributed among the poor. He also began to travel over the whole Sudan and soon realized the bad feelings of the population against the Egyptian–Turkish government and their hopes that a Mahdi might appear to free them from this oppression. His travels also helped to increase ever more his followership. He began to study books to find out the characteristics and signs of the Mahdi, and found that he himself fulfilled all the necessary traits. He himself reported that he did not know anything about this matter, until he received the calling from above, from the Messenger of God, Muhammad, without having merited it.

Muhammad Ahmed believed that the Turkish dominated Egyptian government and her officials were the worst infidels. They were the most abject men since they were not believing and hypocritical, whose law codes had destroyed Islam. According to his belief, religion went at that time through a period of suffering, since people did no longer believe in the after-life and were possessed by greed for money and reputation. Science apart from the Koran was objectionable and scholars had sold their souls to the government and were drunk from love of this world.

Thus, he admonished the warriors of faith that they should rush forward into the Djihad, the holy war, and massacre without pity the unbelievers, the Turks.

It is thus not surprising that the Mahdi interpreted his victories as miracles of Heaven and as proof of his heavenly message, and was able to assemble a growing fanatical followership, who was prepared to die in the holy war as martyrs believing in the promise of splendid rewards in after-life (Oeser 2012, pp. 25–29). His army succeeded to defeat all the troops of the government including the expeditions sent to crush it, and this although in the beginning the believers owned only primitive weapons. In the end of this successful holy war the army of the Mahdi was able to take Khartoum, the capital, in 1885, defended under the command of the British General Gordon, and thus had conquered about the whole of the Sudan. An expeditionary force meant to break the ring around the beleaguered city arrived too late. After having conquered Khartoum, incredible atrocities rook place. The capital of the heavenly kingdom was established in Omdurman on the other side of the Nile.

However, already a few months later the Mahdi died on June 22, 1885, and his successor, Caliph Abdullahi lacked the charismatic traits of Muhammad Ahmed, so that his rule soon turned into a kind of military dictatorship (Churchill 1899, vol. 1, p. 58). After some years, he was defeated by the army of the later Lord Kitchener in the battle of Omdurman; the city was conquered and afterwards the rest of the Sudan taken. Caliph Abdullahi and some of his followers escaped and dominated Kordofan for about a year, but he was finally defeated and killed in the battle.

4.6 The Rule of the Taliban in the Islamic Emirate of Afghanistan

The rule of the Taliban in Afghanistan was a direct consequence of the successful fight of several factions in this country against the Soviet Russian occupation. In the following civil war after the Soviet forces had been withdrawn, the Pakistani-trained Taliban got the upper hand and established their capital in Kandahar. Mohammad Omar was their founder and spiritual leader. They finally controlled the greatest part of Afghanistan from 1996 to 2001, when they were defeated by the Western Alliance led by the USA. Since then they employ terrorist activities to regain power with no small probability of success after the retreat of the main Western forces.

The Taliban movement grew out of students studying Islamism in religiously run schools for Afghan refugees in Pakistan. When their forces advanced in Afghanistan thousands of people fled. During their rule, ten thousands of homes were destroyed. The Taliban follow a strict ideological interpretation of the Sharia, the Islamic law. Girls are not allowed to go to school, and women are forced to wear the burqa in public. If somebody was caught in forbidden education of women, he or she faced execution. It is estimated that 80% of marriages were forced (see file:///E:/Taliban%20-%20Wikipedia%20the%20free%20encyclopedia.htm).

4.7 The Islamic Caliphate in Syria and the Levant

The group, which since June 14, 2014 calls itself a worldwide Caliphate, was founded in 1999 by Jordanian radical Abu Musab al-Zarqawi as "The Organization of Monotheism and Jihad." It developed under different names and first considered itself to be a part of al Qaeda, a relationship which has meanwhile been ended. After al-Zarqawi was killed in 2006, and the two next leaders suffered the same fate through US forces, Abu Bakr al-Baghdadi became the new leader of the group in April 2010. Meanwhile the state spread by military force to several regions in Syria and Iraq including the city of Mosul, and also created dependencies in Libya and the Egyptian Sinai. The Islamic movement of Boko Haram in Nigeria has declared itself to be a part of the Caliphate.

The ideology followed is based on a radical Sunnite Islamic creed based on the Sharia with a strong eschatological trait. Many Shiite and Christian unbelievers have been killed, and people transgressing the strict rules of the Sharia are severely punished. Martyrs dying in suicide attacks for the good cause enjoy the fruits of paradise after their death. Heathen idols and monuments have been destroyed in the former capitals of Assyria and in Palmyra (https://en.wikipedia.org/wiki/Islamic_State_of_Iraq_and_the_Levant).

4.8 The Bloody Trails of Totalitarian Regimes

It follows from the Supreme Values of totalitarian regimes that especially in-convertibles, but also recalcitrant nonbelievers have usually to suffer a bitter fate. For they have either to be used as slaves to reach the implied goals, or to be persecuted, driven into emigration or even to be eliminated since they are considered a permanent danger for the regime. But not only in-convertibles and nonbelievers are threatened to suffer. For as has been pointed out, believers have also to be prepared to sacrifice their lives for the noble and absolutely true aims. Moreover, if the Supreme Values of the ideocracy ask for expansionary policies, for instance to convert all people on earth to the true creed, or to subject the whole globe to Communism or the dominance of the Aryan race, it becomes probable that many believers will die in the following imperialist wars. It is thus not surprising that totalitarian regimes have left a bloody track of death, usually not characteristic of other oppressive regimes (Table 4.1).

Table 4.1 Number of deaths caused by totalitarian regimes

Country	Period	Number of deaths (in thousand)	Sources
Mongols	13–15th ctr.	29,927	Morgan (1986)
Incas	Until 16th ctr.	n.a.	Conrad and Demarest (1988)
Aztecs	Until 16th ctr.	1000	
Calvin's Geneva	1534-35	0.058	Choisy (1902), Zweig (1936/1983)
Anabaptists in Münster	16th ctr. 102	n.a.	van Dühlmen (1974)
French revolution (Jacobin Terror)	1789–96	263	Greer (1935), Ladouce (1988)
Taiping revolution	1851–64	20–34,000	Shih (1972), Chesneaux (1973)
Soviet Union	1917–87	61,911	Rummel (1990), Courtois et al. (1997)
Nazi Germany	1933–45	20,946	Rummel (1992)
Communist regimes			
China	1949–87	35,236	Rummel (1991)
Vietnam	1954–87	1678	Rummel (1996)
Cambodia (Khmer Rouge)	1975–79	2035	Kiernan (1996)
North Korea	1948–87	1663	Rummel (1990)
Poland	1946–48	400	Checinski (1983)
Eastern Europe	1917–89	1000	Courtois et al. (1997)
Cuba	1959–96	15–17	Courtois et al. (1997)
Ethiopia	1974–91	2000	Human Rights Watch (1991)

Additional sources for numbers: Elliott (1972), Dobrowski and Walliman (1992: 167)
Rummel (1996: 12); completed and corrected by Heinsohn (1998)
For Calvin's Geneva: Meyers Grosses Konversationslexikon (1903)
Remark: in some cases, the figures presented by other authors differ widely. For instance, for the Soviet Union even by a factor of 0.5. But all estimates agree concerning the order of magnitudes

References

Baudin L (1956/1944) Der sozialistische Staat der Inka. Rowohlts Deutsche Enzyklopädie. Hamburg: Rowohlt. Appeared first in French in Paris 1944, Librairie de Médicis

Bernholz P (1993) Necessary conditions for totalitarianism: supreme values, power and personal interests. In: Radnitzky G, Bouillon H (eds) Government: servant or master? Amsterdam and Atlanta, Rodopi, pp. 267–312

Calvin J (1887) Institutio Religionis Christianae. English translation by Battles FL (1960) Institutes of the Christian Religion. Westminster Press, Philadelphia

Checinski M (1983) Terror and Politics in Communist Poland. Jerusalem, The Soviet and East European Research Center, Hebrew University

Chesneaux J (1973) Peasant revolts in China, 1840–49. W. W. Norton, New York
Choisy (1902) L'Etat chrêtien calviniste à Genève. Paris
Churchill WS (1899) The river war. A historical account of the reconquest of the Sudan, 2 vols. London
Conrad GW, Demarest AA (1984) Religion and empire. Cambridge and New York: Cambridge University Press
Conrad GW, Demarest AA (1988) Religion and empire. Cambridge University Press, Cambridge and New York
Courtois et al (eds) (1997) Le livre noir du communisme: Crimes, terreur, répression. Robert Laffont, Paris
de Rachewiltz I (1973) Some remarks on the ideological foundations of Chingis Khan's empire. Papers on far eastern history, vol 7, pp 21–36
Dobrowski MN, Wallimann I (1992) Genocide in our time. Ann Arbour, MI, University of Michigan
Elliott G (1972) Twentieth century book of the dead. Allan Lane, The Penguin Press, London
Goertz HJ (1980) Die Täufer. C.H. Beck, München
Greer D (1935) The incidence of terror during the French revolution: a statistical interpretation. Harvard University Press, Cambridge (Mass.)
Heinsohn G (1998) Lexikon der Völkermorde. Rowohlt Taschenbuch, rororo, Reinbeck bei Hamburg
Human Rights Watch (1991) Evil days: thirty years of war and famine in Ethiopia. Human Rights Watch, New York
Kiernan B (1996) The Pol Pot Regime. Race, power and genocide in Cambodia under the Khmer Rouge, 1975–79. Yale University Press, New Haven and London
Larouse I (1988) Was France the fatherland of genocide? The World and I, 683–690
Meyers Grosses Konversationslexikon (1903) Calvin, vol 2, 6th edn. Bibliographisches Institut, Leipzig and Wien, pp 108–109
Morgan D (1986) The mongols. Blackwell, Oxford
Oeser E (2012) Das Reich des Mahdi. Aufstieg und Untergang des ersten islamischen Gottestaates. Wissenschaftliche Buchgesellschaft, Darmstadt
Rothmann B (1970) In: Stupperich R (ed) Die Schriften Bernhard Rothmanns. Aschendorff, Münster 456 pp
Rummel RJ (1990) Lethal politics: soviet genocide and mass murder since 1917. Transaction Publishers, New Brunswick, NJ
Rummel RJ (1991) China's bloody century: genocide and mass murder since 1900. Transaction Publishers, New Brunswick, NJ
Rummel RJ (1992) Democide: Nazi Democide and Mass Murder. Transaction Publishers, New Brunswick, NJ
Rummel RJ (1996) Death by government. Introduced by I-L. Horowitz. Transaction Publishers, New Brunswick, NJ
Shih VYC (1972) The taiping ideology: its sources, interpretations and influences. University of Washington Press, Seattle
Stayer JM (1976) Anabaptists and the sword. Colorado Press, Lawrence (Kansas)
van Dühlmen R (1974) Das Täuferreich zu Münster 1534–1535. Reports and documents. Deutscher Taschenbuch Verlag, München
Voegelin E (1941) The mongol orders of submission to European powers, 1245–1255. Byzantion, vol XV, 1940–1941, pp 378–413
Zweig S (1983/1936) Castellio gegen Calvin oder Ein Gewissen gegen die Gewalt. Fischer, Frankfurt/Main

Chapter 5
Mature Ideocracies

We have already shown that ideocracies need not but can be totalitarian regimes. We thus have to differentiate between totalitarianism and mature ideocracies as subspecies. What are then mature ideocracies? In a mature ideocracy, the goals of the ideological movement have been broadly reached, whereas this is not true for a totalitarian regime. Good examples of mature ideocracies are the Puritan state in Massachusetts and the Jesuit state in Paraguay, both founded at the beginning of the seventeenth century. Further examples may be Tibet under the Dalai Lama, modern Saudi Arabia and Iran. Even Egypt under the Pharaohs may be an example, though in this case I have not looked closely enough at the evidence. Today even Iran may be considered to be a mature ideocracy, for after a totalitarian period in which according to empirical estimates 20–30,000 nonbelievers or opponents were killed, now mainly only Shiite believers in the supreme values remain, with probably quite some people only pretending to do so.

Subsequently Puritan Massachusetts, Jesuit Paraguay, Tibet, Shiite Iran, and Saudi Arabia will be analyzed as examples of mature ideocracies. Some people may doubt whether the first two really fit into our category, since they were dominions of the English and Spanish crowns, respectively. But the domination by England and Spain was mainly nominal. The two colonies were actually self-ruling, could mobilize armed forces, and had thus combined spiritual and secular forces. Both were founded with the explicit intention of preserving the purity of creed and to admit and tolerate only true believers.

5.1 The Puritan State of Massachusetts

The Puritans

> … had undertaken to establish a society where the will of God would be in every detail a kingdom of God on earth (Morgan 1958, p. 68).

P. Bernholz, *Totalitarianism, Terrorism and Supreme Values*,
Studies in Public Choice 33, DOI 10.1007/978-3-319-56907-9_5

From the beginning, except for some necessary craftsmen, only believers were admitted for emigration from England to Massachusetts. And later arriving "heretics" of differing protestant beliefs like Roger Williams and Anne Hutchinson were exiled to Rhode Island under threat of the death penalty should they return (Morgan 1958, Chaps. IX and X). Thus, from the very beginning, the contents of the supreme values were implemented, since nearly all the population shared or, at least, acquiesced to the tenets of this democratic theocracy. The whole private and public life was regulated according to the commands of God. Sins had to be punished.

> And punish they did, with the eager cooperation of the whole community, who knew that sin unpunished might expose them all to the wrath of God (p. 71).

Within these limits, a democracy including all freemen developed. But only those could be freemen who were members of the Puritan church.

5.2 The Jesuit State in Paraguay

The "state" of the Jesuits was organized to convert and to civilize the Indians of the region who were, until then, still earning their living by hunting and foraging. The Jesuit fathers also wanted to save them from the encomienda, a kind of serfdom, where they were badly treated and exploited by their Spanish masters. The Indians were settled in villages called "reducciones", reductions, which are referred to sometimes also as misiones. They were mainly occupied with agriculture and with raising cattle. Some were busy as craftsmen and artisans. Their everyday life, including religious duties, was strictly regulated. One can, in fact, speak of a kind of planned economy. Only Indians converted to Catholicism were admitted as permanent members of the reductions. Scarcely any whites were admitted by the fathers to prevent obnoxious influences on their Indian sheep. It is true that some exceptions existed for white traders and for gauchos. But the latter lived outside of the settlements and the former were only allowed to stay for a few days (Ezran 1989, pp. 129–133). Moreover, both groups were at least Catholics. Indians who fled the reductions and possibly reverted to paganism or caused unrest, both rare events, were caught and whipped. Women were shaven, rebellious shamans sometimes hanged if no other means helped (pp. 82 and 132). But on the whole, this use of force was rare, since only believers constituted the population. Thus little use of secular force and no terror were necessary to reach the supreme values of the creed. But the form of government was strictly oligarchic since it was totally in the hands of the two Jesuit fathers in each mission, who again had to strictly follow the orders of their superiors. The local Indian chiefs were only employed in executing the decisions taken by the fathers and to monitor the people. But it was a benevolent oligarchy since it was, in fact, a theocratic regime dominated by Catholic Christian values. In time the Jesuits built up an efficient army, which several times rescued the Spanish viceroy. This army had become necessary because of attacks by still uncivilized Indians, but much more because of the raids of "Paulistas" from Sao Paulo in Brazil looking for slaves and booty (Ezran 1989).

5.3 The Rule of the Dalai Lama in Tibet

Tibet enjoyed most of the time of its history, only limited self-rule under the sovereignty of the Mongols, and later of the Chinese. In 1578, Altan Khan of the Tuemed Mongols gave Sonam Gyatso, a high lama of the Gelugpa School, the name of Dalai Lama. Dalai being the Mongolian translation of the Tibetan name Gyatso "Ocean".

The fifth Dalai Lama (1617–1682) is known for unifying the Tibetan heartland under the control of the Gelug school of Tibetan Buddhism, after defeating the rival Kagyu and Jonang sects and the secular ruler, the Tsangpa prince, in a prolonged civil war. His efforts were successful in part because of aid from Güshi Khan, the leader of the Khoshuf Khanate. With Güshi Khan as a largely uninvolved overlord, the fifth Dalai Lama and his intimates established a civil administration which is referred to by historians as the *Lhasa state*. This Tibetan regime or government is also referred to as the Ganden Phodrang.

Following the Xinhai Revolution against the Qing dynasty in China in 1912, Qing soldiers were disarmed and escorted out of the Tibet Area. The region subsequently declared its independence in 1913 without recognition by the subsequent Chinese Republican Government. Later, Lhasa took control of the western part of Xikang, China. During this time, Tibet has to be considered to have been a pure theocracy under the Dalai Lama. The region maintained its autonomy until 1951 when, following the Battle of Chamdo, Tibet became incorporated into the People's Republic of China, and the previous Tibetan government was abolished in 1959 after a failed uprising (file:///E:/Tibet%20-%20Wikipedia,%20the%20free%20encyclopedia.htm.).

5.4 Saudi Arabia

The development of Saudi Arabia is intimately connected with the strict Islamic Creed reinvigorated by Muhammad ibn Abd al-Wahhab. The aim of this movement was the restoration of the true Sunna, in which the worship of the Prophet Muhammad, of saints, graves and reliquiae is frowned on, and alcoholic drinks, coffee and tobacco are forbidden. The duty for the holy war, djihad, and the tax helping the poor played also an important role.

Al-Wahhabi succeeded to win the ruler Muhammad ibn Saud of Darija in Nedjd for his religious ideas, whose son and grandsons succeeded to conquer from 1801 to 06 Kerbela, Medina, and Mecca. But at the order of the Sultan of the Ottoman Empire in Constantinople armed forces of Mehmed Ali of Egypt succeeded to throw the Saudis back to their original territory, where they established Er Riad as their capital. Later efforts of them to expand their territory during the nineteenth century failed.

Only after World War I and the end of the Ottoman Empire their leader Ibn Saud was able to defeat his old enemies in Nejd in 1919, and finally conquered Mecca, Medina, and Djidda against the Hashimids. Since then the rule of the House Saud has been consolidated in the greatest part of the Arabian Peninsula (Saudi Arabia), and no further expansion has been aimed at. The rule of the government and the rules for the behavior of the population are still based on the Wahhabite ideology, so that a Mature Ideocracy has been established. At the same time, the huge income from the natural oil resources has led to a strong economic development. (Compare Der Grosse Brockhaus, vol. 12, Wahhabiten, p. 290; for the present situation Imsand 2013)

5.5 The Iranian Shiite Islamic Republic

The Islamic Revolution in Iran forced Shah Mohammad Reza Phalavi, who had ruled an absolute monarchy, to flee in January 1979 after strikes and demonstrations had paralyzed the country. The final collapse of the Pahlavi dynasty occurred on February 11, when Iran's military declared itself neutral after guerillas and rebel troops had overwhelmed troops loyal to the Shah in armed street fighting. Already on February 1, the spiritual leader of the Islamic movement, Ayatollah Ruhollah Khomeini returned from his exile in France greeted by millions of Iranians and soon founded the Islamic Republic. This meant that a constitution was introduced following the ideas of the supreme leader Khomeini that Muslims require guardianship in the form of supervision by a leading Islamic jurist or jurists. This implies that though Iran is ruled by a civil government headed by a president, the last decisions remain with the Islamic Shiite leadership, that is until his death in 1989 of Ayatollah Khomeini. In December 1979, this new constitution was approved in a referendum which established a clerical Council of Guardians with power over legislation and elections, headed by Khomeini. After his death, Ali Khamenei took the position of supreme leader.

In the new republic, the rapidly modernizing capitalist economy of the Shah was replaced by populist Islamic economic and cultural policies. Many industries were nationalized, laws and schools Islamized, women had to be properly clad in public and Western influences were banned.

For the initial years, the new Islamic Republic has to be characterized as a totalitarian regime, in which the consolidation of the revolution into a theocratic republic took place. Until 1982–83 protests and uprisings by secularists, leftists, and more traditional Muslims were effectively suppressed and many opponents executed. Revolts by federalist parties and Marxists beginning in 1979 in several regions were lasting up to one year and were suppressed by force. The Kurdish uprising was the most violent one, lasted until 1983 and resulted in about 10,000 casualties.

Beginning in July 1988 and lasting for about 5 months, the regime systematically executed thousands of political prisoners. Estimates of the number executed vary greatly from 1400 to 30,000. Since this time only believers in the Islamic Republic or people pretending to believe in it were left. No further bloody terror was necessary and the country can be considered to be since this time a Mature Ideocracy. Several presidents were elected who usually were more open minded for economic and other reforms—with the exception of Mahmoud Ahmadinejad—than the clergy, who had the last word (https://en.wikipedia.org/wiki/History_of_Iran, Scholl-Latour 1988, pp. 93–203).

5.6 Conclusions for the Theory of Totalitarianism and of Mature Ideocracies

In all the historical cases discussed in this chapter, the introduction or the decisive change of an ideology was a necessary factor for the development of a totalitarian regime or of a mature ideocracy. Also in all these cases, secular and spiritual power were combined and used to stabilize and to extend the totalitarian rule and to enforce the supreme values contained in the ideology. Moreover, crises played a role in the early development of the Aztec, Inca and Münster Anabaptist ideology, and in its interpretation and in the consolidation of spiritual and secular power. There is also no doubt that the revival of Islamic ideology played a decisive role in the development of the Islamic Caliphate in the Sudan, the Taliban Emirate in Afghanistan and the Islamic Caliphate in Syria and the Levant. The same is true for all cases of mature ideocracies discussed. And in these three cases of totalitarian regimes too, crises played a decisive role: The Turkish overlordship in the Sudan, the Soviet occupation of Afghanistan, the American invasion in the Iraq and the civil war in Syria.

Whether crises played a central role in the Mongolian and Calvinist Geneva cases has still to be studied carefully. But Geneva banned Calvin and Farel, the preacher who had called Calvin, in April 1538. Recalled in 1541, Calvin had to struggle against aristocracy and the "mob" to succeed in introducing his new system. Both facts seem to point to a possible crisis. Concerning the Mongols, it is known that during the time in which Genghis Khan slowly rose to power, they were threatened to be subdued by the Tartars whose power had strongly increased at the end of the twelfth century. Only by combining his forces with those of another non-Mongolian nomad tribe, could the Tartars be defeated. In fact, Genghis Khan had to acknowledge its prince for some time as his feudal Lord before he was finally able to defeat him (Hambly 1966). Thus, in the Mongolian case, too, a crisis seems to have been present.

Let us stress, moreover, that the Mongols had a universal dominance ideology, whereas the Mexica and Inca ideologies were expansionist. The Münster Anabaptist ideology also called for universal domination, however ridiculous this may seem, given their very limited forces. We may even attribute a universal ideology to Calvinist Geneva, and in both of these two latter cases the goals of the ideology were certainly not reached domestically at the moment when spiritual and secular power were joined. Thus in all these five cases, totalitarian regimes were established since the preconditions for a mature ideocracy were not given. In conclusion, the empirical evidence shows that our general theory is capable of explaining the development towards totalitarian regimes as well as their important characteristics. The latter may, however, be different to a certain degree for each case because of the different substantive contents of the supreme goals of the respective ideologies.

The analysis of the historical examples should also have shown that totalitarianism regimes are not confined to modern experiences as asserted, e.g., by Friedrich (1953, p. 27) or implied by those who think like Linz (1975, pp. 193 sq.) that a single mass party is a necessary building block of such regimes. For, as we have seen, a party can be substituted by a priesthood or by an ideologically indoctrinated warrior class or aristocracy. We thus agree with Andreski (1965, p. 319) that "The empire of the Incas … although it was the most totalitarian state of the past … rested on technological foundations which were more primitive than those of any state of Asia or Europe."

On the other hand, the evidence for Geneva and the Mongols shows that the requirement of a planned economy as a characteristic of a totalitarian regime (Friedrich and Brzezinski 1965, p. 27) has been rightly dropped by Linz (1975, p. 191). Thus it is well known that Max Weber thought that Calvinist ideology strongly favored the development of Capitalism. We can also agree with Linz and others that mass participation is important (p. 194), that expansionism is dependent on the content of ideologies (p. 194 sq.) and that terror is in contrast to Arendt's (1951) view, not a necessary but a highly probable event in totalitarian regimes (Linz 1975, pp. 195 and 211). But we have to stress that our theory, which is confirmed by the empirical evidence discussed, demonstrates that these and other characteristics are a consequence of the driving forces of totalitarian movements and regimes: namely the supreme values of the ideology, crises, and the combination of spiritual and secular power under one leadership.

References

Andreski S (1965) The uses of comparative sociology. University of California Press, Berkeley and Los Angeles

Arendt H (1968/1951) The origins of Totalitarianism. Harcourt, Brace and World, New York

Der Grosse Brockhaus (1957): Wahhabiten, vol. 12. Wiesbaden

Ezran M (1989) Une colonisation douce: Les missions du Paraguay. Editions L'Harmattan, Paris

Friedrich CJ (1953) The unique character of Totalitarian society. In: Friedrich CJ (ed) Totalitarianism. Proceedings of a conference held at the American academy of arts and sciences, Harvard University Press, Cambridge (Mass.)

Friedrich CJ, Brzezinski ZK (1965/1956) Totalitarian dictatorship and autocracy, Harvard University Press, Cambridge (Mass.)

Hambly G (ed) (1966) Zentralasien. Fischer Weltgeschichte, vol. 16. Frankfurt/Main: Fischer, chapters 6–7

Imsand L (2013) Unverschleiert in Saudi–Arabien: Erlebnisse am Golf und in der Wüste. Axel Dielmann, Frankfurt

Linz J (1975) Totalitarian and Authoritarian regimes. In: Greenstein, Fred I, Polsby NW (eds) Handbook of political science, vol. 3, Macropolitical Theory. Reading (Mass.) and London: Addison-Wesley

Morgan ES (1958) The Puritan Dilemma. The story of John Winthrop. Harper Collins, New York

Scholl-Latour P (1988) Allah ist mit den Standhaften. Begegnungen mit der islamischen Revolution. Ullstein, Frankfurt/M und Berlin

Chapter 6
The Theory of Totalitarian Regimes, Part II: Stability, Further Development, and Demise

6.1 Development of Totalitarian Regimes Depending on the Universalism of Their Aims

Let us now turn to the question which developments have to be expected for totalitarian regimes in the long run once they have been established. In studying this question, we have to take into account that each ideology provides a more or less coherent and comprehensive Weltanschauung, or view of the world; and that this Weltanschauung may come into conflict with the true empirical nature of the world.

Thus it should be obvious that universal or universal dominance ideologies face nearly unsolvable problems in implementing their goals. Only in case they should gain secular power in a state belonging to the Great Powers or in very many states does a certain chance exist to conquer the world. But even then, as the examples of Nazi Germany and the Soviet Union show, the probability for such an event remains rather low.

The situation is similar for expansionary ideologies if their goals are not sufficiently limited. Rather unlimited expansionary goals were typical of Mexica and Inca ideologies and led their empires into deep trouble during the final decades of their existence

> The problems that beset the Mexica and Inca in the early sixteenth century were unforeseen long term consequences of the reforms instituted by the first imperial regimes. As the Aztec and Inca armies found themselves fighting farther and farther from their capitals, logistic difficulties arose. Overextended, vulnerable lines of supply and unfamiliar terrain… swelled the costs of long-distance campaigns while decreasing the rewards. In the mountainous Tarascan homeland of western Mexico and the Amazonian jungle east of the Andes, the imperial armies suffered appalling losses and came away with nothing (Conrad and Demarest 1988, p. 183).

Thus both empires were already severely weakened when they were conquered by the Spanish.

P. Bernholz, *Totalitarianism, Terrorism and Supreme Values*, Studies in Public Choice 33, DOI 10.1007/978-3-319-56907-9_6

But what happens to totalitarian regimes if the goals implied by their supreme values cannot be realized? In this case, four different paths may be taken (see right-hand side of Fig. 6.1). First, the totalitarian regimes may be defeated on the battlefield. In fact, this alternative is not improbable. For an ideology often engenders by its very nature in leaders and followers, especially of the first generation, the belief that supernatural powers, fate, or the forces of history are on their side and will guarantee victory over all enemies. Thus the leaders may take incredible risks in their foreign and military policies. Nazi Germany, the Khmer Rouge, and the Münster Anabaptists provide examples for such defeats of totalitarian regimes.

The second alternative is to postpone the realization of the ideological goals into a more distant future and to prepare militarily and by diplomacy for more auspicious days. This route will be taken probably by leaders of the second and following generations, who have distanced themselves from the ideology and thus taken a more realistic outlook. They may be encouraged to pursue such policies not only because they want to stay in power but also by the ideological belief that the opponents of the true creed must run into ever more severe difficulties and crises with the passing of time. The Soviet Union under Stalin and Brezhnev may serve as an example for such a reinterpretation of ideology implying a postponement of goals.

The third alternative which can only be taken after a long passage of time, or in a crisis, consists in a substantive reinterpretation of the supreme values of the ideology. This may happen, e.g., when it is realized by the leadership that the state(s) controlled by them is (are) too weak to ever having a chance of universal domination. Or leaders of a great power belonging to the second or to a later generation may perceive that they cannot defeat their opponents militarily or with the help of their ideology presently, and that the balance of military power is shifting against them because of an inferior performance of their economy. Note that the latter is probable to happen if the supreme values of the ideology call for much state intervention, a centrally planned or directed economy and/or the abolishment of private property, for price and profit controls, prohibition of interest, etc. In this case, leaders may want to engineer reforms from above, which is, however, not possible without a reinterpretation of the contents of the ideology. Examples are the reforms begun in China since 1979 by Deng and later by Gorbatshev. It should be mentioned, however, that the reform steps taken may not be adequate and thus remain without the intended success.

Finally, we should mention a fourth alternative which refers to a rather slow historical process. If the totalitarian regime is surrounded by economically more successful regimes (with free markets, rule of law and strong property rights), and if the regime cannot shield its inhabitants from the information coming from the outside world, then an erosion of the ideological values will take place. It seems obvious that this is especially likely for totalitarian regimes, which have already postponed their goals into the distant future. Such a development (corresponding to the fourth alternative) may also help to initiate the third alternative (Fig. 6.1).

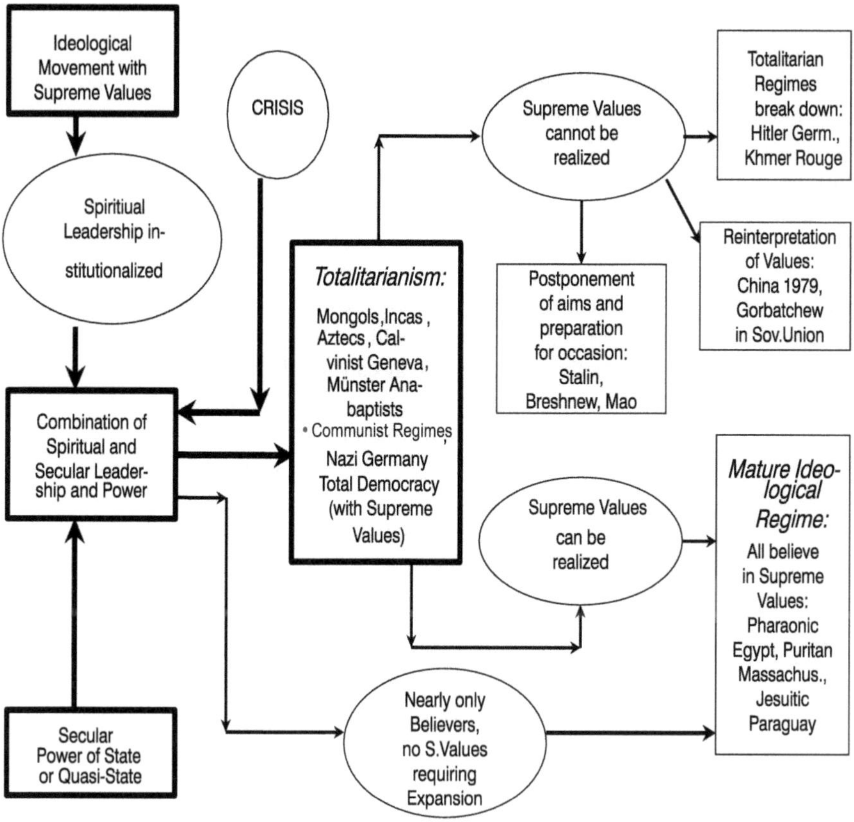

Fig. 6.1 The creation and development of totalitarian regimes

6.2 Development of Totalitarian Regimes After Reaching Their Aims

But what happens if the aims implied by the ideology can be and are realized after some time? It should be clear that in this case a situation will be reached which corresponds to a Mature Ideology. For then no expansionary goals remain which have still to be reached domestically as well as internationally. Thus the totalitarian regime turns into a rather stable, peaceful and mature ideocracy, if allowed by the outside world.

We have shown that the theory of totalitarianism presented can explain how and under which conditions totalitarian regimes arise, and what are the driving forces responsible for their establishment, their internal development and their characteristics, but also for their eventual demise. This theory has also allowed to show how mature ideocracies may develop out of totalitarian regimes or instead of them.

It has enabled us, moreover, to explain a number of historical cases which seemed for most researchers to lie outside the field of totalitarian phenomena.

In the end, we return to the question of what happens to ideological movements which do not succeed in gaining secular power or lose it. The answer is not difficult. If they are not totally suppressed, they may either still try to secure secular power by turning to terrorism or guerilla warfare. Or they have to adapt to the surrounding states and societies. In this case, they will become strong proponents of ideological tolerance (Bernholz 1994) and try to isolate themselves as much as possible from influences of their environment to preserve the purity of their creed. Even then an adaptation of some elements of their ideology which are strongly frowned on by society may be necessary. An example would be the polygamy of the Mormons.

Terrorist or guerilla activities after defeat can be observed, e.g., for the Khmer Rouge in Cambodia, but also for some branch of the Anabaptists after the Münster kingdom had been routed. On the other hand, Menno Simons, founder of the Mennonites, firmly (re)established the peaceful traditions of the Anabaptists (Stayer 1976, Chaps. 12 and 13).

The theory of terrorism inspired by supreme values will be discussed in Chap. 8.

References

Bernholz P (1994) Supreme values, tolerance and the constitution of liberty. In: Radnitzky G, Hardy B (eds) Values and the social order. Avebury Publishers, England

Conrad GW, Demarest AA (1988) Religion and empire. Cambridge University Press, Cambridge and New York

Stayer JM (1976) Anabaptists and the sword. Colorado Press, Lawrence (Kansas)

Chapter 7
The Constitution of Totalitarianism

7.1 Introduction

Can totalitarianism have a constitution or is this not a contradiction of terms? For does totalitarianism not substitute the rule of terror for the rule of law? (Arendt 1951). In the present chapter we are going to show that totalitarianism constitutes a rational system (as already discussed by Brzezinski 1956) which binds population and leaders by stable long-lasting rules, which form an unwritten or written constitution. It is exactly this constitutional trait of totalitarianism which is one of the main differences distinguishing it from dictatorship or tyranny, since the latter are characterized by the uncontrolled discretionary power of the tyrant.

If we abhor or distrust the idea that totalitarianism can have a constitutional system, this is due to our habit of equating constitutions with the constitutions of free societies deriving their legitimacy from the rights of sovereign individuals. Such constitutions protect the human rights of individuals and guarantee to citizens a domain free from interference within which they can decide according to their own preferences. A constitution of totalitarianism, on the contrary, is not derived from and legitimized by the postulate of sovereign, autonomous citizens. Its legitimacy and its rules are derived from supreme values which transcend individual freedom and individual preferences. Such a constitution does not lack reliable rules and even the rule of law is possible, or in certain respects, even necessary (this fact has been stressed by scholars studying constitutional law; see Böckenförde 1969, Sect. 3). But in contrast to the rule of law in a free society, this does not preclude terror. For the supreme values embodied in the constitution may demand individual sacrifices and the sacrifice of individuals. And individuals not prepared to suffer

This chapter is republished with permission from J.C.B. Mohr (Paul Siebeck). Original Publication: Bernholz, Peter (1991): The Constitution of Totalitarianism'. Journal of Institutional and Theoretical Economics 147(3), 425–440.

P. Bernholz, *Totalitarianism, Terrorism and Supreme Values*,
Studies in Public Choice 33, DOI 10.1007/978-3-319-56907-9_7

these sacrifices would violate the constitution or the laws consistent with it and might have to be forced by terror to comply.

The discussion of the constitution of totalitarianism not only allows to stress its differences from dictatorship and to demonstrate that there may be a whole range of more or less severe degrees of totalitarian regimes. For by contrasting such a constitution with that of a free society, it also allows light to be thrown on the necessary ingredients of the latter. The discussion of a totalitarian constitution may help us, moreover, to detect totalitarian traits in societies, and in their constitutions, which are presently considered to be free societies, but which may be in danger, because of these traits, of restricting or even losing their freedom in the future.

7.2 Supreme Values as a Basis for a Constitution

It has been shown in earlier chapters that an ideology postulating supreme values to which everything and everybody must be subordinated is a necessary condition for the development and existence of a totalitarian regime. Or as stated by Drath

> Thus the goal emerges as a primary phenomenon of totalitarianism to enforce a new social value system, which will be based even on metaphysics, and which determines its character and shapes its specifics (Drath 1958, 346).

The values postulated by the respective ideology or creed have to be preferred in the corresponding belief system to any other goal. They rank first on a lexicographic preference function, no substitution with other values or goals being allowed. As has been stated above, the supreme values may be of a religious or non-metaphysical nature.

As already mentioned before, the importance of an ideological system for totalitarianism has been early and widely stressed in the literature (Arendt 1951). Friedrich (1954) made it the first of five characteristic traits by which he defined a totalitarian society. The importance of this characteristic for a constitutional development in a totalitarian regime has, however, been overlooked and neglected. A totalitarian movement must, as its aim, achieve the goals postulated by its ideological system of supreme values. In consequence, after having gained governmental power, it has to introduce a written or unwritten constitution incorporating the corresponding aims and to construct a legal system requiring subjects to do everything necessary to promote them and to abstain from everything which hinders their fulfillment. Punishments and fines incorporated in the penal code must be severe enough to break any resistance. Since the basic ends and principles implied by the supreme values, such as the superiority of the Aryan race or of Communism, and the dangers threatening the goals of a "perfect" society, because of the machinations of the Jewish race or of Capitalists are indubitable and of a long-term nature, they must be crystallized into permanent and unchangeable rules of a constitution and legal system.

Some of these ideas were clearly expressed by Schmitt (1934, 203), when he defended Hitler's measures suppressing and eliminating the SA-leadership under Röhm in the so-called Röhm Putsch in 1934

> If the Führer demands … the liquidation of a gloomy period of German history, then this is also of juridical importance for our legal thinking, legal practice and the interpretation of laws. We must consider anew our traditional methods and ways of thinking, the dominant doctrines and the earlier decisions of the highest courts in all fields of law. We cannot follow blindly the legal concepts, arguments and precedents formed by an old and sick age.

Schmitt thus asks for a new legal and constitutional system incorporating supreme values. The latter becomes quite clear in the following quotation:

> II. The Führer protects law against the worst abuse if he directly creates law as the supreme judge by using the force of his leadership in the moment of danger … Indeed, the measures of the Fuhrer were genuine jurisdiction not subject to revision by the courts but themselves supreme jurisdiction. They were not the action of a republican dictator creating a fait accompli in a space free of law during a moment in which law closes her eyes … The jurisdiction of the Führer springs from the same source of law from which flows all the law of every people. In the strongest emergency the supreme law proves itself and there emerges the highest degree of a revenging realization of this law by jurisdiction. All law stems from the right of a nation to live. Each law of the state, each decision of a judge contains only so much law as flows into it from this source (Schmitt 1934, 200–201).

Moreover, the constitution of a totalitarian regime must define which people can be members of the community according to the supreme values. People who are not convertible to the creed, such as non-Aryans or capitalists, cannot be members. Rather, they are nonpersons who may only be tolerated as long as they, their possessions and their work, are useful for the attainment of the supreme values and as long as they do not endanger these goals. Also, constitutional rules must limit the rights and determine the duties of the members of the ideological community. The members must do everything necessary to promote, and avoid doing anything to harm, the goals postulated by the supreme values. They may even have to sacrifice their lives, not to speak of their possessions. Any loyalty to other people, creeds, or organizations must be subordinated to their loyalty to the true belief. All acts making it more difficult to promote the goals of the ideology are forbidden. Organizations, institutions, firms must if necessary be reshaped, to be founded or even to be dissolved to comply with and to further these goals. Members of the society are thus not citizens in the sense of a free society.

They enjoy freedom to decide according to their own wishes only in so far as their acts are neutral relative to the supreme values and do not limit their ability to serve the goals implied by these values. Individual freedom and human rights are subordinate to supreme values. Even more, individuals as members of the ideological society only have rights as far as they do not conflict with these values.

But this statement does not imply that an ideological society is a lawless society without a constitution. Quite the contrary: There are reliable rules and fundamental unchanging principles embodied in the constitution. Even the leaders of a totalitarian regime must comply with these fundamental principles, since the legitimacy of their rule rests on the acceptance of the supreme values (but see Sect. 7.4 for reasons of discretionary powers of leaders under totalitarianism). Leaders of totalitarian regimes thus face the danger of losing their powers if they do not comply with constitutional rules.

People not following the constitution or the laws implementing it face severe penalties. Each action hindering, or not dutifully promoting, the goals implied by the supreme values must be a severe crime. For it endangers the very ends of the ideological society which are sacrosanct and on which the legitimacy of rulers and the self-understanding of society is resting. Heretics to the creed are often worse than inconvertible pagans, since they may pose a great danger to the purity of faith and the coherence of society. Thus a different penal code may be applicable to them than to nonmembers of society. If the latter are inconvertible they even cannot become members. For the constitution and the laws, they may, but need not to be, merely objects. Specific laws may be applicable to them.

7.3 Islam and Christianity as Examples of Such Types of Constitutions

It is interesting to look at an example of such a legal system. In Islam, we find the following situation:

> … the country of this community was called the country of Islam … a country which should stretch over the whole world according to the commandment to fight all non-Muslims. The law of this state is the commandment of God as taught by Islam; its officers must protect and safeguard Islam. Everybody is a member of the Islamic community who has been born to Islamic parents or who professed to belong to Islam by speaking the testimonial word: 'I testify that there is no god besides the one God (Allah) and that Muhammad is his prophet…'
>
> The basic law from which all others derive is the organization of one's entire life according to the commandments of God. The actions committed or omitted by the mature Muslim in the possession of his full senses belong in each case to one of five classes: 1) Commands whose non-compliance will be punished; 2) meritorious acts, which will be rewarded, but the omission of which will not be punished; 3) forbidden actions which will be punished; 4) actions which are frowned upon but which are not punishable, and whose omission will be rewarded; 5) neutral acts which are neither punished nor rewarded (Meyers Konversationslexikon [1905, vol. 10, 48–49]).

Here we find all the elements discussed above: a legal system deriving its status from supreme values and with a permanent nature of basic rules and thus of a constitutional nature; a definition of members of the community; a different legal status for nonmembers; legal obligations and duties of members in the service of supreme values; a neutral domain, not covered by laws derived from supreme values, within which members are free to take their own decisions. Christian authorities took similar positions. For example, St. Augustin explained in one of his letters to the Donatists, who were North African heretics

> 5. As you see, you rise with force against the peace of Christ. Thus you are not suffering for Him but for your misdeeds. What a delusion that you can claim the glory of martyrdom in spite of your wicked life and your criminal acts, for which you are rightly punished. Consequently, if you coerce people in arbitrary audacity - how much more are we obliged to resist your frenzy with the help of the legal authorities, which God has subordinated to Christ in accordance with his earlier pronouncements. We are obliged to resist so as to free pitiable souls from your despotism, to cure them from a very old delusion and to accustom them to the light of the most manifest truth. For though you assert that we force people against their free will, it is true that many like to be forced, as they confess before and afterwards, since by this fact they escape from your oppression ….
>
> 12. Take note, that God Himself has truly spoken in this law through the heart of the king which rests in his hand. He has spoken in this law of which you assert that it has been enacted against you. Though, if you want to understand it, it has been enacted for your sake … (Augustinus [1878, vol. 7, 438–439, 444])

St. Ambrose has similar convictions. Concerning religious matters, the church is placed above imperial competence, and not vice versa. The emperor, as son of the church, owes obedience to it. He does not stand above the church, but is a member within its community. He is not allowed to assign churches to heretics (Epistulae 21, 4.9 ff.; 21, 36; 51, 12; 41, 27; 21, 2); for a general discussion, see Schilling 1923).

An episode which took place between St. Ambrose and the Roman Emperor Theodosius I, is revealing. In Callinicum in Mesopotamia, Christians had burned a synagogue. The emperor ordered the criminals to be severely punished and commanded the local bishop to restore the synagogue. Ambrose heard about this and wrote a lengthy letter to Theodosius asking him to pardon the guilty. A Christian emperor was not allowed to act as an advocate of the synagogue and to help the Jews to win a triumph against the Church (Ambrose, Epistula 40). When the emperor went to church the next time, St. Ambrose preached as to the necessity of what had been done, the glory of the Church, the abjectness of the synagogue and asked for pardon. He only continued the holy service after Theodosius had promised complete amnesty (Lietzmann 1976, 120; Jones 1966, 69). The attitude of St. Ambrose meant, of course, that Christians have the right or even the duty to destroy synagogues.

This interpretation is supported by a letter written some years earlier to emperor Valentinian III, in which St. Ambrose attempted successfully to prevent the reinstallation of the pagan Victoria altar in the Curia (the Roman Senate)

> Whereas all men … serve you, the emperors and masters of the earth, you yourself serve God and the holy creed … Everybody serves this true God. And he who accepts Him to honor Him with deep love, is not indifferent and tolerant, but zealous in his belief and his piety. If he is such a person, he cannot consent to the worship of the images of pagan gods and the cultivation of pagan customs (Ambrose, Epistula 17 in Klein 1972).

These positions were confirmed by Thomas Aquinas. According to him, stubborn *heretics* not prepared to repent and to forswear, must be left to the secular power, i.e., to be eliminated. For if their lives were saved, they might pervert others by infecting them with their beliefs or by returning to their heretical practices (Summa Theologica 2, 2 q. 11, a. 4; Chapter 9 X; De Haereticis 5, 7; see de Aquino

1933 sq.). Though milder against pagans, St. Thomas speaks out against tolerating the pagan cult (Summa Theologica 2, 2 q. 10, a. ll).

In these statements, proposals for a legal system derived from supreme values can once again be detected. The system is also supposed to be permanent and thus of a constitutional nature. Members of the community are defined and a different legal status given to nonbelievers, namely pagans, Jews and heretics. Members are supposed to have legal obligations and duties in the service of supreme values. It thus seems that the proposed system was never fully realized only because neither the pope nor the emperor, kings, or princes ever succeeded in uniting spiritual and secular power, and because their interests were usually in conflict.

In concluding this section, it should be stressed that all that has been demonstrated is that states dominated by a supreme value society will have a constitution and a reliable legal system, if the time in power allows their development. And since ideologies with supreme values are a necessary condition for a totalitarian regime, it follows that totalitarianism also will develop a constitution and a reliable legal system if its time in power permits. But it should also be obvious that the existence of a constitution and a legal system dominated by the supreme values of an ideological system do not imply the presence of totalitarianism. For the latter to exist, other conditions must be fulfilled, as has been discussed in earlier chapters.

7.4 The Importance of the Totalitarian Domain

A legal system and a constitution oriented toward supreme values are necessarily totalitarian in the sense that all human action or inaction relating to the ideological goals are subordinated by them to those supreme values. Persons have no rights which might conflict with these goals. So far as their behavior or inaction refers to supreme values they are merely instrumental in fulfilling their goals; they are totally dominated by them. But this is not true of actions which are neutral relative to the supreme values of their society. With respect to this "neutral domain," the constitution and the legal system are not dominated by ideological goals and may even grant individual freedom similar to that in a free society. Relative to this neutral domain, the legal system and the society are thus not totalitarian. Or, put differently, the "totalitarian domain" dominated by supreme values may be limited. This is an important insight. It shows that the degree of totalitarian dominance of supreme values in a society depends on the range of personal activities related to the goals implied by the former. We conclude that the very nature of supreme values in a society determines the extent of the "totalitarian" domain and that of the "neutral domain." From this viewpoint, a society may be more or less totalitarian. In fact, there may exist a continuum reaching from an absolutely free society with zero extent of the totalitarian domain and with a neutral domain covering the whole constitutional and legal system, to a regime in which no neutral but only a totalitarian domain exists and where the entire legal system and constitution and every aspect of human activity is dominated by an all-inclusive supreme value system.

Obviously, some previous students of totalitarianism have had a system in mind approaching the latter extreme when they spoke about this regime, e.g., Friedrich (1954, 52) refers to "an official body of doctrine covering all vital aspects of man's existence,..." And Leibholz (1954, 125–127) states

> The principle of total states knows of no limitation. There is no human being within the reach of the total state who can escape the grasp of this political power. All individuals are subjugated in all spheres of life to the leadership and control of the state no individual can possess any rights in a total state... The right to life also does not exist in a total state.

It should be clear from the above that the extension of the totalitarian domain is of the greatest importance for the question whether a totalitarian regime exists in a country or not. But it follows also that it may be difficult or even impossible to state at which point the extension of the totalitarian domain has passed the borderline towards a totalitarian regime.

7.5 Supreme Values and the Separation of Powers

The difficulties just discussed are increased by the fact that there exist at least two further dimensions which are also relevant for the degree of totalitarianism in a system. These are, first, the degree of the separation of powers in a country with a supreme value ideology; and second the substantive content of the respective supreme values. If there exists a separation of powers in the de facto constitution, the conflicts among different power holders may still limit the possibility of a total domination of people and of their use according to the supposed commands of supreme values, even in case of an unlimited totalitarian domain.

And if the respective supreme values imply the preservation of all human life and the well-being of all human beings, the obnoxious consequences attributed to totalitarianism need not follow, even if the totalitarian domain is unrestricted and no division of powers exists. In fact, such a situation may even be better than a benevolent dictatorship since the dictator is only bound by his own good intentions, whereas, in the benevolent regime with an unlimited totalitarian domain, the discretionary power of leaders is restricted by a constitution and a legal system embodying as rules the benevolent goals inherent in the supreme values.

To guarantee the rule of law to the fullest extent possible, a separation of governmental powers into legislative, administrative, and judicial authority seems to be necessary. Also, a division of powers in a federal system should be helpful. It is true that the concentration' of legislation, administration, and jurisdiction into one agency does not preclude that this agency is formally bound by and must follow, to a greater or lesser degree, the rules contained in the constitution. Especially if many of the members of a community share the values expressed by the constitutional rules, the agency risks losing legitimacy and popular support and encountering resistance if it openly violates the constitution.

This controlling force should be important in a society with a strong belief system in which the constitution embodies the goals of supreme values. But if all governmental powers are concentrated in one authority, this authority has the right to interpret the meaning of constitutional rules. It can promulgate new laws and change those laws and possibly those parts of the constitution which are not well-sanctified by the ideology. And in the absence of an independent judiciary, nobody can litigate to test whether administrative acts and orders or new laws are in compliance with the laws and constitutional rules. Thus without a separation of powers, the rule of law may still exist especially in a supreme value society, but this rule of law is severely limited.

Apart from the classical separation of powers, there may be another important division of power in societies dominated by supreme values. This is a division between priesthood or "ideology board" concerned with the correct interpretation of supreme values and a secular power pursuing the "ordinary" business of government. A system of supreme values consisting of sentences expressed in words can always be interpreted in different ways. This is already true for ordinary texts but acquires an additional importance in the lofty and abstract statements which make up ideological systems. But if there exists an ideology board wielding the spiritual monopoly power of correctly interpreting the supreme values, which is independent of the secular power, it must of necessity fulfill judicial functions and review not only the activities of ordinary members of society but also of the holders of secular power. For since supreme values are embodied in constitutional rules and laws, the board's interpretation of supreme values implies that it must also interpret the respective constitutional rules and laws. But if this is true, it must also judge whether the government has acted in a way corresponding to the correct interpretation of ideological goals.

A separation of powers in a society governed by supreme values is certainly a possibility. Historically, however, it seems to have developed only when a stalemate between different contenders for unlimited power emerged. For example, according to Canon Law "from the time of Gregory VII, the pope was the supreme legislator, the supreme administrator, the supreme judge" (Berman 1983, 206). And the pope also strove for secular power. Pope Boniface's famous bull Unam Sanctam claims

> … we learn from the words of the Gospel that in this church and in her power are two swords, the spiritual and the temporal. …Both are in the power of the Church … But the latter is to be used for the Church, the former by her; the former by the priest, the latter by kings and captains but at the will and by the permission of the priest… (quoted from Weber 1972, 226).

The popes, however, did not succeed in subordinating the princes and governments in Europe, and thus a separation of power between spiritual and secular authorities was maintained in Catholic medieval Europe. A similar separation of power seems to have existed in ancient Egypt, where the society was strongly oriented by supreme values and where a strong priesthood was influential and checked the power of the Pharaoh who, however, retained some religious functions.

In Sparta, we find a strong separation of powers in the (unwritten) so-called constitution of Lycurgus. Power was divided in an elaborate system of checks and balances between a popular assembly (apella), a council of elders (gerousia), a body of overseers (ephors) and two kings. On the other hand, the constitution seems to have been dominated by supreme values aiming at the preservation of the Spartan state and the dominance of the minority of Spartans as a ruling class. The majority of the population was either slaves (the helots) or at least not members of society (the perioeci), though the latter were free to engage in trade and commerce. This was not permitted to the members of society, the Spartans, whose whole life was regulated to make and keep them efficient members of the ruling military caste. Their personal interests were totally subordinated to those of the state and they lived most of their time in a kind of military camp (Rostovtzeff 1941, 218–227). It thus appears that Sparta provides the perfect example of a state and a constitution dominated by supreme values and with an extended totalitarian domain, but with a fully developed separation of power and even a democratic popular assembly with restricted powers reserved to Spartans.

We have seen that a society adhering to supreme values may develop a constitution providing for a separation of powers. But it is important to realize that there are several factors working strongly against this in such a society. First, there is a goal of preserving the purity of the creed. True believers among the leaders are very much concerned to preserve this purity. For this purpose, a unified authority (an "ideology board" or "spiritual college") is necessary to prevent different and wrong interpretations of the creed. But then this board must also be interested in suppressing and punishing heretical statements and actions. Nothing worse could happen than negligence on the part of the secular power in executing the demands of the ideology board or than itself engaging in heretical activities. Thus the members of the board have good reasons to strive for control of the secular power. Second, members of government holding secular power must be unhappy about what they may often perceive as unwarranted interference by the ideology board. Thus they have good reasons for trying to subordinate it to their control. Third, members of both authorities may simply want to extend their powers and thus try to combine them into one agency or to be in control of both. Fourth, if the supreme values call for an extension of the creed to other countries, or for expansionary policies, the concentration of power in one office may increase the potential of the state for expansion (unity of command). Fifth, the danger of a possible splitting-up of society into groups favoring different interpretations of supreme values (heretical movements) make a unified approach necessary in the eyes of both the spiritual and the secular leaders. To achieve this unified approach, both strive for control of the ideology board and secular government.

Finally, the more extended the totalitarian domain in a country, the more important it becomes for secular leaders to secure the right to interpret the contents of the supreme values. We have seen that leaders are bound by constitutional rules and laws oriented by supreme values. It follows, then, that their discretionary powers are the more limited, the more extended the totalitarian domain. As a consequence, the right to interpret supreme values becomes the more important for securing discretionary powers, the larger the totalitarian domain. Thus the more extended the latter, the more secular leaders will strive to control the ideology board.

Let us consider some examples. We have already seen that the popes attempted in vain to attain a concentration of powers. By contrast, the early Caliphs as successors of Muhammad as spiritual and temporal heads of Islam seem to have reached such a concentration of powers in their hands. Obviously no real separation of powers was preserved under National Socialism in Germany and under Communism in the Soviet Union.

Let us sum up: The greater the degree to which powers are separated, the less totalitarian is a regime and the stronger is the rule of law, even given an extended totalitarian domain. But societies instructed by supreme values show a tendency to remove or not to allow a separation of powers in their constitution. This tendency is the more pronounced the more extended the totalitarian domain and, because of the fourth point, the more the goals implied by the supreme values call for an outward expansion. A more or less pronounced separation of powers can only develop if a stalemate develops between different power centers in the country.

7.6 The Intensity of Ideocratic Demands

Even if the whole legal system, including the constitution, belonged to the totalitarian domain in a supreme value society, and even if no separation of powers were to exist, the substantive contents of supreme values could be such that no totalitarian regime would result. For if these substantive contents were not malevolent, in the sense that they did not ask for the sacrifice of the lives of members of the community, the persecution and/or killing of nonmembers or heretics, the conquest of foreign countries or the conversion by force of nonbelievers, then not all the characteristics usually used to define totalitarianism would be present.

> A system of terroristic police control … characteristically directed not only against demonstrable 'enemies' of the regime, but against arbitrarily selected classes of the population… (Friedrich 1954, 53) would not exist or would do so only to a limited extent. For less brutal means than outright terror, such as peer group pressure, fines, ideological propaganda, excommunication and threat of losing one's career, would be usually sufficient to achieve compliance with such less demanding goals of supreme values, at least if no other competing belief system strengthened the resistance of sectors of the population. In fact, a Mature Idiocrasy would have developed.

It follows that what we may call the "intensity of totalitarian demands" is another factor determining how totalitarian a regime is. Here, again, all degrees of intensity are possible, from zero intensity in a free society to the highest intensity measured for the respective individuals by certainty of death. For example, in the later years of National Socialism, in Communism under Stalin and in the Aztec Empire (compare Conrad and Demarest 1988) the probability of being killed approached certainty for Jews, for Capitalists or Bourgeois and for prisoners of war, respectively. The same was true for city dwellers under the Khmer Rouge in Cambodia. Except for the case of the Aztecs these people had to be eliminated to reach the supreme values, since they were inconvertible and dangerous to the implied goals. For the Aztecs, they had to be sacrificed to keep the world going (Conrad and Demarest 1988, 52).

Loss of life was also a probable event for opponents of these regimes. And even ordinary male members capable of military service faced a high risk of death in the expansionary wars fought by National Socialists and Incas to secure the territory for the selected race or needed for the ruling Inca (Conrad and Demarest 1988, 51) according to the supreme values of their ideologies. Similar dangers were faced by the Aztec warriors in the wars necessary to secure a sufficient supply of prisoners of war (Conrad and Demarest 1988, 52 sq.). Even Christians fought the crusades and killed tens of thousands of heretics and pagans (Lea 1988), whereas Muslims had to wage Holy Wars for the sake of spreading or defending the supreme values of their religion.

We are now able to identify again the necessary elements of the

Constitution of Totalitarianism: A totalitarian constitution is dominated by rules embodying the permanent goals of supreme values. It does not contain or contains only a weak separation of powers. Thus the rule of law is limited by the right of leaders to interpret the true meaning of constitutional or other legal statements. The totalitarian domain dominated by supreme values is nearly all-inclusive and the intensity of totalitarian demands sanctified by penal laws very strong.

Our analysis has shown that no clear-cut borderline exists telling us exactly where a totalitarian regime and a totalitarian constitution begin. The extent of totalitarian domain and the intensity of totalitarian demands are variables which can change nearly continuously. And even the separation of powers and, consequently, the rule of law can be stronger or weaker. This implies also that no revolution may be necessary to introduce totalitarianism, but that it can develop not only by a revolutionary change but also by a gradual or even a slow transition from a free or unfree society. More and more totalitarian elements may enter the constitution and legal system of a formerly free society, and the totalitarian domain and the intensity of totalitarian demands may slowly grow over time. But such a development is only possible if a supreme value system exists or comes into being, and if the implied goals are consciously or unconsciously adopted by a sufficient part of the population and in time preferred to individual freedom and autonomy.

7.7 Conclusions

It this chapter, we have shown that totalitarianism constitutes a rational system which binds population and leaders by stable long-lasting rules, which form an unwritten or written constitution. It is exactly this constitutional trait of totalitarianism based on supreme values which is one of the main differences distinguishing it from simple dictatorship or tyranny, since the latter are characterized by the uncontrolled discretionary power of the tyrant. Moreover, necessary elements of the Constitution of Totalitarianism are identified.

References

Arendt H (1951) The origins of totalitarianism. Harcourt, New York

Augustinus A (1978) Ausgewählte Schriften des hl. In: Augustinus A (ed) Valentin Thalhofer, Köln

Ambrosias, Sancti Ambrosia Mediolanum's Opera, Turnholti: Typogr. Brepols Editores Pontifici, Corpus Cristianorum, Series Latina

Berman HJ (1983) Law and revolution. Harvard University Press, Cambridge and London

Bernholz P (1992) Necessary Conditions for Totalitarianism. In: Radnitzky G, Bouillon H (eds) Ordnungstheorie und Ordnungspolitik. Springer, Heidelberg und Berlin

Böckenförde W (1969) Entstehung und Wandel des Rechtsstaatsbegriffs, pp 53–76, in: Festschrift für Adolf Arndt zum 65. Geburtstag, Frankfurt/Main 1969

Brzezinski Z (1956) Totalitarianism and rationality. Am Polit Sci Rev 50:751–763

Conrad G, Demarest A (1988) Religion and empire. Cambridge University Press, Cambridge

de Aquino T (1933 ff.) Die deutsche Thomas Ausgabe. Summa Theologica, Salzburg

Drath M (1958) "Einleitung" zu Richter E Macht ohne Mandat. Köln und Opladen, Westdeutscher Verlag. Reprinted in : Seidel B, Jenkner S (1968) Wege der Totalitarismus-Forschung. Darmstadt, Wissenschaftliche Buchgesellschaft, 310–358

Fiedrich CJ (1954) The unique character of totalitarian society. In: Friedrich Carl J (ed) Totalitarianism. Harvard University Press, Cambridge and London

Forsthoff E (1964) Begriff und Wesen des Sozialrechtsstaates. In: Rechtsstaat im Wandel, Stuttgart

Jones AHM (1975) The Decline of the Ancient World. Routledge, London and New York

Klein R (1972) Der Streit um den Victoriaaltar. Übersetzung und Erläuterungen, Darmstadt, Einführung, Text

Lea HC (1988) A history of the inquisition of the middle ages, 3 vols, Russel and Russel, London

Leibholz G (1954) Das Phänomen des totalen Staats. In: Festschrift für Herbert Kraus, Mensch und Staat in Recht und Geschichte, Kitzingen. Holzner

Lietzmann H (1976) Das Problem Staat und Kirche im Weströmischen Reich. In: Ruhbach G (ed) Die Kirche angesichts der konstantinischen Wende, Darmstadt, pp 112–121

Meyers Konversationslexikon (1905) Article "Islam;" Bibliographisches Institut·tut (vol. 10), Leipzig und Wien

Mussolini B (1929) Article "Fascismo". In: Enciclopedia Italiana, vol XIV, 7th edn. Milano and Roma

Rostovtzeff M (1941) *Geschichte der Alten Welt,* Wiesbaden. Dietrich. English: History of the Ancient World

Schilling O (1923) Die Staats- und Soziallehre des hl. Thomas von Aquin, Paderborn

Schmitt C (1934) Der Führer schützt das Recht. Reprint in: Schmitt. Carl [1940], Positionen und Begriffe, Hanseatische Verlagsanstalt, Hamburg

Weber E (1972) The western tradition. B.C. Heath & Co, Lexington and Toronto

Chapter 8
Terrorism as a Means to Win or to Regain Secular Power

8.1 Changes in the International Environment Furthering Terror

In our view, there have been two important developments in recent decades, which are bound to increase the probability of terrorism: First, technological innovations in the instruments of warfare, and second, changes which occurred in the international political system. The development of nuclear weapons and of intercontinental missiles makes it impossible for rational leaders of countries owning them to employ them against each other. This is also often true for their application against states not possessing such weapons. For they may be supported by other essential actors such that the risk of an escalation into an atomic war is too high. As I pointed out 20 years ago (Bernholz 1985, 201):

> ...because of this stalemate wars against non-essential states, possibly not with an actor's own troops but with those of a satellite, guerilla wars, ideological and economic warfare, terrorism and revolution will be more and more prominently employed by members of the new balance of power system [the rise of which I then envisaged and even now envisage as a future possible development].

Because of the superiority in modern arms, even excluding atomic weapons, of leading industrialized countries, it is also true that other states, and even more so organized non-state actors have no other possibility than to turn to revolution, guerilla warfare, and terrorism to promote their aims or to seek relief for their grievances in the face of superior powers. In doing so, weaker states have to camouflage such activities, and non-state actors have to hide in the general population or in inaccessible areas to preserve their striking capabilities. On the other hand, modern technological developments have provided such states and organi-

---

This chapter is republished with permission from Elsevier. Original Publication: Bernholz, Peter (2004): "Supreme Values and Terrorism". European Journal of Political Economy 20(2), 2004, 317–333.

P. Bernholz, *Totalitarianism, Terrorism and Supreme Values*,
Studies in Public Choice 33, DOI 10.1007/978-3-319-56907-9_8

zations with several kinds of cheap arms capable to work terrible local destruction. Moreover, highly developed countries are rather vulnerable against terrorist acts. Networks of electricity or water supply, of transportation and communication can be badly hurt if they are centrally organized, that is if they are connected in central knots. Any strong centralization of activities offers a valuable target. And the development of modern means of communication provides the organizers of such acts not only with a broad echo through the mass media, but also with an easy way to coordinate their actions.

Next, let us consider the changes in the international political system furthering terrorist activities. Before the two world wars, an international Balance of Power System comprising seven great powers existed. This ended with World War II, which led to a Bipolar System containing the USA and the Soviet Union. Finally, the Soviet Union broke down around 1990 because of the inferiority of its economic system and its closed state-dominated society, so that the USA remained as the only superpower.

But why did these events change the direction and the kind of terrorism? First, in a system of several great powers the grievances perceived by smaller states or by specific groups and organizations are usually referring to one or the other of these powers. Even if the groups and organizations direct their complaints against their own nation or against neighboring countries not belonging to the great powers, they often see a relationship of them to the latter, and believe that their own governments are dominated by or are just puppets of them. But since there exist several essential actors, the repugnance, hate, and ill-feelings are not concentrated on just one of them. This changed already with the development of the bipolar system. Here the temptation was great to identify with the ideologies of one of them, and to direct the hateful actions against the other. It is thus not surprising that many governments, like Nasser's in Egypt, and organizations accepted and adopted the communist or socialist ideology of the Soviet Union, or followed a path more related to the USA. Consequently, it was true until 1970s that

> Although terrorists are found among adherents of almost every brand of left-wing or right-wing ideology, the overwhelming majority of today's terrorists can be described as leftist. Most have a New Left or Trotskyist character (Sobel 1975, p. 6).

This changed at least with the breakdown of the Soviet Bloc. The communist ideology has lost much of its attractiveness because of its failure. This provided a chance for other ideologies to become influential in states supporting terrorist groups or in organizations willing to use terrorism.

Moreover, with only the USA remaining as a superpower with an average per capita income far above that of most other countries, it is not surprising that most of the grievances of the elites of many countries and of many organizations are now directed against this country and its supporters. It remains to be seen how a future change to another balance of power system with several new Great Powers like China will change this situation.

8.2 How to Apply Terrorism to Reach the Desired Aims

The changed conditions for terrorism because of the superiority of leading countries in modern arms have been early recognized by terrorists:

> The old method of guerilla warfare, as carried out from the hills and countryside, would be ineffective in a powerful country like the USA … The new concept [of revolution] is to huddle as close to the enemy as possible to neutralize his modern and fierce weapons. The new concept creates conditions that involve the total community, whether they want to be involved or not. (American black militant Robert Williams, February 1964 issue of his publication The Crusader, quoted from Sobel 1975, p. 4.)

First, however, it has to be explored what should be understood by terrorism:

> Terrorism is an action, usually involving the placement of a bomb or fire explosion of great destructive power, which is capable of effecting irreparable loss against the enemy…. (Brazilian revolutionary Carlos Marighella in his 1967 Minimanual of the Urban Guerilla, quoted from Sobel 1975, p. 5)

A more general definition of terrorism is attempted by Hoffman after a discussion comprising a whole chapter (Hoffman 1998, p. 43 f.):

> All terrorist acts involve violence or the threat of violence. Terrorism is specifically designed to have far-reaching psychological effects … It is meant to instill fear within, and thereby intimidate, a wider 'target audience' that might include a rival ethnic or religious group, an entire country, a national government or political party, or public opinion in general. Terrorism is designed to create power where there is none or to consolidate power where there is very little.

We are interested in what happens to ideological movements that do not succeed in obtaining secular power. Or to those which do not accomplish their goals, or lose secular power. In a previous paper (Bernholz 1997), I have argued that:

> First, some [ideological movements] may turn to armed resistance, intimidation of the population or to terrorism, especially if they are suppressed or persecuted by government(s). They may do so either just to preserve their existence or in the hope of conquering government power later on…. Second, especially if armed resistance, intimidation and terrorism prove unsuccessful or/and if the societal environment is more beneficial, the ideological movement may change or reinterpret some of its values so that it is tolerated…. Third, the ideological community may decide to emigrate to more favorable environments if they see no end to suppression and persecution in their homeland….

Let us turn now to terrorism, given these perspectives. We note first that in the self-understanding of the ideological movement, acts branded by the outside world as acts of terror are altruistic deeds to serve the aims implied by the supreme values. It follows that true believers are not criminals but self-denying idealistic or holy men or women sacrificing a comfortable life, a career or even their lives in the service of the most valuable and truthful goals. The reward will be reaped either in the world beyond or consists in the knowledge that they contribute to a future better world. An individual following the supreme goals of an ideocratic movement is therefore often considered to be an idealist, or even a saint. Most outsiders, in particular as victims, will however regard adherence to the goals as sinful and/or following the lexicographic preference ordering for the supreme values as irrational or insane.

Terrorism based on an ideology with supreme values usually leads into deep, fundamental conflict. For the true believer, fighting is not just about some other human beings, but about the embodied forces of evil who are bent to resist or even to obliterate the true creed and its beneficial consequences promised by the ideology. The true believer tries to prevent the victory of these forces, to overcome them, and to establish the supreme values embodied in the ideology.

Third, the world view contained in the ideology depicts an image of the outside world that may be strongly at odds with a scientific perception and also with the understanding of the common people who are not believers of the creed. And if two or more ideologies vie with each other, they may all have a distorted view of each other, which embitters more the conflict between the different movements and often makes reconciliation impossible.

Fourth, the distorted world view of the ideological movement may also lead to an exaggerated vision of its capabilities to overcome the forces of organized states, and of achieving the ideological aims. This increases willingness to use terrorism, and leads to extended resistance by the true believers before the victims can wipe them out.

The use of terror by ideological movements oriented by supreme values is not a new phenomenon. The *assassins*, a Shiite Muslim sect, who fought the Seljuq Empire and the Christian Crusaders, were an early example. The same is true for the *thugs,* an Indian sect sacrificing human beings to the goddess Kali, who were finally suppressed by the British in India in the first half of the nineteenth century. The Jewish Zealots and Sicarii should also be mentioned. They played leading roles in the insurrection against the Romans which ended with the Roman occupation of Jerusalem and the fall of Masada after the defenders had committed suicide (for an excellent description of these sects, their religious motivation and methods see Rapoport 1984).

The *Red Army Fraction* in Germany and the *Red Brigades* in Italy are more recent examples. In more recent times, Maoists were fighting the government in Nepal. Islamic fundamentalists oppose the governments of Algiers and Egypt. Islamic terror is being used against Jews in Israel, against Christians in Pakistan, the southern Philippines and in different parts of Indonesia, and by Hindus against Muslims in Northwestern India. Islamic terror has been used against the United States on a number of occasions, culminating in the events of September 11, 2001.

8.3 Supreme Values as a Basis for Terror

Several writers have well described the use of terror-based on religious beliefs (Rapoport 1984; Hoffman 1998, Chap. 4; Hubback 1997). But these authors do not offer a general theory comprising terrorism, ideocracies, and totalitarianism as all are based on secular and non-secular ideologies with supreme values. Hoffman even differentiates between religiously and ideologically motivated terrorism (p. 90). Hubback mentions Communism and Nazism only just in passing:

> In the 20th century political ideology adopted the language of doomsday religion with catastrophic results around the world (p. 2).

Rapoport rightly rejects the view that terrorism is a modern phenomenon caused by the developments of technology,

> since weapons are cheaper, more destructive, easier to obtain and to conceal. (1984, p. 658 f.)

He also realizes that

> Since doctrine, rather than technology, is the ultimate source of terror, the analysis of modern forms must begin with the French, rather the Industrial Revolution." (p. 672)

But in spite of these insights Rapoport, like the other political scientists mentioned above, does not see the relationship between totalitarianism or, more generally, ideocracies and terrorism as being both based on ideologies with supreme values, though he even mentions that the assassins were supported by a kind of state they had created. Not surprisingly, all these scholars have no idea of a lexicographic preference ordering demanded by the respective religious or secular creeds.

Historically, there have been terrorist or guerilla activities after the defeat of a totalitarian regime, e.g., by the *Khmer Rouge* in Cambodia and by a branch of the *Anabaptists* after the Muenster kingdom had been routed (Stayer 1976, Chaps. 12 and 13). The defeated Taliban in Afghanistan have been able to maintain an ideological movement that commits terrorist acts.

Quite independently of ideological movements based on supreme values, an increase of terrorist activities has to be expected, for another reason. The effectiveness of modern weapons limits warfare opportunities,[1] and terrorists hide for protection among the general population. It was a mistake of the Taliban government that it committed itself to the protection of Osama bin Laden, though it had no nuclear weapons available and dominated a country that could be the target of modern weapons.

The empirical evidence seems to show that the number of terrorist acts in the period from 1968 to 2002 moved cyclically (Sandler and Enders 2002, Table 1, with figures provided by the US State Department). But the local maxima of the number of deaths caused by terrorist acts increased with the passage of time. They amounted to 311 in 1974, 697 in 1979, rose to 2272 in 1987, and to more than 3000 in 2001.

[1]Nuclear weapons can only be used if the attacker cannot be wiped out after using them himself (Bernholz 1985, 200 f.). This was the basis of the Cold War stalemate and absence of war between the Soviet Union and the USA.

8.4 Religious Fundamentalism as a Source of Terror

Until the 1970s it was true that

> Although terrorists are found among adherents of almost every brand of left-wing or right-wing ideology, the overwhelming majority of today's terrorists can be described as leftist. Most have a New Left or Trotskyist character (Sobel 1975, p. 6).

This has changed since then, and Hoffman (1998, 90 f.) states that

> … while the re-emergence of modern religious terrorism was initially closely associated with the Islamic revolution in Iran, within a decade of that event none of the world's major religions could claim to be immune to the same volatile mixture of faith, fanaticism and violence.…
>
> Significantly, during the 1990s the growth in the number of religious terrorist groups as a proportion of all active international terrorist organizations has not only continued but increased appreciably. In 1994, for example, a third (sixteen) of the forty-nine identifiable international terrorist groups active that year could be classified as religious in character and/or motivation; and in 1995, the most recent year for which complete statistics are available, their number grew yet again, to account for nearly half (twenty-six, or 46 per cent) of the fifty-six known, active international groups.

Today many people are especially afraid of terrorist attacks based on Islamic ideology. Islam has seen several revivals of fundamentalism during history, in which its supreme values were reinterpreted as demanding a holy war against pagans, and even against the Jewish and Christian book religions. It is, however, important to stress that this is not a specific trait of Islam. An example is the sarin nerve gas attack by the Aum sect in the Tokyo subway system in 1994. The Aum sect was founded in 1988 and combines Buddhist and Hindu beliefs (Hubback 1997, 19 f.). Christianity has seen similar fundamentalist revivals during its long history, which led to the persecution of pagans after the Roman emperors had been converted, to the crusades, to the persecution of the Cathars, and to the bloody religious wars among different Christian denominations, as between Catholics and Huguenots in sixteenth century France, or the Thirty Years War between Catholics and Protestants. One quotation from the famous speech of Pope Urban II to crusaders at the Council of Clermont in 1095 reveals the aims implied by the respective interpretation of the supreme Christian values:

> Let the deeds of your ancestors move you … and of your other kings, who have de-stroyed the kingdoms of the pagans, and have extended in these lands the territory of the holy church. Let the holy sepulcher of the Lord of our Savior, which is possessed by unclean nations, especially incite you, and the holy places which are now treated with ignominy and irreverently polluted with their filthiness. …But if you are hindered by love of children, parents and wives, remember what the Lord says in the Gospel, 'He that loveth father or mother more than me, is not worthy of me.' … Enter upon the road to the Holy Sepulcher; wrest land from the wicked race, and subject it to yourselves. … undertake this journey for the remission of your sins, with the assurance of the imperishable glory of the kingdom of heaven (quoted from Weber 1972, p. 248 seq.)

Not only religious ideologies call for a holy war against infidels and opponents and for the application of terror, if necessary. The same is the case for ideologies with non-metaphysical supreme values like Communism. It is interesting that Lenin called for acts of terrorism after the Communist revolution in Russia of 1905 had failed:

> It horrifies me to find that there has been talk about bombs for over six months, yet not one has been made! … Form fighting squads at once everywhere, among the students, and especially among the workers, etc. Let groups be at once organized at three, ten, thirty, etc., persons. Let them arm themselves at once as best they can, be it with a revolver, a knife, a rag soaked in kerosene for starting fires. …Some may at once undertake to kill a spy or blow up a police station, others to raid a bank to confiscate funds for the insurrection, others again may drill or prepare plans of localities, etc. (Letter of October 5, 1905, to the St. Petersburg Committee).

Let us turn now to Islam, and begin with a classical statement by the famous scholar Ibn Khaldûn, who lived around 1400:

> In the Muslim community, the holy war is a religious duty, because of the universalism of the (Muslim) mission and (the obligation to) convert everybody to Islam either by persuasion or by force. Therefore, caliphate and royal authority are united in (Islam), so that the person in charge can devote the available strength to both of them at the same time (Ibn Khaldûn, vol. 1, p. 473, 1967).

This interpretation of the supreme values of Islam has been sharpened by other scholars, including modern ones. Let us first quote the scholar Ibn Taymiyyah, who lived from 1263 to 1328, when the Mongols under Timur attacked Damascus:

> The command to participate in jihad and the mention of its merits occur innumerable times in the Koran and the Sunna. Therefore, it is the best voluntary [religious] act that man can perform … Jihad implies all kinds of worship … Since lawful warfare is essentially jihad and since its aim is that the religion is God's entirely and God's word is uppermost, therefore according to all Muslims, those who stand in the way of this aim must be fought. (Quoted in Peters 1996, pp. 47–49)

The Indian Islamist Mawdudi (1903–1979) expressed his interpretation as follows:

> Islam … wants and requires the entire inhabited world. It does not want this in order that one nation dominates the earth and monopolizes its sources of wealth, after having taken them away from one or more other nations. No, Islam wants and requires the earth in order that the human race altogether can enjoy the concept and practical program of human happiness, by means of which God has honored Islam and put it above the other religions and laws. In order to realize this lofty desire, Islam wants to employ all forces and means that can be employed for bringing about a universal all-embracing revolution. … This far-reaching struggle that continuously exhausts all forces and this employment of all possible means are called jihad. (Quoted by Peters 1996, p. 128.)

We finally quote Sayyid Qutb, 1906–1966, an Egyptian and a member of the Muslim Brotherhood, who was a prominent Islamic figure, and was tortured and executed by Nasser's regime:

> If we look at the sources and foundations of modern ways of living, it becomes clear that the whole world is steeped in Jahiliyah (pagan ignorance of divine guidance), and all the marvelous material comforts and high-level inventions do not diminish this ignorance. This Jahiliyah is based on rebellion against God's sovereignty on earth: It transfers to man one of the greatest attributes of God, namely sovereignty, and makes some men lords over others. It … takes the form of claiming that the right to create values, to legislate rules of collective behavior, and to choose any way of life rests with men, without regard to what God has prescribed. … The Islamic civilization can take various forms …, but the principles and values on which it is based are eternal … the worship of God alone, … the supremacy of the humanity of man over material things, … and the control of animalistic desires, respect for the family, the assumption of the vice-regency of God on earth according to His guidance and instruction, … the rule of God's law [al-Sharia] …

Given these interpretations of the Islamic creed, the following statement by Osama bin Laden should not come as a surprise:

> In the name of Allah Most Gracious Most Merciful, Sunday, 6 Rajab 1422 (Sep. 23, 2001). … To our Muslim brothers in Pakistan: Peace be upon you and the mercy of Allah and his blessings; I received with great Sorrow the news of the murder of some of our Muslim brothers in Karachi while they were expressing their opposition to the American crusade forces and their allies … We ask Allah to accept them as martyrs and include them with prophets, their followers, martyrs, … It is no wonder that the Muslim nation in Pakistan would rush to defend its Islam, since it is considered the first line of defense for Islam in this area, just like Afghanistan was the first line of defense for itself and for Pakistan before the Russian invasion.
>
> We hope that these brothers are among the first martyrs in Islam's battle in this era against the new Christian-Jewish crusade led by the big crusader Bush under the flag of the Cross, this battle is considered one of Islam's battles, …The Prophet, Peace Be Upon Him, said: 'Whoever did not fight, or prepare a fighter, or take good care of a fighter's family, Allah will strike him with a catastrophe before Judgment Day'.
>
> I announce to you the good news … that we are steadfast on the path of Jihad for the sake of Allah … with the heroic faithful Afghan people, under the leadership of our fighter emir, who is proud of his religion, the prince of the faithful. Mullah Mohammed Omar. We ask Allah to make him victorious over the forces of infidels and tyranny, and to crush the new Christian-Jewish crusade on the land of Pakistan and Afghanistan. If Allah makes you victorious, none will defeat you and if He fails you, who after Him will make you victorious and on Allah the faithful shall trust.

Your brother in Islam, Osama bin Mohammad bin Laden

(Wall Street Journal Europe, September 25, 2001. Provided to Qatar's El-Jazeera satellite channel Monday, September 24, 2002.).

Several points in this statement merit attention:

1. There is a Jewish-Christian crusade that is taking place led by President Bush under the flag of the cross against Afghanistan and Pakistan.
2. Even the adherents of the book religions, that is, Jews and Christians, are called infidels.

3. The jihad has to be fought against them and all faithful dying in this fight are martyrs for the sake of Allah.
4. The phrase "If Allah makes you victorious, none will defeat you" shows a certain unrealistic evaluation of the relative power of the parties involved in the Afghan war.

8.5 Terrorism and Supreme Values

The presence of ideologies with supreme values greatly increases the danger of terrorism for several reasons:

First, true believers are prepared to sacrifice not only the lives of others but also their own lives in following the demands of their creed. This makes it very difficult to protect targeted objects or persons against terror attacks.

Second, true believers are idealists and experience no guilt feelings when planning to commit terrorist acts. The absence of guilt makes them more determined to execute their or their leaders' designs.

Third, true believers are convinced that their good cause will eventually win since the supreme values of their ideology are superior to anything else and absolutely true.

Fourth, they believe that "innocent victims" are pagans or heretics, for as such are the victims defined through the supreme values of their ideology. As a consequence, they feel no qualms in killing their victims.

Fifth, the evidence is clear from recorded interviews that the families of true believers are pleased that their children have had the opportunity for martyrdom, and that mothers offer other children as candidates for achieving the same glory.

Sixth, the core of the true believers and their intellectual leaders come mostly from middle class or wealthy families. They have studied, know the ways of their opponents, and have the economic and technical means to prepare efficiently their terrorist acts. It is therefore not poverty that breeds the ideologies,[2] their inventors and innovators, and their leading personalities, though a crisis stemming from increasing poverty may attract a mass following for the ideology.

Finally, the way of life of nonbelievers often contradicts the demands of the true creed. The secular nature of Western countries, their materialism, the taking of interest, the viewed immoral behavior of women through mode of dress, and open interaction with men in conversations and personal meetings, and other unwarranted freedoms given to women, and the toleration of homosexual practices are for instance anathema to Islam.

Democratic rule is only tolerable if it is used by true believers to fulfill the commands of God. Otherwise it implies

> Jahiliyah (which is the Islamic term for any system not based on Divine revelation) (Qutb 2001, p. 31).

[2]Compare the empirical study by Krueger and Maleckova (2002).

For

> Jahiliyah means that people are ruled by people, because this signifies that they submit to one another. They refuse to submit to God alone and reject His Godhead, acknowledging instead that some human beings have qualities of Godhead and hence they submit to their authority (p. 133).

And now the West, with its superior economic and military strength, its domination of the mass media, is even invading the earlier strongholds of Islam and corrupting its adherents. Moreover, many rulers of Islamic countries are not following the commands of the sharia, and have introduced secular law. It follows that true believers have not only the right and the duty to fight the infidels, but also their own heretic governments.

The tasks to be accomplished are thus extensive. Not only heretic governments have to be overthrown and their supporters to be killed. Besides that, the Western powers have to be broken, their economies to be wrecked, and their governments to be revealed as impotent to protect their citizens, with the aim to turn them into true believers.

All this asks for decisive terrorist acts, against important symbols of the enemy and against the very centers of their political, military, and economic strength. All attacks that are highly visible and covered by the mass media are very attractive.

8.6 An Economic Model of Ideologically Based Terrorism*

8.6.1 The Model

In this section, an economic model is presented to deduce certain characteristics of terrorism and its consequences. But in contrast to other economic models, it includes a utility function of a representative believer which takes into account the aims of terrorists to change society. This means that we assume that all believers have identical preferences and are potential terrorists. It is well known that lexicographic preferences as well as utility have been widely discussed in the literature. In the subsequent approach a Cobb-Douglas utility function is introduced. Given this function, it is possible to asymptotically approach the lexicographic ordering postulated by a supreme value by increasing the respective power asymptotically to one. As documented above, Islamic like (formerly) Christian or Communist ideologies demand that all people on earth are converted to the right creed or that people which cannot be converted are subjugated or removed. As a consequence, these ideologies aim at increasing the share of believers in total population, a fraction which we may call y and define as B/N, where B is the number of believers and N that of the total population. Alternatively, y could describe the probability to reach secular power and to establish an ideocracy.

The size of y depends on the application of terrorist acts committed with two different kinds of instruments, whose quantities are denoted by T_1 and T_2. Two production functions describe the technical relationships and efficiency in influencing y with these instruments. For simplicity, we will call the application of the quantities of these instruments the number of the corresponding terrorist acts committed. T_1 and T_2 are produced with the help of capital C_i and labor $L_i (i = 1, 2)$ by using a Cobb-Douglas production function and can be bought in the markets by terrorists at prices p_1, p_2. The prices of capital and labor are denoted by r and w, respectively. The costs K for buying the terrorist instruments have to be borne by the B believers out of their identical incomes v, out of which they have also to buy the only consumption good x at the normalized price 1. This is done by applying a voluntary tax rate t. Perfect competition is assumed for the markets. From these assumptions we can formulate the following model:

$U = Ax^{1-\beta}y^{\beta} = \max!$ Utility function of representative believer which has to be maximized. (8.1)

$x = (1-t)v$ Expenditure of believer on consumption good; (8.2)

$K = Btv$ Expenditures spent by all B believers on buying terrorist instruments in quantities. T_1, T_2. (8.3)

$\mathrm{K} = p_1T_1 + p_2T_2$ Costs of buying terrorist instruments (= expenditures of believers) (8.4)

$y_1 = (1 + T_1^{\varepsilon})b$ Influence on ideological aim by applying first terrorist instrument. (8.5)

$y_2 = (1 + T_2^{\mu})b$ Influence on ideological aim by applying second terrorist instrument. (8.6)

Both influences determine the size of

$$y = y_1 + y_2 \tag{8.7}$$

If y is interpreted as the share of believers in the population B/N after the terrorist acts have been performed, then b has to be thought of as the share $B(0)/N(0)$ of believers before the acts are taken. This means that this share remains constant if no terrorist acts are implemented.

Let us turn now to the production functions for the terrorist instruments:

$$T_i = k_iL_i^{1-\alpha}C_i^{\alpha} \quad (i = 1, 2) \tag{8.8}$$

$$E_i = wL_i + rC_i \quad \text{Expenditures for labor and capital} \tag{8.9}$$

$$G_i = p_i T_i - E = \max! \quad \text{Profit functions to be maximized.} \tag{8.10}$$

This system of equations can be solved and used to derive demand and supply curves for the consumption good and the ideological aim, and also for the terrorist instruments (or acts). By using comparative statics, the influence of the intensity of ideological beliefs and of the efficiency of the terrorist instruments, for instance because of defensive measures, can be deduced.

8.6.2 The Demand for the Ideological Good and the Consumption Good

Let us first examine, how the intensity of ideological beliefs influences the demands for the ideological good and the consumption good of the representative believer. We can do this by increasing beta in Eq. (8.1) and by consolidating restrictions (8.2)–(8.7) into a budget curve. If beta is moving closely to one, we are approaching a lexicographic preference ordering for the supreme value denoted by *y*. For if beta equals one, a zero amount of the consumption good is demanded. This can be interpreted as the believers' willingness to sacrifice his life in the terrorist acts. Figure 8.1 sketches the corresponding relationships. *y* is depicted on the vertical, *x* on the horizontal axis. The second figure after the *x* in the *j* functions denotes the value of beta. With increasing values for beta the demand for *y* rises and that for *x* falls. The blue indifference curve is sketched with a beta = 0.999, a figure which closely approximates a lexicographic preference function. The believer is prepared to sacrifice his life in this case, since he foregoes to demand any amounts of the consumption good.

It is interesting to see the demand curve for terrorists instruments (acts), let us say for the first of them, T_1, depending on its price in the market, p_1 and the intensity of the ideological belief, as represented by β. If we add the supply curve, derived from Eqs. (8.8) to (8.10), we also get the corresponding equilibrium values for T_1, p_1 as depending on β.

As a consequence, the number of terrorist instruments demanded and supplied, and thus the number of terrorist acts committed, increases with the intensity of ideological belief. The equilibrium price for the instrument rises. It also follows also that the demand for terrorist acts decreases with a rising price of the instrument, even for high intensities of the ideological belief.

It is another important question, how demand for the ideological aim *y* and for terrorist instruments (acts) develops with income. As can be seen from Fig. 8.2, both rise with the income of believers (given by the numbers in the *g* function).

As can be seen from Fig. 8.2, the demand rises with income both for the consumption good and the ideological aim. Our assumptions imply that none is an inferior good. The figures after the *x* in the *g* function denote the size of the

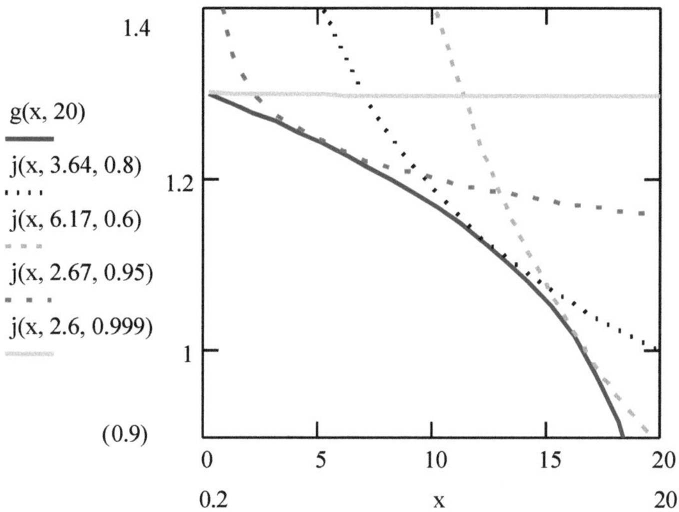

Fig. 8.1 Demand for *x* and *y* depending on strength of ideological belief, represented by size of β

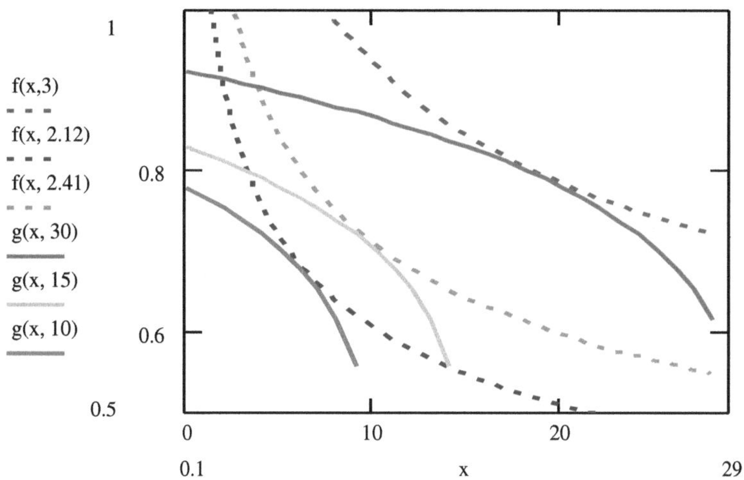

Fig. 8.2 Demand for the consumption good and the ideological aim depending on the size of income

individual income. It follows that with rising demand for the ideological good, the demand and therefore the equilibrium values for the terrorist instruments (acts) rise, too (Fig. 8.3). This result contrasts strongly with the usual assumption that terrorism is the result of abject poverty.

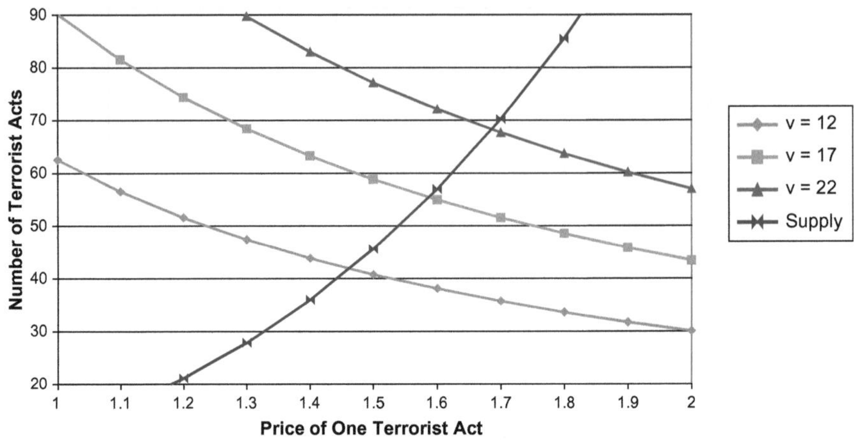

Fig. 8.3 Number of terrorist acts depending on income *v*

8.6.3 Measures to Defend Against Terrorism

Several economists have presented valuable contributions to the question of defensive measures against terrorism and their consequences and problems (for contributions see Sandler and Enders 2002). Not surprisingly, our model replicates some of these results. We do, however, not go into the strategic, game theoretical aspects of the interplay between terrorists and defenders. On the other hand, out model helps to draw attention to the widely neglected spiritual battle.

Defensive measures can first be directed against the efficiency of terrorist acts in reaching their aims by making the targets less vulnerable, by better guarding them and by reducing their psychological effect by reducing the coverage they get through the mass media. The measures can, secondly, be aimed at reducing the availability of terrorist instruments, for instance by controlling their production or by export controls. Finally, efforts can be made to change the preferences of present and especially potential future believers of the ideology, and to reduce their capabilities to win converts.

The first set of measures can be analyzed in the model by reducing ε, μ in Eqs. (8.5) and (8.6). It is sufficient to look at the consequences of decreasing the former (Fig. 8.4). As would be expected by any economist, the number of terrorist instruments bought and applied decreases with a reduced efficiency or rising difficulty of their application, as measured by lowering ε.

As would be expected by any economist, the number of terrorist instruments bought and applied decreases with a reduced efficiency or rising difficulty of their application, as measured by lowering ε.

But let us not forget that an important cause for the number of terrorist acts is income. According to the economic model, a reduction of income would decrease

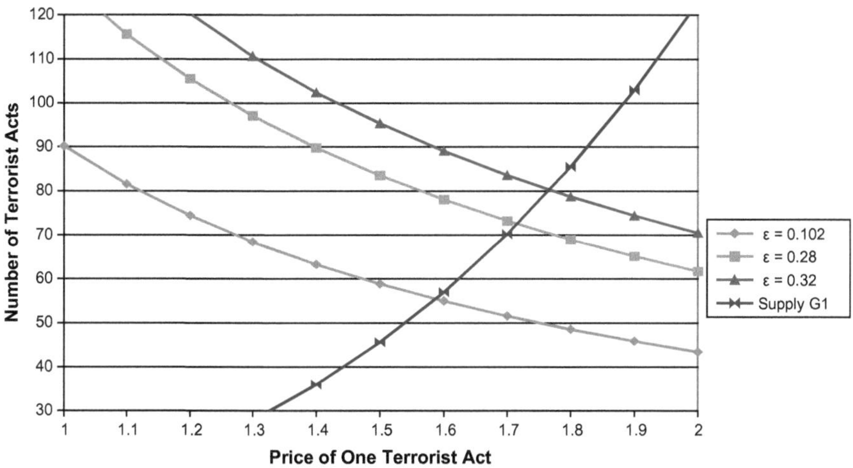

Fig. 8.4 Demand depending on efficiency of delivery and supply of terrorist acts

the demand for terrorist acts (Figs. 8.2 and 8.3). From this result one of the reasons for the rise of religiously motivated acts could thus be the huge oil incomes of the last decades. It is probably not by chance that many of the terrorists in recent years have come from Saudi Arabia, where high oil revenues are combined with a strong fundamentalist Islamic creed of the Wahhabite observation.

More interesting than the result of decreasing ε for the first kind of terrorist acts is the result concerning the second kind. For it shows that a successful effort to reduce terrorism of the first kind will lead to increasing terrorism of the second kind (Fig. 8.5). Note that similar results follow if the defensive efforts are directed to the other instrument and the terrorist acts committed with it by reducing ε.

Let us turn now to the second way of fighting terrorism by reducing the availability of the instruments of terror. In the model this is reflected by lowering the value of $k_i(i = 1, 2)$ in Eq. (8.8). We confine ourselves again by considering only the first case (Fig. 8.6). Obviously the equilibrium value of the number of instruments bought and thus of terrorist acts of the first kind decreases with lower k_1, that is with making the supply or production of the good more difficult. But again, since the price for this first terrorist instrument rises there should be some substitution through the second one and thus an increase of the terrorist acts committed with it.

A second way refers to keeping $b = B/N$ and also y small. We have already shown by which measures the latter aim can be reached. To succeed to reduce B/N in time means two things. First the immigration of fundamental believers has to be prevented as far as possible (this aspect is not included in the model). Second, since old fundamental believers are dying, the winning of new converts should be made more difficult. The third way of fighting terror may be the most important one in the long run. It consists in winning the spiritual battle by influencing present and especially potential future adherents of the ideology, and by preventing an increase

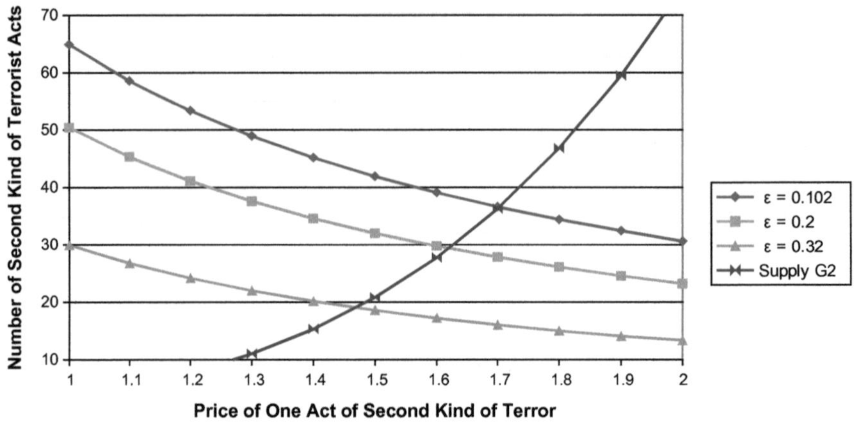

Fig. 8.5 Rise of the second kind of terror because first kind becomes more difficult

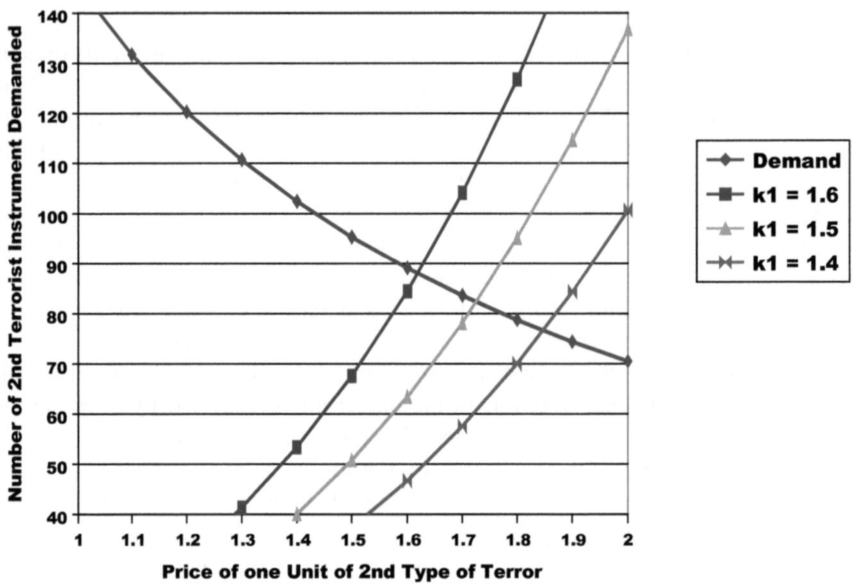

Fig. 8.6 Demand for and supply depending on restriction of first terrorist instrument

of the number of believers. The first way to do so in our model is to spend efforts to decrease the intensity of the believe β. This would reduce the number of terrorist acts committed, as shown by Figs. 8.1 and 8.7. Since old believers die, it is important to educate the next generation in a way that they do not become (strong) fundamental believers. We can fit this idea into the model by reinterpreting the production function for the second terrorist instrument into a production function for educating new fundamentalist believers. The function given by Eq. (8.8) would have to be changed into:

$$\frac{\partial b}{\partial t} = k_2 L_2^{\alpha} C_2^{1-\alpha} - a. \tag{8.11}$$

The deduction of $a > 0$ is necessary since just to keep constant the present number of believers in the ideology requires efforts because of the natural mortality of the population. The defensive measures require to keep the first expression on the left-hand side of the equation smaller than the second. This may, for instance be reached by requiring all students to attend secular schools where they have to learn the principles of a free society, and where religious instruction is controlled to prevent fundamentalist inculcation. Equation (8.11) does change our model into a dynamic system. It is, however, not our intention to discuss the further results of this change in our present approach.

8.7 Measures to Protect Against Supreme Value Terrorism

Since it is a "holy" duty of true believers fighting in good faith the "devilish" forces of darkness to spare nothing and nobody, even their own lives for the good case dwarfing all other aims, good or bad, it is difficult to prevent supreme value terrorism. Nonetheless political and economic damage can be contained.

The danger from terror does not so much arise directly from the military and political potential of states, which have an interest in hiding their support and involvement. For the leaders of these states have to follow widely the prescriptions of the ideology, which are at odds with a favorable economic development and the freedom of a pluralistic system. As a consequence, such societies cannot keep up with the developed nations and remain inferior in their economic and military capabilities.

This implies that a main danger for Western and "Westernized" countries arises from immigrant believers. Only people who are true believers and have the chance to study, to become informed about the Western way of living, and to acquire the necessary technical expertise, are able to commit the most conspicuous terrorist acts.

It follows that much can be done by limiting the influx of strong believers. Also, where the strong believers are already present, terror can be contained by preventing that they can win proselytes under the mantle of religious or other tolerance. An early screening of the respective movements and their adherents can help much to limit the possibility of terrorist acts.

Also, the attention and the reports of mass media about the successful acts of terrorists are not only spreading the news of their success, but are also contributing

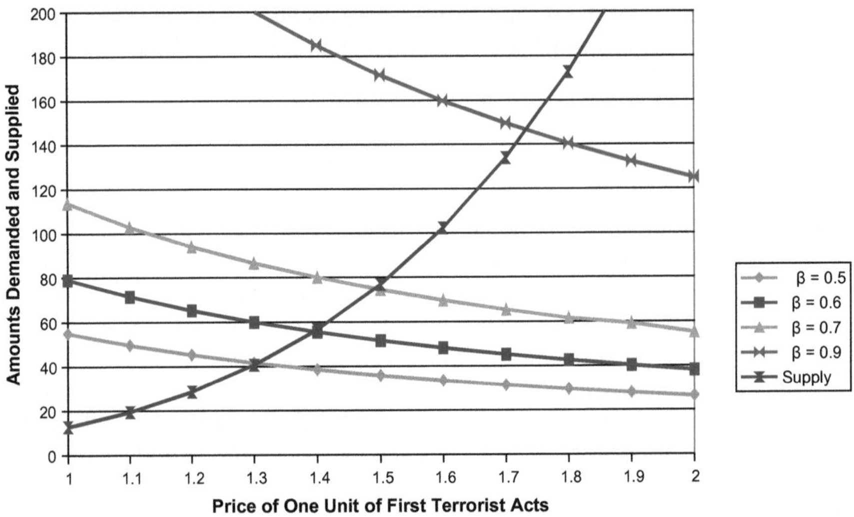

Fig. 8.7 Demand depending on intensity of ideological belief and supply of first instrument (terrorist acts)

to their fame and to attract new believers as potential imitators. It should thus be examined whether a case might exist for restricting sensationalist reporting by the mass media, although this is of course a delicate task in a free society.

The centralization of technical and economic facilities is bound to attract highly devastating attacks. If financial and other activities had not been concentrated in the two towers of the World Trade Center and instead been decentralized in the suburbs of New York, which could have been the case given modern computers and information networks, the damage would have been much smaller. From this perspective, an idea like that of the Swiss Railway Authorities to concentrate their switching system in one location, seems not to be a good one. Decentralization is therefore part of the solution. Also, a decentralized federal political system is less vulnerable than a highly centralized one.

8.8 The Spiritual Battle

To overcome the threat posed by supreme values movements, the war about spiritual values has to be won. At the moment the West has scarcely entered this fight, and is even immobilized by a dogma of granting cultural diversity or favoring a "multicultural society". Indeed, the Western position in this conflict seems to be rather weak, because secularization has left no substantive supreme values that could be opposed to those of other ideologies, especially if they are based on the "absolute truth" revealed by God. The adherence to Christian believes is waning, and some of its doctrines like the trinity appear to be inferior to the rational mind to the strict monotheism of Islam.

Moreover, it is not obvious how a confrontation among belief systems with conflicting *substantive supreme values* believed to be absolutely true by the adherents can be resolved by argument and discussion.

If it is believed or acknowledged that the Quran is the definitive word of God, then it is difficult, if not impossible to contradict the results deduced by thinkers like Sayyid Qutb. In this case, there can only be a discussion about interpretations. The argument can then no longer be accepted that everybody should have the right to make his own decisions as long as he does not violate the same right of others. For his decisions might be contrary to the commands of God. This means that another approach has to be taken.

This different approach has to be based on the very observation that different movements or groups of people may believe in different ideologies (including religions) with conflicting supreme values and that this will lead to hatred and violence if they try to win proselytes by more or less pressure, by threats or force. The only way to finally prevent such developments, is provided if all such movements or groups agree that no pressure or force, but only peaceful missionary work is allowed to convert others (Bernholz 1995). This implies, as far as the commandments of the different supreme values diverge or conflict, that secular law has to be established and to be acknowledged, but only in the cases in which action by the state is inescapable. It also implies that secular law has to be promoted by a legislature, executed by an administration and monitored by a judicial system, and not based on one of the supreme value systems. Moreover, the legislature and the government have to be elected by free citizens, with no one belonging to different creeds excluded from participation. A constitution has to provide for the protection of minorities and the right of everybody to select his or her own creed or convictions. A free society implies the *formal supreme value* that everybody has the right to take his or her own decisions.

This is, however, all what can be done, given the situation in western democracies. Yet the very values of western democracies contradict the supreme values of Islam, including the idea of a secular, non-theocratic democracy itself, and the freedom of women to participate equally in a society. In this sense a fundamental conflict is present.

This conflict can also not be prevented by separating the world into different territories, each dominated by only one ideology. For this is not a solution as long as the supreme values of Islam imply a universal mission. Moreover, the West also has *formal* supreme values expressed in the right of individual freedom of everybody, and of women as equals to men and not in a state of subordination as required by the supreme values of Islam. They are *formal* since they allow each individual to have his or her own *substantive* supreme values, *provided* that they are not forced on others.

8.9 Conclusions

Supreme values allow no compromise, and one weapon available to Islamic as to other fundamentalist ideological movements to accomplish them is terror. The options for ending terror based on supreme values are rather limited. A first option is to contain the damage by technological, economic, and political decentralization. A second option is military preemption of terror or its prevention by intelligence and police actions, both difficult tasks since terrorists hide in the general population. Moreover, some of the latter measures may restrict the very freedoms they should protect. A third option is to ensure that children are taught values of tolerance and self-improvement, rather than values of supreme values demanding to sacrifice oneself and the lives of others, and promising glory and future rewards for doing so. How the third option can be achieved in several non-Western or not Westernized countries is of course another question.

The conclusions of this chapter, and of the corresponding model are valid for any terrorism based on supreme values, and not only for the more recent terrorist acts based on Islamism. The model describes as well the terrorism of the National Socialists, especially the SA (Storm Troops), before the Nazis grasped power in Germany in 1933, and also for the Soviet troops in Russia before they consolidated their despotic rule in the Soviet Union. But history experienced also Christian terrorism. This was especially the case for the People's Crusade, when the crusaders on their march to the Holy Land killed thousands of Jews in the so-called Rhineland massacres of 1096. Another example are the damages wrought by the Christian sect of the Hussites in Bohemia and Germany from 1420 to 1431, after their spiritual leader, Jan Hus, ad been condemned and executed at the Council of Constance.

References

Bernholz P (1985) The international game of power. Mouton Publishers, Berlin and New York

Bernholz P (1995) Supreme values, tolerance and the constitution of Liberty. In: Radnitzky G, Bouillon H (eds) Values and the social order, vol 1: values and society. Aldershot, Brookfield, xxx and Avebury xxx, pp 235–250

Bernholz P (1997) Ideology, sects, state and totalitarianism: a general theory. Forum für osteuropäische Ideen- und Zeitgeschichte 1(1): 51–84. Also In: Maier H. und Schaefer M (eds) Totalitarismus und politische Religionen. Konzepte des Diktaturvergleichs, Vol. II. Ferdinand Schoeningh, Paderborn, Muenchen, Wien und Zuerich, pp 271–298

Hoffman B (1998) Inside terrorism. Columbia University Press, New York

Hubback A (1997) Apocalypse when? the global threat of religious cults. Conflict Studies 300, New Delhi

Krueger AB, Maleckova J (2002) Education, poverty, political violence and terrorism: is there a causal connection? Princeton Discussion Paper, Draft of July 2002

Peters R (1996) Jihad in classical and modern islam. Markus Wiener Publishers, Princeton, N.J

Qutb S (2001) In the Shade of the Quran. Vol. IV: Surah 5. Translated and edited by Salahi, A and Shamis, A Markfield (Leicester): The Islamic Foundation

Rapoport DC (1984) Fear and trembling: terrorism in three religious traditions. Am Polit Sci Rev 78:658–677
Sandler T, Enders W (2002) An economic perspective on transnational terrorism. Internet: http://www.ecaar.org/Articles/SandlerDIW.pdf
Sobel LA (ed) (1975) Political terrorism. Clio Press, Oxford
Stayer JM (1976) Anabaptists and the sword. Colorado Press, Lawrence, Kansas

Chapter 9
Economic and Political Problems Facing Ideocracies

We have shown that Ideocracies, that is, Totalitarian Regimes and Mature Ideocracies are political regimes based on the Supreme Values, which are considered to be absolutely true. Science, however, cannot pretend to be able to find absolute truths, but hopes to develop a sequence of theories about reality, which allows it to slowly get an always better understanding of it. To quote Sir James Jeans (1954, p 364):

> It was supposed [by the physicists of the last century] that a model which reproduced all the phenomena of science, and so made it possible to predict them all, must in some way correspond to the reality underlying the phenomena. But obviously this cannot be so. After one perfect model had been found, a second of equal perfection might appear, and as both models could not correspond to reality, we should have at least one perfect model which did not correspond to reality. Thus we would never be sure that any model corresponded to reality.

Jeans goes on to explain what he means by presenting several examples from the history of science. To quote only one of them (p. 375f.):

> The Newtonian theory of gravitation, which required the planets to move round the sun in elliptical orbits, gave an excellent account of the movements of the outer planets, but failed with the inner. Attempts were made to remedy this by slightly altering the Newtonian law of gravitation, by supposing the sun to be surrounded by clouds of gas or dust which impeded the free motion of the inner planets, and in a variety of other ways. The relativity theory of gravitation [by Einstein] then cleared up the whole situation at one stroke by rejecting Newton's force of gravitation altogether, and impressing a curvature on the space-time unity in which the motions of the planets were depicted. … The whole motion of planets and other bodies, as well as of rays of light, could now be described by the simple statement that they all described geodesics – i.e. took the shortest possible course from point to point – in the new curved space-time unity.

What has been quoted concerning the fact that the natural sciences cannot aspire to reveal absolute truths about physical relationships, is also true for the sciences of economics, political science, and sociology. Here, too, we can only hope that we move asymptotically to better and better insights. But, this means that the supreme values believed to be absolutely true must necessarily provide a distorted view of reality and thus lead in time to negative consequences if applied. In the following sections, we will discuss some of these problems.

P. Bernholz, *Totalitarianism, Terrorism and Supreme Values*,
Studies in Public Choice 33, DOI 10.1007/978-3-319-56907-9_9

9.1 Negative Economic Consequences if Supreme Values Are Demanding a Planned Economy

> … in economies of about the same degree of development it must be stated that the power relations of the market also deeply affect the revolutionary production development. It should be noticed that with the exception of a few initiatives no socialist country figures among those introducing the product in question for the first time.
>
> (Hungarian economist Janos Kornai 1971, p. 288)

At least since the work of Ludwig von Mises (Socialism/Die Gemeinwirtschaft 1981/1919) and Friedrich A. von Hayek (Collectivist Economic Planning 1935; see also Bernholz 1987; de Soto 2013) it has been shown that planned economies cannot deliver the goods necessary to guarantee and to enhance the well-being of the population. Though both agreed—but Hayek to a lesser degree—that it might be possible to solve the problem of rational calculation in such a system if it were characterized by a stationary economy, this would never be possible in a growing economy. Other economists, however, like the well-known Paul A. Samuelson doubted this conclusion, probably exactly because they thought in terms of a system of equations typical for a stationary system. As Samuelson (1976, p. 92) formulated it:

> Around 1900 Pareto showed that an ideal socialism would have to solve the same equations as competitive capitalism. Around 1920, Ludwig von Mises, perhaps unaware of Pareto's proof, set forth the challenging view that rational economic organization was **logically** impossible in the absence of free markets. Fred Taylor of Michigan, A. P. Lerner of England and California, and Oskar Lange of Poland answered Mises with the view that socialism could conceptually solve the problems of economic organization by a decentralized process of trial and error.

Samuelson stuck to his view until shortly before the breakdown of the Communist System of a so-called planned economy in 1989. And, Oskar Lange (1972, 401–402) strengthened his similar position after the development of computers.

> Not quite thirty years ago I published an essay "On the Economic Theory of Socialism". Pareto and Barone had shown that the conditions of economic equilibrium in a socialist economy could be expressed by a system of simultaneous equations. The prices resulting from these equations furnish a basis for rational economic accounting under socialism (only the static equilibrium aspect of the accounting problem was under consideration at that time). At a later date Hayek and Robbins maintained that the Pareto–Barone equations were of no practical consequence. The solution of a system of thousands or more simultaneous equations was, in practice, impossible, and consequently the practical problem of economic accounting under socialism remained unsolvable.
>
> In my essay I refuted the Hayek-Robbins argument by showing how a market mechanism could be established in a socialist economy which would lead to the solution of the simultaneous equations by means of an empirical procedure of trial and error. …
>
> (Today) my answer to Hayek and Robbins would be: so what's the trouble? Let us put the simultaneous equations in an electronic computer and we shall obtain the solution in less than a second. The market process … may be considered as a computing device of the pre-electronic age.

However, Enrico Barone had not been as confident in his 1908 paper. He concluded concerning the Central Planning Board (CPB) in summing up his arguments.

> If, for a moment, we assume that the variability of the technical coefficients may be neglected and we take account of their technical variability only, it is not impossible to solve on paper the equations of the equilibrium. It would be tremendous – a gigantic work (work therefore taken from the productive services): but it is not an impossibility (Barone 1935, p. 287).

It seems to follow that Barone does not expect a solution to be possible if technical coefficients are variable, that is, in a dynamically developing economy, and this is certainly the case in real economies in which new products and production processes are created and in which consumer demand is also variable. But, Hayek is even skeptical concerning the solution for a stationary economy. Though he admits like Barone, Mises, and Lange that a solution of the equilibrium equations would be logically possible if the necessary information were available to the central planning board (CPB) (Hayek 1935, p. 207), he doubts that this would be the case. For he points out that kinds of knowledge exist, that are not readily available and/or are not transferable to the CPB. We might add that chess, though it is – as game theory has proven – a trivial two-person zero sum game with a definite solution, neither the best chess players nor the best computers have been able to find this solution until now because of the sheer complexity of the problem.

Mises and Hayek agree that problems become absolutely unsolvable in a dynamic environment, where new kinds of goods and new production processes are invented. Since they are not invented by the CPB, a complete and detailed description has to be given to the CPB, a requirement, which is even often beyond the capabilities of language. The same is true for new kinds of labor skills developed. How could the new capabilities of a new kind of cellular biological engineer and of his possible uses in different lines of production be transmitted to the CPB and its computers? Moreover, the members of the CPB would probably not understand the microbiological terminology used to transmit the message.

Similar problems arise if the quality and quantity of inputs, especially of labor, are variable. Moreover, such variations may even be consequences of the economy's administrative organization and of the nature of its plans.

It is obvious that these were some of the problems envisioned by Mises and Hayek. But there are others. Let us just give one more example. Mises points out that it is nearly impossible for the CPB to decide which firms and industries should produce which amounts of which goods, which firms and industries should be created, and which should be closed. He denies that these problems can be solved in a developing economy without capitalists and a capital market (1981, pp. 119–123). With new goods and production processes, the size of firms and the structure of industry become a problem. Changing preferences of consumers also pose the problem of which firms or industries to expand, to contract, to abolish, or to create. But, under these conditions the CPB will not be able to get the information necessary for reliable ex ante planning because of the nature and complexity of the situation. Rational calculation breaks down if central planning is used.

All this means that the plans worked out by the CPB on the basis of such unreliable, incomplete and partly distorted information cannot not fully correspond to reality. This has the consequence that firms may often find themselves either unable to fulfill the plan or able to easily overshoot its targets. It obviously depends on how the CPB or the leading politicians sanction or reward deviations of individual firms from planned targets. Since the CPB itself is aware of the inadequacy of its targets, it will probably apply a graduated response: premiums increasing with the degree of the over-fulfillment of the plan; no premiums it the plan targets have not been reached, but degradation, removal, or imprisonment of managers if the targets have been missed by substantial degrees.

Given this situation, managers will react in several ways: First, it is advisable to understate production capabilities and available capacities. Second, it is helpful to ask for more current inputs than probably needed. Third, investment requirements may be overstated. But, here the management has to be careful not to demand too much, since otherwise the CPB may increase the plan targets for the firm too much in the next period. Somewhat to understate the firm's capabilities and to ask for too high inputs could also make it possible to set aside part of the production for getting required inputs in exchange with other firms if the requested inputs are not sufficient, are not granted or are inadequate.

We conclude that a planned economy must lead to rather inefficient plans because of the existing information and information problems and thus lead to an inferior supply of goods compared to a market economy working within an adequate institutional setting of safe private property rights, well-working legal systems and not too high burden of taxes and regulations.

In a long-run dynamic setting, however, the obstacles to innovations may even be more obnoxious for the economic development in a planned economy. For whereas in a market economy innovations are encouraged by possible profits and for business firms by threatening losses, if competitors are more successful in introducing new goods and production processes, this is not the case in a planned economy. For here firms would first have to convince the bureaucrats of the CPB that the proposed innovations would work and not need too many inputs. And, why should managers try to do so, since their firms and they themselves would usually not profit from such innovations. For they would probably be used by the CPB in creating new firms or even a whole new industry. And would the bureaucrats of the CPB always have the knowledge and courage to introduce all newly proposed untested goods and production processes, whose success may be highly uncertain? By contrast, in market economies private inventors could either try to get venture credit from banks or in financial markets besides their private capital to try to accomplish their ideas, or even sell their invention to entrepreneurs whom they can convince of the promises of their invention. All this is impossible in a planned economy, where the bureaucrats have to be convinced of the value of inventions and innovations.

The experiences in the communist countries of the Soviet Bloc during the decades before its breakdown have demonstrated that these conclusions of economic theory correspond to reality. The efficiency of the system in providing goods has been very low, most of the time a scarcity of the goods wanted by consumers dominated. And what is more, nearly all path-breaking innovations took place in capitalist Western countries. Already in the 1970s the Hungarian economist Janos Kornai quoted above listed 79 revolutionary new products, of which only five were developed or codeveloped in communist planned economies (Kornai 1971, Table 20.3).

Communist countries are not the only ones whose ideologies contained supreme values demanding a centrally planned economy. The ideology of the Nazi Regime also demanded planning, as exemplified by the so-called Four Year's Plans. Though private property of business firms was maintained, these firms were subjected to the requirements of central plans aiming especially towards self-sufficiency of the German economy and the development of the arms industry. The negative influences and inefficiencies of this planning system have been well described by the Italian economist Bresciani-Turroni (1948, Italian ed. 1942, especially Chap. 8). Let me just quote one example (p. 156; my translation from the German):

> New agencies have to be created to issue licenses for exports and imports, which are controlling each foreign exchange transaction, distribute raw materials to different industries, fix prices for wages and goods, control the cost of production of individual firms, organize the distribution of the labor force among business plants, issue cards permitting to get consumer goods … The fixing and control of prices which first began for agricultural products, was slowly extended in Germany to more and more segments of the economy, so that in 1937 already two thirds of all goods sold were controlled. 1935 these controls were executed by 49 agencies, to which had to be added the 19 committees of the Agricultural Union (Landwirtschaftliche Vereinigung) and the 27 agencies controlling foreign trade. Already 1935 700 orders controlling prices had been issued—a number which increased significantly later.

Until now, we have supposed that the aims of the planned economy prescribed by the ideology are followed rationally. But, this is not always the case, first because leaders may distort their policies to strengthen their own position, and second because of other aims implied by the respective supreme values, or third since they themselves act following an even more distorted view of reality. A telling example is the Great Jump Forward announced by Chairman Mao in China in December 1958 (Margolin 1998, pp. 539 ff.). According to this plan the lives of peasants should be changed within 3 years. They were forced to combine into cooperatives of thousands or even ten thousands of families. Everything should be done together, beginning with common meals. Agricultural production should be increased enormously with the help of gigantic irrigation projects and new methods of cultivation. Moreover, the differences between agricultural and industrial work should be abolished by creating industrial units, especially tiny blast furnaces everywhere. All these efforts had the aim to secure the self-sufficiency of all village communities and to accelerate industrial growth by the new firms in the countryside, and the agricultural surpluses, which had to be delivered by the cooperatives to the state-owned heavy industry. In this way, a communist system would be approached; and capital accumulation and a rising standard of living would be reached at the same time.

For 1958, the plan asked for a cereal production of 375 million tons, an increase of more than 92% compared to the 195 million tons produced in 1957. All these ambitious plans could only lead to a catastrophe, which was initially hidden by falsifying the statistics. Economically, the misallocation of resources had the bad consequences to be expected. Capital accumulation reached 43.4% of Gross Domestic Product in 1959, but the capital was invested into big dams never completed or of bad quality and into a massive extension of industry in the city agglomerations. And, this misallocation of capital also led to a misallocation of labor: Government-owned big firms hired 21 million new workers in 1958, an increase of their employment by 85%. The share of the population not working in agriculture grew from 15 to 20% of the population within 1957–1960. At the same time people in agricultural regions were kept busy in constructing new buildings, tiny blast furnaces, destruction of old villages and the creation of new accommodations instead of being employed in agriculture. Instead of the planned 199,000 t of grain planned for the model region Feng yang (Anhui) in 1959 only 54,000 t were produced compared to 89,000 t in 1958. But, the government insisted to receive its part in the planned amount, namely 29,000 t. This meant that nearly all the population was starving on only water soup with some rice in the following year.

The resulting starvation hit the whole country. The harvest of 1960 amounted only to 143 million tons of cereals, 26% lower than in 1956, with a population grown by 100 million. Even cases of cannibalism occurred. In absolute numbers, the worst period of famine in all Chinese history took place, with an estimated number of deaths between 20 and 43 million.

9.2 Consequences of Other Supreme Values for Economic Development

The damages wrought by government interventions with the aim to plan the economy were not the only ones following from the Nazi ideology in Germany. The persecution of Jews proved also detrimental to science and economy, because it turned out to be a factor decreasing the rate of new scientific discoveries and thus the growth of new successful industries. This can be best measured by looking at the number of Nobel Prizes won by German scientists compared to the United Kingdom and the USA (Table 9.1).

Table 9.1 Number of Nobel Prize winners in three countries

	Germany	United Kingdom	USA
1901–1939	34	23	14
1940–1974	15	36	104

Sources Encyclopedia Britannica, 15th edn. Chicago and London 1976, Micropedia, vol VII, pp 369–372, and Grosser Brockhaus, 18th edn., vol 8, 1979

Whereas, the number of Nobel Prize winners has increased strongly in the United Kingdom and especially in the USA, it has been halved in Germany, certainly at least to a great part because of the emigration of numerous scientists, among them many Jews, as a consequence of the policies of the Nazi regime.

Not only the German but also the Soviet economy has suffered from the persecution of in-convertible minorities, in this case the bourgeois and the kulaks (the rich peasants), determined as such by the prevailing supreme values.

These two examples show that other factors contained in the supreme values of ideologies besides central planning may exert an influence on economic well-being, efficiency, innovation, and development. Several Islamic Totalitarian Regimes and Ideocracies provide also interesting cases. The prohibition of interest by their supreme values is perhaps the least damaging fact, since it can be circumvented without high costs, for instance by turning the providers of capital into shareholders receiving part of the profits. Much more important are the strict regulations hindering girls to be educated adequately, of women participating productively as workers or entrepreneurs in business firms, not to speak of not allowing them to appear in public without male company of close relatives. Moreover, rules how women have to dress in public, for instance veiling their heads and bodies (e.g., by the Burka) are not helping business activities. Examples of this kind abound. The Taliban in Afghanistan did not allow girls to be educated in school. Other Islamic countries at least demand a strict separation of girls and boys during their education. In SaudiArabia, women are not allowed to drive. And, the separation of women and men in universities and business firms is a common characteristic of several Islamic countries. By such measures, about half of the population is hindered or at least limited to participate in the production process. It is thus not surprising that societies with such Islamic ideologies are lagging in economic development, except if they have been benefitted by natural resources like big oil reserves.

But economic development has probably also suffered in totalitarian regimes characterized by different supreme values. The steady expansion of their territories by warfare in the cases of the Mongols, Aztecs, and Incas must have been a heavy burden on their economies. Moreover, the human sacrifices postulated by Aztec ideology to maintain the world running, as well as the destruction of flourishing cities and the slaughtering of their populations by the Mongols could not have but negative effects on economic well-being.

9.3 Negative Domestic Political Consequences of Supreme Values

The negative domestic political consequences of supreme values characterizing the respective ideologies are often dramatic. This is especially the case concerning in-convertible enemies and convertible people who stubbornly object to accept the true creed. Jews and Capitalists have to be persecuted, robbed of their property, forced into immigration, put into concentration camps, or even to be eliminated. This has been the case for the Nazi and Communist regimes.

In Islamist regimes of a Sunni conviction Christians, Jews, and Shiites have often been killed if they were not prepared to convert. Even if Christians and Jews were willing to pay the tax demanded from adherents of book religions, they were certainly not allowed to participate in the political decision process. Since God's laws are always superior to secular human law, it is even in democratic settings necessary that only true believers control that the legal system corresponds to His commands. Similarly, in Shiite Iran Christians, Jews and Sunnites are a suppressed minority. In Calvin's Geneva, more than 50 people were killed because they adhered to a different protestant creed (Meyers Universallexikon 19, article).

Apart from such extreme measures postulated by different ideologies it is clear that private life is strongly regulated following the contents of the supreme values. Correspondingly, the press and the mass media are not allowed to criticize these values. Even private conversations have to be in agreement with them. As already mentioned, the dressings of women have to follow Islamic standards. And, a quite similar attitude dominated Calvin's Geneva. Thus no local costumes were allowed. Bachelors and virgins had to live with families to prevent their moral corruption. In certain Islamic countries, visitors are not allowed to see the women of the house. Alcoholic drinks and tobacco are forbidden.

More importantly, it has to be decided who has the right to interpret the supreme values of the ideologies. This is usually a very restricted group like a number of priests, a Politburo or even a single leader like a Mahdi, Caliph, or a Führer like Hitler. Such a system, of course, prevents even a true democracy of believers like in Iran. This is especially pronounced in systems, which are expansionary, since in this case spiritual and secular powers have to be combined to prepare the holy war.

9.4 Consequences of Supreme Values for International Policies

All Totalitarian Regimes in contrast to Mature Ideocracies have not yet reached the ends postulated by their supreme values. If this is the case concerning foreign countries, as is typical for ideologies asking for the domination of the whole world or of certain territories abroad, and for those whose aim is the conversion of potential believers all over the globe, international conflicts cannot be prevented. Given such a situation, it is of the utmost importance how pliable and patient the leadership of these regimes are in waiting for a favorable situation to promote their goals, and how prepared they are to postpone into the future the efforts demanded by their supreme values. This may to a large degree depend on the character of the leaders and on whether they still believe into the supreme values of their creed. Since especially leaders of the first generation are mostly true believers, they are usually less prepared to compromise and to wait. Moreover, they may be inclined to believe that the forces of fate or God's will be on their side. This may be the reason that they are prepared to incur great risks internationally and to act prematurely. Another factor working in this direction may be their concern to finish the tasks demanded by the supreme values before their own death. In this sense, Hitler was obviously not hesitating to take incredible risks and to act too early instead of waiting for better chances. To attack the Soviet Union before Great Britain had been defeated and before securing Japanese support for a common attack was certainly a big mistake.

The situation may look quite different for leaders belonging to the second generation. They may no longer believe in the supreme values of the ideology but only have pretended this to use it to gain power. And, even after they have succeeded in reaching the top they are trapped by the ideology in having to pretend that they are still true believers. Here Stalin provides a valuable example of this attitude, for it seems that in contrast to Lenin, he did no longer believe in the Communist ideology, but used it ruthlessly for his own advancement. And he still had to pretend that his former comrades were traitors of true socialism, when he had them condemned in the purges of 1936–38.

On the international scene, Stalin did not hesitate to conclude the Hitler-Stalin pact with the ideological enemies of Bolshevism in 1939 to get the control of Eastern Poland, the Baltic States and Bessarabia. And when the Nazis invaded the Soviet Union in 1941, he had no problems to form an alliance with the Western Capitalist countries Britain and the USA, only to deceive them, especially Roosevelt, in Yalta about his final plans, and in the end to force the Western allies in Potsdam to deliver Eastern and parts of Central Europe to his rule without any hope of establishing democratic regimes in these countries (Kennan 1967).

His successors in the Soviet Union followed a similarly realistic foreign policy when they were confronted by American containment policies. Whenever dangerous tensions like during the Cuban Crisis threatened war and the Soviet leaders were convinced that the US President would not give in, they withdrew from their positions. Thus, Soviet ballistic missiles with atomic weapons were withdrawn from Cuba when the USA instituted a blockade. On the other hand, Soviet leaders did not hesitate to crush the uprisings in East Germany in 1953, in Hungary in 1956 and in Czechoslovakia in 1968, when they were convinced that the USA would not intervene.

Finally, because of the bad performance of the planned communist economy, Soviet foreign policy was again adapted by President Gorbatchev in the late 1980s. Even before having been elected as General Secretary of the Politburo he stated that economic reforms were unavoidable if the Soviet Union wanted to enter the next century as a leading international power and to reach a better supply of goods for its population. And in 1988, he revealed at the Plenary Session of the Central Committee of the Communist Party that the Soviet economy had not grown for the last 20 years (Communique 1988, 1; see also Roberts 2002). This meant that the Soviet Union would loose the arms race with the USA if did not change its economic and its international policies. It is thus not surprising that Gorbatchev agreed to the German unification, and to the end of Soviet domination of Eastern Europe, and then, but now against his intentions, was instrumental in furthering the breakdown of the Soviet Union.

Similarly, I suspect that Mao Zedong was a true believer in his version of the Communist doctrine, especially as long as it helped him to maintain his power position. Otherwise, one can scarcely imagine why he did promote the Great Jump Forward as well as the Cultural Revolution, for they not only damaged the economy incredibly, but also weakened the international position of China as a Great Power. This changed with Deng Xiaoping and his successors since 1978, who obviously realized that he and they had to introduce market reforms not only to provide the population with more and better consumption goods, but also to turn China by increasing its economic strength into a valiant international power. That the Communist ideology had to be adapted and changed in this process could be covered as much as possible by an adequate propaganda effort. I still recall when traveling in China in the 1990s, that I read in "China Daily" that since Marx had speculated in the stock markets, such markets were compatible with socialism.

Let me just mention in passing some other true believers who obviously hoped the forces of history would help them to reach their aims. Pol Pot of the Khmer Rouge and Ceaucescu of Communist Romania obviously belonged to this category. Otherwise, it would not be understandable that they stuck to their positions in the face of international opposing forces. The same seems to have been true for Honecker and his wife in East Germany. As a result of these policies, the Khmer Rouge were overwhelmed by Vietnamese troops, whereas Ceaucescu and the Honecker's lost their positions as Communist leaders in Romania and East Germany by Gorbatchev's policies leading to an agreement with the Western Powers.

It also seems to be obvious without further comment that the Caliphate of the Sudan in the nineteenth century as well as the Islamic State of Iraq and the Levant had or have not the economic and military power to withstand in the long run their non-Islamist opponents, among them Great Powers. And some centuries ago the expansionist policies of the Aztecs and Incas had no real chance to conquer the North or South American continents in face of their opponents and with their supply lines increasing when their armies advanced into more distant and difficult mountainous or jungle territory.

References

Barone E (1935) The ministry of production in the collectivist state. In: Hayek FA (ed) Collectivist economic planning, George Routledge & Sons, London. Originally published in Italian in Il Giornale degli Economisti, 1908

Bernholz P (1987) Information, motivation, and the problem of rational economic calculation in socialism. In: Pejovich S (ed) Socialism: institutional, philosophical and economic issues, Kluwer Academic Publishers, Dordrecht, London & Lancaster, pp 147–174

Bresciani-Turroni C (1948) Einführung in die Wirtschaftspolitik. Bern A, Francke AG (eds) Originally published in Italian as Introduzione alla Politica Economica, Giulio Einaudi, Torino, 1942

Communique of the Plenary Session of the Central Committee of the Communist Party of the Soviet Union (1988) Pravda, February 18, 1

Hayek FA von (1935) Collectivist economic planning. George Routledge & Sons, London

de Soto, JH (2013) Sozialismus, Wirtschaftsrechnung und unternehmerische Funktion. Stuttgart: Lucius und Lucius

Der Grosse B (1955) Nobelstiftung, Bd. 8, 428-30. Wiesbaden, F. A. Brockhaus

Sir James Jeans (1954) Some problems of philosophy. In: Commins S, Linscott RN. (eds) The philosophers of science. Man and the Universe, The Pocket Library, Pocket Books, New York, pp 361–410

Kennan GF (1967) Memoirs (1925–1950). Little, Brown & Co, Boston

Kornai J (1971) Anti-equilibrium. North-Holland, Amsterdam and London

Lange O (1972) The computer and the market. In: Nove A, Nuti DM (eds) Socialist Economics, Penguin Books, Harmondsworth, Middlesex

Margolin J-L (1998) China: Ein langer Marsch in die Nacht. In: Courtois S et al (eds) Das Schwarzbuch des Kommunismus. Unterdrückung, Verbrechen und Terror. Piper München und Zürich. Original in French Le livre noir du communisme, Robert Laffont, Paris, 1997

Mises L von (1981) Socialism. Indianapolis: liberty fund. First German Ed. Die Gemeinwirtschaft: Untersuchungen über den Sozialismus, 1922, Gustav Fischer, Jena

Roberts, PC (2002) My time with soviet economics. The Independent Review 2, Fall, 259–264

Samuelson PA (1976) Economics, 10th edn. New York

Chapter 10
Art and Science in Totalitarian Regimes and Mature Ideocracies

Corresponding to the nature of their Supreme Values, most Ideocracies develop rather specific attitudes to literature, arts and sciences. Everything which contradicts the aims contained in these values has to be banned or destroyed, whereas all artistic endeavors positively commemorating these values or celebrating their spiritual and secular leaders will be favored. Let us begin with the former, that is, the destruction or prohibition of everything violating the supreme values. We can distinguish two relevant kinds of ideologies. One in which the supreme values are of a secular nature, and a second group of supreme values determined by religion. National Socialism states that the Aryan Race has to dominate the globe and that all literature and art opposing this aim has to be banned. Communism tries to eradicate any capitalistic exploitation and thus promotes atheism, since religion detracts from the suffering of the masses caused by capitalism. The radical view of Christianity and Islam condemns any pictures and sculptures of God and of demons (gods or holy objects venerated by nonbelievers), since God is way above any human comprehension. The Aztec religion believes that the Earth comes to an end if the Sun God is not nourished with human blood. Thus pictures of sacrificing human victims are presented.

10.1 The Destruction and Prohibition of Works and Ideas Violating the Supreme Values

10.1.1 National Socialism

The relevant supreme values of National Socialism were formulated by Adolf Hitler in his book "Mein Kampf" which first appeared from 1925–1927.

P. Bernholz, *Totalitarianism, Terrorism and Supreme Values*,
Studies in Public Choice 33, DOI 10.1007/978-3-319-56907-9_10

> It is not by chance that the first civilizations (Kulturen) originated where the Aryan subjugated and subdued to his will lower populations when meeting them. They became the first technical instrument of a nascent culture (p. 69).

In this way, the path to be followed by the Aryan was predetermined. As a conqueror, he subdued the lower human beings and then organized their practical work under his command, will and for his aims. But by leading them to a useful but also strenuous work, he not only saved their lives, but perhaps even a future which was better than that during their earlier "freedom". As long as he recklessly pursued his position as Lord, he remained not only the real lord, but the propagator and preserver of culture. For this reason civilization was based on his creativity and his presence (pp. 323–324).

> The Jewish doctrine of Marxism rejects the aristocratic principle of nature and substitutes the eternal prerogative of power and strength by the sheer mass of numbers and their dead weight. She denies thus the value of the human personality, and disputes the value of national traditions and race. By doing so she is removing humanity's basis of existence and culture (p. 69).
>
> The bolshevism of art is the only possible form of life and spiritual expression of bolshevism. To whom this seems to be strange, has only to examine the art of the nations fortunately turned to bolshevism to realize in horror the morbid outgrowths of insane or depraved men, which have emerged under the labels of Cubism and Dadaism since the turn of the (twentieth) century, and which we can admire as officially government acknowledged art (p. 283).
>
> (Hitler 1933, my translation from the German)

The consequences to be expected because of these supreme values were soon unveiled after the Nazis had come to power in 1933. First, a burning of all un-German writings occurred, and later the sale to foreigners or the destruction of paintings and sculptures belonging to degenerate art took place.

The burning of un-German books took already place in May 1933, four months after the Nazis had taken power in Germany. As reported by the Neuköllner Tageblatt of May 12, 1933:

When the books were burning bands of the SA and the SS played national tunes and March music, until nine representatives of the students, to whom their tasks had been assigned corresponding to several subjects, flung the books of un-German spirit into the fire.
1st Shouter: *Against class struggle and materialism, for national community and an idealistic life! I hand over to the flames the writings of Marx and Kautsky.*
2nd Shouter: *Against decadence and moral decline! For discipline and morality in family and state! I hand over to the flames the writings of Heinrich Mann, Ernst Glaeser and Erich Kästner.*
3rd Shouter: *Against shabby principles and political treason, for devotion to people and state! I hand over to the flames the writings of Friedrich Wilhelm Förster.*
4th Shouter: *Against soul-tearing overestimation of sexual drives and for the nobility of the human soul! I hand over to the flames the writings of Sigmund Freud.*

5th Shouter: *Against falsifying our history and discrediting her heroes, for reverence concerning our past! I hand over to the flames the writings of Emil Ludwig and Werner Hegemann.*
6th Shouter: *Against unpopular journalism of Democratic-Jewish character, for responsible participation in the work of national reconstruction! I hand over to the flames the writings of Theodor Wolff and Georg Bernhard.*
7th Shouter: *Against literary treason of the soldiers of the World War, for education of the people in the spirit of military training. I hand over to the flames the writings of Erich Maria Remarque.*
8th Shouter: *Against arrogant deformation of the German language, for care of the most valuable accomplishment of our nation! I hand over to the flames the writings of Alfred Kerr.*
9th Shouter: *Against impudence and arrogance, for respect and deference concerning the eternal spirit of the German nation! I hand over to the flames the writings of Tucholsky and Ossietzky!*

The burning of un-German books was not limited to Berlin, but took also place in several other German cities. No surprise that Dr. Goebbels lauded the work of the students:

If you students take to yourself the right of throwing the spiritual muck into the flames, then you have also to carry the responsibility to free the path for a sincere German thinking replacing this filth. And therefore you are doing well in entrusting these perverse ideas of the past to the flames during this hour of midnight (quoted by Wulf 1966, p. 51).

At about the same time, all Jews were excluded from the Dichterakademie (Academy of Poets), Sect. 3 of the Preussische Akademie der Künste (Prussian Academy of Arts) as from all other Sections. Some non-Jewish members like Thomas Mann, Max von Schillings, Alfred Döblin, and Ricarda Huch decided not to remain in the Academy, given its new National Socialist direction (Wulf 1966, pp. 15–41).

The policies of the Nazis were not confined to burn the books of un-German contents. Already during the night from April 26–27, the monument of the Jewish-German poet Heinrich Heine in Frankfurt was overturned, much to the satisfaction of the Hessian Minister of Culture, Dr. Werner. (Wulf 1966, pp. 42–43). This was only the beginning of the Nazis' suppression of *Entartete Kunst* (Degenerate Art) that is of art which did not correspond to the Aryan race.

Hitler's first gesture after his assumption of power was to lay personally the cornerstone of "The House of German Art" (Haus der Deutschen Kunst) in Munich which was to become the main center of the official art exhibitions of the Third Reich. Later he explained the symbolism of this: *"When we celebrated the laying of the cornerstone for this building four years ago, we were all aware that we had not only to lay the cornerstone for a new home but also the foundations for a new and genuine German art. We had to bring about a turning point in the evolution of all our German cultural activities."* (Golomstock 2011, p. 81).

If a genuine German art had to be developed, then it follows that the Degenerate Art and the artists responsible for it had to be fought and the museums cleansed of their works. Already in a speech in the German Reichstag on March 23, 1933 Hitler explained:

> Simultaneously with this political purification of our public life, the Government of the Reich will undertake a thorough moral purging of the body corporate of the nation. The entire educational system, the theatre, the cinema, literature, the Press, and the wireless – all these will be used as means to this end and valued accordingly." (Baynes 1942, Vol. I, p 568).

On November 27, 1936, a committee headed by Prof. Ziegler was authorized to select for an exhibition of German Degenerate Art in 1937 all paintings and sculptures found in the collections of the German Reich. The commission toured the Reich and removed 15,997 works by German and foreign artists from 33 museums. Besides the most important German modernists the list of confiscations contained works from van Gogh, Braque, Derain, Rouault, Kandinski, Chagall, de Chirico, Vlaminck, Ensor, Lissitzky, and van Doesburg. On May 31, 1938 a law was passed confiscating all works of Degenerate Art from all German collections. The majority of them were sold abroad, Goering appropriated the finest of them, and the remainder (about 5000 paintings, water colors, and drawings) were burned by the Berlin fire brigade. (Golomstock 2011, pp. 103 f.).

The authors of Degenerate Art were usually called Jews, Bolsheviks or Bourgeois, though this was often a fiction. Thus Lyonel Feiniger, a "degenerate artist", complained in a letter in 1935 that he had to prove that he had no Jewish ancestors, though all of them had been Aryans since immemorial times. The same happened to Barlach, Pechstein, and Nolde, though the latter was even a member of the National Socialist Party. (Golomstock 2011, p. 110).

10.1.2 Communism

The relevant supreme values of Communism were already formulated by Karl Marx:

Religious suffering is, at one and the same time, the expression of real suffering and a protest against real suffering. Religion is the sigh of the oppressed creature, the heart of a heartless world, and the soul of soulless conditions. It is the opium of the people.

The abolition of religion as the illusory happiness of the people is the demand for their real happiness. To call on them to give up their illusions about their condition is to call on them to give up a condition that requires illusions. The criticism of religion is, therefore, in embryo, the criticism of that vale of tears of which religion is the halo.

Criticism has plucked the imaginary flowers on the chain (of capitalism) not in order that man shall continue to bear that chain without fantasy or consolation, but so that he shall throw off the chain and pluck the living flower. The criticism of religion disillusions man, so that he will think, act, and fashion his reality like a man who has discarded his illusions and regained his senses, so that he will move around himself as his own true Sun. Religion is only the illusory Sun which revolves around man as long as he does not revolve around himself (Karl Marx 1820).

In the Soviet Union, the application of atheism as supreme value as postulated by Marx varied over the years. Common tactics applied were the confiscation of church property, harassing believers, and educating atheism in schools. Orthodox priests and believers were persecuted, tortured, or imprisoned in labor camps. During the first years of Soviet rule, 28 orthodox bishops and over 1200 priests were killed. Sometimes the Soviets experimented with mind control to force believers to give up their religion. Churches were closed or destroyed.

These policies were not limited to the Orthodox Church but also extended to other religions like Protestant Christians. But in the long run, the government never formally outlawed the churches, and especially allowed them more leeway during the Second World War. The few places of worship left to the Orthodox Church were state property and permitted to be used by the church.

Let us begin to demonstrate Soviet repression of literature by quoting Solzhenitsyn, who had been condemned to years of forced labor in a labor camp:

> In this way I wrote: During winter in the warming room [of the forced labor camp], in spring and summer on the scaffolding when laying bricks. In the breaks between two troughs of mortar I put the sheet of paper on a brick and jotted down with the stump of a pencil, (so that the neighbors) could not see it, the lines condescending on me, when it appeared as if I cleaned the trough which I had finished. I lived like in a dream. When I sat over the holy camp soup in the canteen, I often did neither smell it nor heard the people around me – I always let my thoughts wander through my lines and ordered them like the bricks in the wall. I was searched, I was counted, driven in the column through the steppe – but in front of my eyes was the stage on which my play was unwinding; I perceived the color of the curtains, the arrangement of the furniture, the patches of light and the steps of the actors. (Solzhenitsyn 1978, Vol. 3, p 101; my translation from the German ed.).

Under such conditions, every piece of written paper was confiscated in the forced labor camps in the Soviet Union and its author heavily punished, so that Solzhenitsyn could only preserve his works written during this time by learning them by heart and by destroying the lines he had written on paper.

This Soviet attitude was not confined to incarcerated inmates of the Archipelago Gulag:

Zhdanov, Gorky, Bukharin and Radek [at the first All-Union Congress of Soviet writers, held in Moscow from 17 to 31 August 1934], together with other important Soviet writers, poets and dramatists, all described socialist culture as the antithesis of the decadent culture of a doomed and criminal world. Rationally organized according to the objective laws of historical development, socialist culture would be a culture of a new type and of the highest stage. From its heights all the preceding cultural activity of humanity would seem like prehistory. Thus it must be imbued with an optimism that expressed the joy of the Stalinist epoch; it follows that every writer and artist must be guided in his work by a love of the people, the motherland, the party and Stalin, and a spirit of hatred towards their enemies. It was this combination of love and hatred that Gorky called true, socialist humanism. (Golomstock 2011, pp. 88 ff.)

The most sinister feature of these totalitarian unions [like the Reich Chamber of Culture and the Union of Soviet Artists] was that they were obligatory: only as a member of a union did the artist have the right to practice his profession in his own country. … In the Soviet Union such legal measures [as introduced in Nazi Germany] were unnecessary: all essential artists' materials were in the hands of the State and could be distributed only amongst members of the Union of Soviet Artists – paints, canvas, paper, plaster, bronze and marble, not to mention lithographs which, like all means of mass reproduction, were strictly accountable to the State. (p. 94).

It is also important that the Bolsheviks in the Soviet Union wanted to abolish religion in favor of atheism, since religious ideas were in strong contrast to their own ideology to create a stateless paradise on earth—the completion of communism. It follows that priests, as already mentioned, especially of the Christian Orthodox Church, and believers were persecuted, killed, or put into Forced Labor Camps. It has been estimated that in 1937 alone more than 85,000 Orthodox priests have been killed. Many Churches and also Synagogues were destroyed or turned into bath houses, granaries, night clubs or museums for atheism.

We turn next to the Chinese Cultural Revolution (1966–1976), engineered by Mao to maintain or regain his power which he had widely lost as a consequence of the Great Jump Forward of 1959–1961, which had led to an estimated number of 20–43 million people dying from starvation (Margolin 1998, p 546). Mao used the young educated generation of frustrated Chinese in the cities as a lever:

> The young people between 14 and 24 were the more enthusiastic instruments in the hands of Mao, since in them a doctrinal fanaticism was combined with great frustration. Their fanaticism was related to the circumstances under which they had grown up. They were the first generation who had been fully educated after the revolution of 1949 and were too young and too influenced by city life to know anything about the horrors of the Great Jump. (Margolin 1998, p 575).

So it was relatively easy for Mao to make them believe that they were the "white, unwritten leaf" on which the glorious heroic drama of the building of communism should be written. (p. 575).

In this way, the Red Guards were formed and officially permitted in factories on November 16 and in the villages on December 15, 1966. Millions of disciples and students organized and found in their teachers, professors, and administrators in local and provincial offices without effort demons fighting the communist development, who had to be humiliated and persecuted. Whereas the number of deaths caused because of these witch hunts was much lower than during the Great Jump Forward (probably around one million victims), the damages for the social system were in certain respects much greater. Moreover, the movement led also to the destruction of a great part of the Chinese cultural heritage, which was considered to be the result of a feudal and bourgeois past.

10.1.3 Christianity

Many Christian Supreme Values are contained in the Ten Commandments in Exodus 20:2–17 (American Bible Society 1977) of the Old Testament:

> "I am the LORD your God, who brought you out of the land of Egypt, out of the house of bondage. You shall have no other gods before Me.
>
> "You shall not make for yourself a carved image—any likeness of anything that is in heaven above, or that is in the earth beneath, or that is in the water under the earth; you shall not bow down to them nor serve them. For I, the LORD your God, am a jealous God, visiting the iniquity of the fathers upon the children to the third and fourth generations of those who hate Me, but showing mercy to thousands, to those who love Me and keep My commandments.
>
> "You shall not take the name of the LORD your God in vain, for the LORD will not hold him guiltless who takes His name in vain.
>
> "Remember the Sabbath day, to keep it holy. Six days you shall labor and do all your work, but the seventh day is the Sabbath of the LORD your God. In it you shall do no work: you, nor your son, nor your daughter, nor your male servant, nor your female servant, nor your cattle, nor your stranger who is within your gates. For in six days the LORD made the heavens and the earth, the sea, and all that is in them, and rested the seventh day. Therefore, the LORD blessed the Sabbath day and hallowed it.
>
> "Honor your father and your mother, that your days may be long upon the land which the LORD your God is giving you.
>
> "You shall not murder.
>
> "You shall not commit adultery.
>
> "You shall not steal.
>
> "You shall not bear false witness against your neighbor.
>
> "You shall not covet your neighbor's house; you shall not covet your neighbor's wife, nor his male servant, nor his female servant, nor his ox, nor his donkey, nor anything that is your neighbor's."

Following the first three of the ten commandments of the Old Testament quoted above, Christianity like Islam originally did not allow to create images of God because of His invisible and supernatural character. But later the veneration of pictures and sculptures of Christ, God Father, the Virgin Mary, and the Saints were allowed by the Christian Church. This was justified by Pope Gregory I, who explained that these images were the books of the poor, needed by them because they could not read. But again and again, the veneration of such images gave rise to steps by religious and political authorities against this wrong position. During the seventh and eighth centuries five Byzantine emperors, influenced by the Eastern

Orthodox Church tried to end the veneration of images (iconoclasm). And later after the protestant reformation of the sixteenth century the reformed church, following the commandments of the Decalogue removed all pictures and sculptures from the churches, though with the exception of Luther who took another attitude (Meyers Konversations-Lexikon 1903, Vol. 2, p 895).

10.1.4 Islamism

The supreme values of Islam concerning literature and arts are stated in the Quran and the Hadiths as follows:

> 52. And indeed We bestowed aforetime on Ibrâhim (Abraham) his (portion of) guidance, and We were well-acquainted with him (as to his belief in the Oneness of Allâh, etc.).
> 53. When he said to his father and his people: "What are these images, to which you are devoted?"
> 54. They said: "We found our fathers worshipping them."
> 55. He said: "Indeed you and your fathers have been in manifest error." (Sure 21).

(Der Koran 1959).

I stuffed for the Prophet a pillow decorated with pictures (of animals) which looked like a Namruqa (i.e., a small cushion). He came and stood among the people with excitement apparent on his face. I said, "O Allah's Apostle! What is wrong?" He said, "What is this pillow?" I said, "I have prepared this pillow for you, so that you may recline on it." He said, "Don't you know that angels do not enter a house wherein there are pictures; and whoever makes a picture will be punished on the Day of Resurrection and will be asked to give life to (what he has created)?"[1]

Whereas in National Socialism Entartete Kunst (Degenerate Art) had to be banned, burned, or sold (for the profit of the true believers), because it did not correspond to the right art feeling of the Aryan Race, and because churches had to be destroyed in the Soviet Union because religious art had to be removed since it conflicted with the atheistic views of Communism; the situation was and is different from the perspective of strictly observed Islam. No pictures and statues of the only and invisible God (Allah) are allowed because they never can grasp his true metaphysical nature. It follows that all such distorting pictures have to be destroyed. The same is true for images and statues of so-called gods venerated by misguided heathens, and of saints or of deceased *holy men* and *women* who are adored by unknowing people. They and their temples or graves have all to be destroyed, since they are at best abominations and at worst pictures and statues of demons.

Examples of such destructions are those of the Bamiyan Buddhas in Afghanistan by the Taliban in 2001 and of the Baalshamin temple committed by the ISIS in Palmyra in 2015.

[1]Hadith of Bukhari, Vol 4, 447–Internet Sacred Text Archive. Accessed January 31, 2017.

10.2 Works of Art and Poetry and Military Parades Celebrating the Supreme Values and the Leaders of Ideocracies

Whereas works of art and poetry condemned by the supreme values of the different ideologies had to be banned or destroyed, all ideocracies have the tendency to glorify their cause and their leaders in poems and works of art. Subsequently we present some of these poems. Works of art include for instance in the Soviet Union pictures of Stalin as a heroic personality and in Nazi Germany of Hitler as a knight. According to the National Socialist and Communist ideologies, leaders are also presented with happy ordinary people. And their power was and is demonstrated by huge parades at the Nuremberg Nazi party gatherings, or victory parades on the Red Square in Moscow, and also by Communist parades in the North Korean capital Pyongyang. Grandiose designs were planned for future buildings in Berlin (Speer's Plan for the New Berlin City Centre called Germania) and in Moscow (Iofan's Plan for the Palace of the Soviets). Even the Aztecs commemorated with pictures the bloody victims sacrificed to keep the Sun going (Codices Tudela and Florence).

Ode an Stalin	Ode to Stalin
Es wird ganz Deutschland einmal Stalin danken, In jeder Stadt steht Stalins Monument Dort wird er sein, wo sich die Reben ranken, und dort in Kiel erkennt ihn ein Student. Dort wirst Du, Stalin, steh`n, in voller Blüte, Der Apfelbäume an dem Bodensee Und durch den Schwarzwald wandelt seine Güte, Und winkt heran zu sich ein scheues Reh Wenn sich vor Freude rot die Wangen färben, dankt man Dir, Stalin, und sagt nichts als: "Du!" Ein Armer flüstert „Stalin" noch im Sterben und Stalins Hand drückt ihm die Augen zu. (J. R. Becher 1953) Was tun? ein Licht und ward Geleit und eine Stimme, die Antwort gab in den Traum, durch den Tag, durch die Zeit. Und die noch gestern die Wirrnis schlug und der Spuk der Dämonen entzweit, trug Lenins Wort wie ein Lerchenflug	All Germans will be grateful once to Stalin, In each town stands Stalin's monument He will stay where vineyards grow, and North in Kiel by students seen There you will stand, oh Stalin, where at Lake Constance bloom the apple trees. And through Black Forest roams his kindness, And waves to him a shy roe deer. And when the cheeks get red because of joy, All people thank you, Stalin, and say only: "You!" A poor man dying whispers "Stalin" and Stalin's hand closes his eyes. Out of the darkness of thousand years was breaking What to do? a light and did escort us to a voice, which gave an answer in our dream, for the day and through all time.

(continued)

(continued)

durch den Traum, durch den Tag, durch die Zeit. Und sie wussten, was tun, und die Frage schwieg, und ihr Träumen ward Wirklichkeit, und das Wort ward Tat, und die Tat ward Sieg, Ruhm und Unsterblichkeit!	And those confusion-beaten until yesterday and divided by the demons' nightmares, Lenin's word now carried like lark's flight through their dream, and through the day, eternity. And the question ended, for they knew their task, and their dream became reality, and to action turned the word, and to victory the action, to fame and immortality

Louis Fürnberg commemorating Lenin's 100th birthday in the East German Neues Deutschland on April 22, 1970

Hitler	Hitler
Einmal nur lassen Götter in Jahrhunderten einmal einen kämpfen, einen gegen Millionen! Einmal nur, in Jahrtausenden schenken die Götter einem die Kraft sich von der Erde ins All zu schrauben, nur durch den Glauben, und alle Brüder, Wir, du und ich erleben die Heimat wieder und finden sich!	Only once within centuries Gods let fight one alone, one against millions! Only once, during thousands of years the Gods bestow the power to one, to rise from the earth high into space, by Faith alone, and all we brothers, we, you and I, enjoy our nation again in finding each other

Carl Maria Holzapfel: "Dem Führer". In Deutsche Bühne, Januar/Februar. 1934, p. 5. Quoted from (Wulf 1966, p. 413)

10.3 Ideocracies and the Sciences

We have already argued that the Supreme Values of ideocracies in contrast to the insights of science are believed to be absolutely true, and therefore are at least partially representing a distorted image of reality. It follows that their belief system must in certain respects contradict the results of the sciences and thus hinder scientific progress. We will demonstrate this by certain examples first referring to National Socialism and Communism, and secondly to religiously anchored supreme values.

10.3.1 National Socialism and Bolshevism

No, the Jew does not possess any gifts allowing him to create culture. For he does not and did never own the idealism without which a further development of humanity is impossible. This means that his intellect will never be constructive, but only destructive, or in rare cases able to whipping up developments. … Not by his efforts any progress of humanity takes place, but in spite of him (Hitler 1933, p 332).

According to Hitler's view embodied in the supreme values of National Socialism the Jews are parasites who are a mortal danger to the only creative race of Aryans. It is thus not surprising that beginning with the "Gesetz zur Wiederherstellung des Berufsbeamtentums" (Law Restoring Professional Public Officialdom) already in April 1933 all Jewish professors (with the exception for some time of Jews who had fought in World War I) were removed from German universities. Besides them some politically unreliable German professors were also dismissed. The consequences for German science were catastrophic:

It has been calculated that about 15% of the professors and assistants of the German universities and research institutes have been lost. This is already purely numerically a grave loss. But the damage was even greater, if the scientific qualifications of the researchers are taken into account, who had to leave Germany. I have already mentioned that in physics Germany lost her leading position, when I spoke about the emigration of the physicists from Göttingen. In my own Department [Law] eight of the ten or eleven internationally renowned scholars left of the generation born around 1880. New Departments like Sociology which had developed before World War I and during the Weimar Republic practically vanished (Kunkel 1966, pp. 117 f.).

According to Beyerchen (1982, p. 75) at least 106 physicists were dismissed in German and Austrian universities and institutes. This amounted probably to a share of about 20% of all physicists. Twenty Nobel prize winners were dismissed or gave up their positions, seventeen of them Jews (p 77). As a consequence of its wrong image of reality, especially concerning Jews, the National Socialist totalitarian system even lowered its own long-term chances of success by such measures.

In the Soviet Union similar problems could be observed. Her supreme values obviously required a rejection of the theory of biological evolution as formulated by Darwin, and thus of the Mendelian laws of inheritance. Biological research was based on the false assertion by Trofim Lysenko that capabilities acquired by individuals during their lifetime would be passed on to the next generation. Stalin supported Lysenko and several geneticists were persecuted or even killed. But the universities also suffered otherwise from the purges initiated by Stalin.

Visas wanted for emigration by Jewish scholars were not granted since it was argued they were needed at home for research. When these restrictions were later removed after Stalin's death, more than one million Jews left the Soviet Union.

10.3.2 Religiously Based Ideocracies

Whatever knowledge man has acquired outside Holy Writ, if it be harmful it is there condemned; if it be wholesome it is there contained.

Saint Augustine (354–430)

Either the books contain what is in the Koran, in which case we do not have to read them, or they contain the opposite of what is in the Koran, in which case we must not read them.

Omar, the Arab conqueror of Alexandria in 640

The Christian attitude expressed by St. Augustine persisted over centuries. Already the rise of Christianity had unfortunate consequences for science. The Roman Christian Emperor Theodosius proscribed the pagan religions and ordered, in 392, the destruction of all Greek temples. In the year that he banned the pagan religions, the Christians destroyed the temple of Serapis in Alexandria, which still housed the only remaining extensive collection of Greek works. It is estimated that about 300,000 manuscripts were destroyed (Kline 1972, Vol. 1, p 171).

Centuries later the same attitude prevailed, as is documented by the fate of Galileo Galilei at the hands of the Roman Catholic Church. He had to revoke his belief in the Heliocentric System under threat of torture in 1633, to proclaim that the sun moved around the earth and was condemned to home imprisonment. But since the Catholic Church did never succeed to combine spiritual and secular power in Europe, Galileo's works were still published, for instance in the Netherlands, so that the Heliocentric Theory could not be suppressed.

Generally speaking, the Christian Churches – except for the cases of Calvin's Geneva and the Münster Anabaptists – were never able to combine spiritual and secular power in Europe. Their last efforts to do so faltered because of the stalemate between Protestant and Catholic princes in the Thirty Years' War. This led to the result that the Christian Churches only succeeded to persecute and eliminate obstinate nonbelievers and their heretic views if they could get the support of the secular power of the rulers. This happened for instance in the war against the Cathars (Albingenses) from 1209–1229 when the Catholic Church under Pope Innocent III. got the help of the French King who wanted to subdue Southwestern France to his rule.

Omar, the Islamic conqueror of Alexandria, followed his believes stated above. All remaining Greek books were destroyed. For six months the baths of Alexandria were heated by burning rolls of parchment (Kline 1972, Vol. 1, p. 171).

But history between about 800 and 1300 shows that Islam can well be compatible with the development of science. The Islamic Caliphates based first in Damascus and later in Baghdad as well as that in Cordova, Spain, followed different policies than the first conquerors. Greek scientific works still available in Syria and Egypt were translated into Arabian, and the cultural resources of Persia and India made available. The Caliphs even bought manuscripts from the Byzantines. As stated by Kline (1972, Vol. 1, p. 191 f.):

> Rather quickly the Arabs became interested in the arts and sciences. Both centers [Baghdad and Cordova] attracted scientists and supported their work, though Bagdad proved to be the greater; an academy, a library, and an astronomical observatory were established there. …
>
> One speaks of Arabic mathematics, but it was Arabic in language primarily. Most of the scholars were Greeks, Christians, Persians and Jews. However, it is to the credit of the Arabs that after the period of conquest, which was marked by religious fanaticism, they were liberal to other peoples and sects and the infidels were able to function freely.

It is thus not surprising that science including astronomy and optics, medicine and philosophy reached a higher level in the two Caliphates than in medieval Europe, which profited later from the transfer of parts of this knowledge, when its own positive development began in the twelfth century.

However, the favorable development in Islamic countries did not persist in later centuries. The Islamic Ottoman Empire hindered the introduction of printing for centuries because the Holy Word of the Koran was only allowed to be copied by hand.

The modern experiences with Islamist states like the Taliban in Afghanistan or even the mature Islamic idiocrasy in Saudi Arabia are discouraging. The Taliban did not allow women to attend school, and even in Saudi Arabia they are not allowed to drive or to move in public unattended by a male relative. Under such conditions, one half of the population is prohibited or at least restricted to work scientifically.

10.4 Caricatures and Underground Jokes as Critique of Totalitarian Regimes

In Totalitarian Regimes,any critique of the leaders of the regime and of the supreme values is strictly forbidden and severely punished. Even to listen to different opinions or to the broadcasts of enemies has the result of heavy imprisonment. My own uncle, Johannes Bernholz, the 24-years older brother of my father, living as peasant in a village in Southeastern Westphalia, was condemned to two years of heavy prison because he had listened during World War II to BBC, the British Broadcasting Corporation. My parents did not tell this to us children until after the war, because they were probably afraid that we might mention it. Similarly, any opposing literature like the Samizdat in the Soviet Union could only be written clandestinely and circulated to trusted relatives and friends.

It was thus typical that the underground opposition took refuge in short jokes criticizing the regime. It is not by chance that Ulsterite (underground jokes) experience their best times in totalitarian regimes.

But as could be observed in most cases, the supreme values of totalitarian regimes are usually, at least during the first years after the introduction of these regimes, not understood, believed or not taken at face value. This was also true for foreign observers and politicians, as shown by how the latter were trying to handle their transactions with totalitarian leaders similarly to those with democratic regimes, as tried by Prime Ministers Chamberlain and Daladier in the late 1930s in their compromises with Hitler's government. Revealing for this lack of understanding of totalitarian regimes is also the following statement by the American Brigadier General Thomas R. Philipps probably written in 1939.

Frederick's (King of Prussia) up building of Prussia determined whether the small German states eventually were to group themselves around Prussia or around Austria. The expansion of Prussia was continued by Bismarck and now has been completed by Chancellor Hitler, making one great nation of all the people of the German race.[2]

And this attitude prevailed in spite of the fact that first steps in explaining the nature of totalitarian regimes had already been taken.[3]Die politischen Religionen. Wien; 2. Ed. Stockholm: Bermann Fischer (1939). Characteristic for this lack of understanding of the nature of totalitarian regimes are also the caricatures in the foreign press, which do not show any apprehension of the ideocratic nature of totalitarian regimes. This lack of understanding has also been demonstrated by the behavior of several foreign sports delegations at the Olympic Games in Berlin during the summer of 1936:

> Some athletes used the Nazi salute in the opening ceremony of the Berlin Olympics as they passed by Hitler in the reviewing stand. This was done by delegates from Afghanistan, Bermuda, Bulgaria, Bolivia, France, Greece, Iceland, Italy and Turkey. The Bulgarian athletes performed the Nazi salute and broke into a goose-step; Turkish athletes maintained the salute all around the track. There is some confusion over the use of the salute, since the stiff-arm Nazi salute could have been mistaken for an Olympic salute, with the right arm held out at a slight angle to the right from the shoulder. According to the American sports writer Jeremy Schaap, only half of the athletes from Austria performed a Nazi salute, while the other half gave an Olympic salute. According to the historian Richard Mandell, there are conflicting reports on whether athletes from France performed a Nazi salute or an Olympic Salute. In football, the England football team bowed to pressure from the British foreign office and performed the salute during a friendly match on 14 May 1938.
>
> (Wikipedia, Article "Nazi Salute.")

10.4.1 Flüsterwitze in the Third Reich (National Socialist Germany)

> Hitler visits a lunatic asylum, where the patients all dutifully perform the German greeting. Suddenly, Hitler sees one man whose arm is not raised. "Why don't you greet me the same way as everyone else," he hisses at the man. The man answers: "My Führer, I'm an orderly. I'm not crazy!"

One of the first measures implemented by the Nazis was making the "Hitler salute" mandatory.

---

[2]Philipps, Thomas R. (1940) Roots of Strategy. Vol 1, Harrisburg, PA., p. 303.

[3]See e.g. Beckerath (1927).

An adjutant bursts into Göring's office: "The Reichstag is on fire!". Göring checks his watch and says: "What, already?"

There was a widespread suspicion that the Nazis themselves had set fire to the Reichstag parliament in order to be able to blame it on their opponents.

Hitler and Göring are standing atop the Berlin radio tower. Hitler says he wants to do something to put a smile on Berliners' faces. So Göring says: "Why don't you jump?"

A factory worker, Marianne K., was executed for telling this joke. Her husband had been killed in Stalingrad.

If Hitler, Göring and Goebbels were on a ship in a storm and the ship would sink, who would be saved? Answer: Germany.

In the end, many Germans wished death to their leadership. Yet in this and other jokes it interestingly isn't a revolution that rids the people of the oppressors, but the forces of nature.

What has gold in its mouth, silver in its hair and lead in its bones? A member of the Volkssturm.

On September 25, 1944, Hitler was forced to call up a "Volkssturm," or "popular offensive." This pathetic militia consisted of Hitler Youths and of men up to sixty who had previously been deemed unfit for military service.[4]

What is the appearance of an Aryan man? Fair-haired like Hitler, slim like Göring and tall like Goebbels.

Here lametta, there lametta,

Our Hermann (Goering) gets always fatter.

Lametta refers to the many medals Goering was wearing on his breast.

The Nazi leaders are standing on marshy ground. Goering has already sunk to his breast, and Himmler to his neck. Only the Führer (Hitler) is still untouched by the swamp. Himmler is asking: „How is he able to remain clean?",„Please be quiet,"Goering responds, „he is standing on the head of Jupp!"(Josef Goebbels, who was rather small).[5]

10.4.2 Political Jokes from the Soviet Union

Three office workers are being questioned during a purge. It turns out that one of them is always a minute late to work, another a minute too early, and the third right on time. All three are purged from the party:

The first for delinquency,
The second for sycophancy,

---

[4]These jokes have been quoted from: http://www.huffingtonpost.com/rudolph-herzog/war-jokes-hitler_b_1798599.html?slideshow=true#gallery/245536/0, Accessed Januar 31, 2017.

[5]These jokes are from the memory of the author, 15 years of age when hearing them in 1944. Compare also Gamm (1966)

The third for bureaucracy.
Three prisoners meet at a transit camp.
The first says:
" I have been in prison since 1919 for calling
Karl Radek a counterrevolutionary."
he second replies:
"I have been here since 1938 for saying that
Radek wasn't a counterrevolutionary."
The third interjects:
"And I'm sorry to say that I *am* Karl Radek."

Stalin's pipe went missing. He calls the NKVD and orders
them to find it. Two hours later, he finds it himself in his own
boot. He calls the NKVD again and says (in heavily accented
Russian):
"Don't worry about it. I've found it."
"I'm sorry, Comrade Stalin, but we've already arrested ten
People on account of your pipe!"
"Let them go."
"But that's impossible sir. All ten have confessed."

Lenin said:
"Communism = Soviet Power + electrification".
By using the most basic laws of algebra,
Soviet engineers have deduced that:
Soviet Power = Communism – electrification
Electrification = Communism – Soviet Power

"Lenin died, but his cause lives on."
An Armenian, having read this slogan, said:
"Eh, Lenin, Lenin … it'd have been better if you had
lived on and your cause had died. "
One day, Stalin unexpectedly orders Poskrebyshev to get him
a copy of the Gospels. When Poskrebyshev returns, Stalin says:
"Find the place where Christ feeds 10,000 people with
Five loaves of bread. I'm curious about how he did it."
A speaker at a meeting goes on and about how "we're going
To catch up to the capitalist countries." Someone asks:
"Once we catch up to them, can we stay there?"
A poster in a peasants' dormitory: "Sleep faster – someone else
Is waiting for your pillow."
A riddle:
Imagine that Stalin, the members of the Politburo, and their whole
entourage were aboard a steamer on the Volga. Suddenly, the steamer
begins to sink. If the steamer were to go down in a moment, who would

be saved?
Answer: All the peoples of the Soviet Union.
Two Soviets are talking:
"What do you think was Adam and Eve's nationality?"
"Soviet no doubt. They had nothing to wear, only a single apple
to eat, and thought they were living in paradise."[6]

10.4.3 *Political Jokes in the Communist German Democratic Republic (GDR)*

What is "Democratic Centralism?" The collective favors it, the individual is against it, and the leadership does whatever it wants.

Wilhelm Pieck and Otto Grotewohl [early Communist leaders of the GDR] drive with a taxi through Berlin. "If I am now throwing cigarettes out of the window, all men will follow us," says Pieck. "And if I now were throwing ladies' stocks out of the window, all women would follow," adds Grotewohl. "And if I threw both of you out of the window," retorts the driver of the taxi, the whole population would be running behind me."

When did Lenin exclaim: Learn, learn and learn again? When he saw the school grades of Walter Ulbricht [Secretary General of the East German Communist party].

Question: What is laying on the stairs and lying? Das Neue Deutschland [the leading Communist newspaper of the GDR].

In Capitalistic countries one is getting everything for money. In Socialism, by contrast, one gets everything which is not available for money.

"Who has been the first man, Fritz?" Fritz shouts: "Our beloved Stalin." "No," explains the teacher, the question was not meant like this. Adam has been the first men." "Yes," answered Fritz astonished, "But only if you also count the capitalists."

Three men are sitting in the train to Siberia. The first is asking his opposite: "Brother, how much did you receive?" "Five years." "And which crime did you commit?" "I was against Popow."

"And you brother, what did you get?" "Also five years." "And what did you commit?"

He answers: "I have been in favor of Popow," and turning to the third: "Brother, what did you receive?" "Also five years." "And what did you do?" "I have done nothing. I am Popow."

---

[6]These political jokes have been quoted from: Brandenberger (2009).

Excerpt from Walter Ulbricht's speech at the 20th anniversary of the GDR:

"Twenty years ago we were standing at an abyss. Now we have moved a great step further."

Somebody steps into a hardware store and asks: "Do you have nails?" "No." "Do you have screws?" "No." "Do you have at least a screwdriver? "No." "Well, what then do you have at all?" "Opened all time." "And why have you opened all the time, if you are selling nothing?" "Because we have no lock."

The children are learning in school that man descended from the apes. But Fritz asks the teacher:

But GDR-citizens have certainly not descended from the apes." "Why not?" "No former ape can live for so long without bananas."

A customer enters a meat store. "Do you have beef olive?" "We don't have it."
"Do you have pork cutlet?" "We don't have it, too."
"Do you have veal cutlet?" "This, too, we don't have."
"Do you have a large Frankfurter?" "Unfortunately not."
Disappointed the customer leaves. Says one sales assistant to the other:
"Astonishing, what a good memory this man had."
Because he remembered the names of these items after years during which they had not been available.

The teacher asks: "Where has Socialism be born?" Fritz raises his hand: "In the Harz mountains."

The teacher surprised: "Why there?" "My father said: "It has been born between Sorge and Elend."

Sorge and Elend are two small cities in the Harz mountains, whose English translation would be "Sorrow" and "Misery".

(All these GDR-jokes have been taken from DDR-Witze 2009).

References

American Bible Society (1977) The Bible. Containing the old and New Testament. Revised Standard Version, New York

Baynes NH (1942) The speeches of Adolf Hitler, April 1922–August 1939. Vol 2. Oxford University Press, Oxford

Becher JR (1953) Danksagung, Zum Tode J. W. Stalins – orlandos.de

Beckerath EV (1927) Wesen und Werden des fascistischen Staates. Berlin, and Voegelin, Erich (1938)

Beyerschen AD (1982) *Wissenschaftler unter Hitler.* Physiker im Dritten Reich. Frankfurt-Berlin-Wien: Ullstein Sachbuch. Original English Edition: Scientists under Hitler. Yale University Press, New Haven and London

Brandenberger D (ed) (2009) Political humor under Stalin. An Anthology of Unofficial Jokes and Anecdotes. Slavica, Bloomington, Indiana

DDR-Witze. Das Original (2009) Berlin: Eulenspiegel Verlag

Gamm H-J (1966) Der Flüsterwitz im Deutschen Reich. List, München

Golomstock I (2011) Totalitarian Art. Overlook Duckworth, New York and London
Hitler A (1933) Mein Kampf. München: Franz Eher Nachfolger. 49th edn
Kline M\ (1972) Mathematical thought from ancient to modern yimes. Oxford University Press, Oxford, New York and Toronto
Koran D (1959) Das Heilige Buch des Islam. München: Wilhelm GoldmannVerlag
Kunkel W (1966) Der Professor im Dritten Reich. In: Die deutsche Universität im Dritten Reich. München: R. Piper & Co
Margolin J-L (1998) China: Ein langer Marsch in die Nacht. In: Courtois S (ed) Das Schwarzbuch des Kommunismus. München: Piper, pp 510–608. Original French Ed: Le livre noir du communisme. Paris: Robert Laffont, 1997
Solzhenitsyn AI (1973) The gulag archipelago. Harper & Row, New York and London
Wulf J (1966) Literatur und Dichtung im Dritten Reich. Eine Dokumentation. Hamburg: rororo Taschenbuchausgabe

Chapter 11
A Formal Model of Totalitarianism

11.1 Introduction: Development and Weaknesses of the Theory of Totalitarianism

After the fall of Communist Regimes, it has become clear that the much criticized theory of totalitarianism has been more successful in explaining events than the alternatives offered by many of its critics. Ballestrem (1992) has shown that one can even demonstrate this with the help of the characteristics used by Friedrich and Brzezinski (1956/1965) to define totalitarianism. Still, it cannot be denied that there are severe weaknesses in the theories developed, e.g., by these authors or by Hannah Arendt (1968/1951), as stressed by Schlangen (1970) and Linz (1975). These theories are too static to account for the rise of totalitarian regimes, their development, and their breakdown or transformation into different political systems.

Since then the theory of totalitarianism has moved further ahead (see, e.g., Linz 1975; Wuthe 1981; Bracher 1970, 1987). But it still lacked a unified and consistent structure capable of explaining a wide range of historical phenomena related to totalitarianism. During the 1990s these gaps have been closed by similar, but independently developed contributions by Piekalkiewicz and Penn (1995) and the present author (1991, 1993, 1994, 1997). Their approaches accept the agreement of earlier authors (e.g., Drath 1963; Schlangen 1970) that totalitarianism can only develop on the basis of an ideology with supreme values, a "political religion" (Maier and Schaefer 1997). But they explain that three other factors besides ideology have to be present to make the emergence of totalitarianism probable. First, an organization has to be founded with a leader or leadership having the monopoly to interpret the ideology. Second, the secular power of a state has to be conquered

---

The greatest part of this chapter is republished with the permission of Springer for the article: Bernholz, Peter (2001): Ideocracy and Totalitarianism: A Formal Analysis Incorporating Ideology?, Public Choice 108, 33–75.

P. Bernholz, *Totalitarianism, Terrorism and Supreme Values*,
Studies in Public Choice 33, DOI 10.1007/978-3-319-56907-9_11

and spiritual and secular leadership to be combined in the hands of the same person or group. Third, this is only possible if the society of the respective state is undergoing a crisis. The authors formulate their (verbal) theories in a way that they can also describe the dynamics of the process: The growth of an ideological movement, its grasp of secular power, the development of a totalitarian state, and its final disappearance. The latter happens, since totalitarian regimes either turn into mature ideocracies, e.g., a theocracy, because of their success in reaching the ends implied by their ideologies. Or they disappear because they are defeated as a consequence of their expansionary foreign policies or since they change the content of their ideology because they realize that they cannot reach their ideological ends.

Apart from these theoretical approaches to totalitarianism, there exists a different type of theory, which has scarcely been influenced by the former. This approach has rather some relationships to the old theory of tyranny, dictatorship and autocracy (see, e.g. Tullock 1987). During the past two decades it has applied the methods of economics to create formal models of dictatorship. In doing so, it has usually assumed that a dictator employs the power of the state to maximize his utility under certain restrictions. The utility depends only on the wealth, income or consumption of the dictator, whereas the restrictions refer, e.g., to the means necessary to maintain his power, or make a distinction between whether the dictator is a roving or a stationary bandit (Olson 1993; McGuire and Olson 1998). This assumption leads to the result, that the latter is more interested in long-term exploitation than the former, so that he has to exploit his subjects less in the present to be able to use their resources for his purposes also in the future.

The most advanced of these formalized economic models has been developed by Wintrobe (1998). He enriches the theory by introducing power besides consumption into the utility function of the dictator and by using a broader set of restrictions. Wintrobe seeks not only to explain ordinary dictatorships (Tinpot dictatorships, tyrannies, and timocracies), but also totalitarian regimes. The latter is the outcome of a great weight given in the dictator's utility function to power as compared to consumption, and of a production function efficiently producing loyalty with the help of a well-organized party and a strong ideology. In spite of the merits of Wintrobe's model it suffers from the assumption that the dictator is mainly interested in power and that ideology is only a means to maximize it. Economists seem to have a hard time to accept that ideologies can be the very aim of totalitarian regimes. To mention just one example: Why should Hitler devote scarce transportation facilities and armed forces to transport people to Auschwitz, which both were badly needed to support the struggling German armies? If power had been his predominant aim, he would never have done so. But his behavior is easily understandable if ideology entered his utility function.

In spite of these weaknesses the formal economic theories of totalitarianism have the advantage of allowing the derivation of unambiguous results. And whereas the other theories mentioned first are clearly more realistic, their results are less compelling because only verbal arguments are used. To remedy this situation, the present paper formalizes this theoretical approach with the purpose to clarify terms and to derive results in a logically compelling way. Also, a clear line can be drawn between exogenous influences and influences represented by the interrelated variables of the model. Another advantage is the possibility to abolish the requirement that the supreme values of an ideology have to be lexicographically preferred to everything else, employed in the verbal model (Bernholz 1997). Though such preference functions are usually demanded by ideologies from their followers, this does not mean that all followers are prepared to sacrifice even their lives or those of others for these supreme values. The formalization allows to express the intensity of feelings for these purposes with the help of parameters, the value of which can be varied in a comparative analysis. On the other hand, some of the richness of the verbal analysis has to be sacrificed, and simplifications to be made to keep the model manageable. For example, the degree of organization of believers as well as the deepness of crises will only be accounted for by using exogenous parameters. Moreover, we will not introduce explicitly the monopoly of interpretation of the ideology and the necessary combination of secular and spiritual power by a leader or leadership. In this sense, we will dismiss possible tensions between divergent views of leaders and other believers by assuming only one representative individual utility function. This can either be interpreted in a way that one leader or a leadership group with identical utility functions is controlling all believers and, after securing secular power, the state, or that all believers have the same representative utility function and control the state. With these two interpretations in mind, we will subsequently speak of the utility function of the representative believer.

An important difficulty in formalizing the theory is how to introduce ideology. For the contents of ideologies are on the whole very different. They can thus, apart from certain general traits, not be included appropriately in a general theory. Consequently, we have introduced ideologies indirectly by taking as variables into the utility function of the representative believer the percentages of believers and of inconvertible people in the population, with the first ratio assumed to be valued positively and the second negatively. This assumption is justified, since about all ideologies want to spread their creed to other people thought amenable to the salvation usually promised. And ideologies want also to fight the forces of evil embodied in in-convertibles (e.g., Jews for National Socialism; capitalists, bourgeois or kulaks for Communism; stubborn non-believers or heretics for certain religions). Now, if the presence of believers has a positive and that of in-convertibles a negative influence on the utility of believers, they will be prepared to spend resources on winning new believers and on removing in-convertibles under certain conditions. In cases in which no in-convertibles are defined in an ideology, the respective parameter can be set to zero. Finally, it will be assumed that, similar to the second set of theories, consumption is another variable in the utility function of the representative believer. But in contrast to Wintrobe's theory, power is not contained there. It is rather implicitly embodied in the restrictions. For it is used to tax and to use government revenues to finance the conversion of believers, the removal of in-convertibles and the effort to increase the probability of spreading the totalitarian regime internationally, which both may imply the use of force (Sect. 11.3).

In the following we proceed as follows. In Sect. 11.2, we describe in a first model under which conditions believers will be successful to spread their creed and finally to secure secular power. Also, the conditions under which a successful ideology will not turn into a totalitarian regime but evolve into a mature ideocracy will be discussed. In Sect. 11.3, the application of secular power within the totalitarian state will be analyzed with the help of a second model. It will also be concerned with the expansionary policies of totalitarian regimes. Section 11.4 will allow a closer look at the possible evolution of totalitarian regimes by using numerical simulations. Moreover, the transformation or demise of totalitarian regimes will be discussed. The chapter will end in Sect. 11.5 with some concluding remarks.

11.2 Gaining Secular Power*

11.2.1 Presentation of Model 1

When the ideological values of a new belief system, a Weltanschauung, have been invented and found their first adherents, or when an old Weltanschauung has been re-established—usually combined with some reinterpretation of its values—these adherents strive to spread it to non-believers and to gain secular power as a means to accomplish their ends. There may also, moreover, be people, who are living in the respective region or state that are not amenable to conversion. They are either not predestined by a higher metaphysical entity to become believers or to be saved, or they are the sworn enemies of the true belief and thus cannot be converted. Thus, secular power may be needed to remove or to "neutralize" these *in-convertibles*. It may also be thought of as an instrument to fight holy wars against infidels in the effort to convert them.

In the following model with a two-period time horizon, we describe the aims of believers with the help of the utility function of a representative believer. According to it, believers are interested in their consumption during the next period t and the following period $t + 1$, C_t and C_{t+1}. Again for simplicity, we may just think of one physical consumption good, *food*. But believers are also concerned about the ratio of the number of believers in the population, B_{t+1}/P_{t+1}, at the beginning of period $t + 1$, to which they attach a positive value. Here B_{t+1}, P_{t+1} are the numbers of the believers and of the total population, respectively. The representative believer also attaches a negative value to the ratio of the number of *in-convertibles* in the population. But since we assume that believers have no influence on them as long as secular power has not been won, we neglect this variable of the utility function for the moment. It will be introduced into the more general Model 2 in Sect. 11.3.1.

We now postulate the following utility function at the beginning of period t for the representative believer:

$$U_t = AC_t^{\alpha} C_{t+1}^{\beta} (B_{t+1}/P_{t+1})^{\gamma}. \quad (11.2.1)$$

All parameters in this as in the following equations are positive. We assume further that it is costly to maintain and to increase the number of believers. These costs amount in period t to

$$K_t = E(B_{t+1}/B_t)^{\varepsilon}. \quad (11.2.2)$$

Costs are measured in units of the consumption good. The value of E is fixed in a way that it describes the costs of holding the number of believers constant, that is for $B_{t+1} = B_t$. These costs are positive because of the opposing influences of other belief systems and of in-convertibles, and since the old and especially the new generation have to be indoctrinated again and again. The costs have to be borne by voluntary contributions by all believers:

$$K_t = B_t Z_t (Y_t/P_t), \text{ with } 0 < Z_t < 1. \quad (11.2.3)$$

Here, we assume for simplicity that everybody in the population receives the same share of national income Y_t, that is Y_t/P_t. The share of the income of the representative believer given as his voluntary contribution to total costs is denoted by Z_t. To get total contributions the individual contribution has to be multiplied by B_t, the number of believers.

Consumption in both periods is limited by gross income, tax, voluntary contributions, savings, and dis-savings. We assume that the rate of the proportional income tax is M and that the representative individual plans so save a share F_t of his income in period t, so that he can spend $(1+r)F_t Y_t/P_t$ additionally in period t + 1. r denotes the rate of interest. Note that the share may be negative, which means that the believer can get a loan in period t and has to repay it with interest in period t + 1. The tax rate in both periods is M. Obviously

$0 < M < 1$, and $-1 < F_t < 1$. Also, $Z_t + M + F_t < 1$. We further make the simplifying assumptions that $Y_{t+1} = Y_t = Y, P_{t+1} = P_t = P$, national income and population are constant over time. As a consequence, we get the following restrictions for individual consumption by believers in the two periods:

$$C_t = (1 - Z_t - M - F_t)Y/P \quad (11.2.4)$$

and

$$C_{t+1} = [1 - Z_t - M + (1+r)F_t]Y/P. \quad (11.2.5)$$

Note that we assume that the share of voluntary contributions is planned at the beginning of period t to remain the same in period t + 1 as in period t, that is $Z_{t+1} = Z_t$ Also, since we have postulated a two-period time horizon of individuals, no savings are planned for period t + 1.

Finally, the influence of an increasing number of believers on the probability π_t to gain secular power during period t is given by:

$$\pi_t = \omega_t \kappa_t B_t / P_t. \tag{11.2.6}$$

ω_t, κ_t, which are assumed to be given exogenously, denote the degree of organization of the believers and the depth of the crisis in period t, respectively. The better organized the believers, the deeper the crisis, and the greater the share of believers in the population the greater the probability to gain power.

Since $B_{t,}P_t$ refer to the beginning of period t, they are historical values which cannot change. We can thus drop subscript t and write B and P subsequently. With (11.2.6) the description of Model 1 is complete.

11.2.2 Presentation and Discussion of Results

In this section, the conclusions following from Model 1 will be presented and discussed. The results, derived in Appendix A, are as follows for the variables of interest to us:

$$(B_{t+1}/B)^{\varepsilon} = \gamma(1-M)(Y/E)(B/P)/[\gamma + \varepsilon(\alpha+\beta)], \tag{11.2.7}$$

$$C_t = [(2+r)/(1+r)]\alpha\varepsilon(1-M)(Y/P)/[\gamma+\varepsilon(\alpha+\beta)], \tag{11.2.8}$$

$$C_{t+1} = [(2+r)\beta\varepsilon(1-M)(Y/P)/[\gamma+\varepsilon(\alpha+\beta)] \tag{11.2.9}$$

We are especially interested in the question, under which conditions the number of believers is growing from period to period. It follows from (11.2.7) that this is the case if

$$\begin{aligned}(1-M)(Y/P)B &> E[1+(\varepsilon/\gamma)(\alpha+\beta)],\\ [(1-M)(Y/P)B]/E &> 1+(\varepsilon/\gamma)(\alpha+\beta).\end{aligned} \tag{11.2.10}$$

The expression on the left-hand side of the first inequality denotes the sum of the disposable income of all believers, so that the greater the resources available to believers the greater the chance to win additional believers. Indeed, the resources have to be sufficient to overcome all the obstacles hindering the expansion of the ideology, corrected by the intensity of the belief in the right creed, which is represented by γ (right-hand side of the first inequality). The obstacles are the intensities of the want to consume in the two periods, $\alpha+\beta$, and the parameters describing the costs of maintaining old and of converting new believers, E and ε. The latter denotes the scale effect on the costs of conversion. If it is >1, then the resistance to the expansion of the new creed increases with its success. This resistance can be explained for instance by repressions against the ideological group, which may be rising with the number of believers, and which are introduced by the government who are afraid to lose their power; and (or) by the growing resistance of other ideological movements. E, on the other hand, describes the costs necessary just to maintain the present number of believers, and (or) the costs if the marginal costs of winning additional believers are zero. For if either $B_{t+1} = B$ or $\varepsilon = 0$, we get $K_t = E$ in (11.2.2). The size of E may be great as a consequence of the permanent opposition because of other virulent ideologies.

Moreover, we conclude from the first inequality that the number of believers will always increase, if E is small enough and if the intensity of ideological feelings, γ, is sufficiently great, or, as we may say, fanatic. But fanaticism alone is not sufficient for spreading the creed, whereas a low level of absolute costs E is sufficient, provided that $\gamma > 0$. For if this latter condition were not fulfilled no proselytizing would take place, as can be seen from (11.2.1).

The second inequality makes these relationships more lucid. Its left-hand side denotes the ratio of resources available to all believers to the costs E necessary to keep the number of believers just constant. It is obvious that this expression must be greater than one, for otherwise the believers would not even be able to maintain their number. But once it is greater than one, it follows, too, from the right-hand side of this inequality, that if intensity of belief as measured by γ is great enough, the number of believers will always increase.

Let us turn now to the probability π to gain secular power, as presented by Eq. (11.2.6). We may assume that levels of $\omega_t = 1, \kappa_t = 1$ represent a normal state of affairs in the following sense: First with respect to the latter parameter, that no crisis is perceived by the population. This means that the crisis is the greater the more the parameter surpasses one. If it is smaller than one this means that the population perceives the situation as the more favorable, the smaller it is. The first parameter has been normalized to one for a state of affairs in which believers are just sufficiently organized to be able to form a government in case a chance turns up to gain power. This means for instance that in a democracy the probability to be able to grasp power under prosperous conditions, that is with $\kappa_t < 1, \omega_t = 1$, is not more than 0.5 if $B > 0.5P$. We assume that the probability is not greater in this case because other factors like the voting system, a coup d'état by the government with the help of the military, or by the armed forces alone, a prohibition and repression of the party of the believers may prevent the ideological movement from gaining government power. On the other hand, with one or both of the two parameters greater than one, that is with a very efficient organization, perhaps with a paramilitary troop, and in a crisis, the probability to win power may be much higher than one half even if $B \ll 0.5P$. The coup d'état by the Bolsheviks in Russia during the crisis in the wake of World War I in 1917, and the grasping of government power by the Nazis by forming a coalition with right-wing parties during the Great Depression in 1933 are examples.

Equation (11.2.6) shows also that under normal conditions $\pi \to 1$ if $B \to P$. But we know that, for $t = 0, 1, 2, \ldots$ this will happen in some later period if condition (11.2.10) is fulfilled and if no in-convertible people are present. If the latter is not true, the probability can only approach $(P - I)/P$ under normal conditions. Thus, a great number of in-convertibles can make it much more difficult if not impossible to gain secular power.

Let us conclude this section by looking at the results for consumption planned by the representative believer for the two periods within the time horizon, as represented by (11.2.8) and (11.2.9). We see at once that consumption is positively related to disposable income $(1 - M)(Y/P)$, and to the intensity of the consumption motivation for the two periods, α, β, respectively. The same is true for ε, that is the scale factor influencing the costs of winning converts. Not surprisingly, the size of γ has a negative influence on consumption. Finally, from (11.2.9) and (11.2.8) we get:

$$C_{t+1} = (1 + r)(\beta/\alpha)C_t. \tag{11.2.11}$$

The relationship between the planned amounts of the consumption good in the two periods is determined by the discount factor $(1 + r)$ and by the relative intensity of the consumption wishes for the two periods. We have good reasons to assume impatience to consume, that is, $\alpha > \beta$. Relationship (11.2.11) is of course well known to economists. $(1 + r)$ is the inter-temporal rate of transformation, with r a real rate of interest, since it is the own rate of interest for food. It follows, moreover, from (A.4) and (A.5) in Appendix A that

$$\frac{\partial U_t}{\partial C_t} / \frac{\partial U_t}{\partial C_{t+1}} = \frac{\alpha C_{t+1}}{\beta C_t} = 1 + r. \tag{11.2.12}$$

The right equation is identical with (11.2.11). This equation implies that the marginal rate of substitution in inter-temporal consumption is equal to the marginal rate of substitution according to the transformation curve.

11.2.3 Simulated Evolution in Time

Though the time horizon of the representative believer in our model comprises only two periods, this does not mean that we cannot look at long-term developments of the number of believers and of the probability that they gain secular power. For with the passage of time the plans for the two periods are revised again and again at the beginning of each new period and executed during this period. We are thus able to simulate a historical evolution for each set of parameters and initial values of Model 1. Note also, that the limitation of the time horizon implies that the representative believer does not form rational expectations, which we think is a realistic assumption.

Subsequently, the model will be simulated for the following parameter and initial values:

$$\alpha = 0.35,\ \beta = 0.3,\ \gamma = 1,\ \varepsilon = 0.4,\ \kappa = 1.4,\ \omega = 1.8,\ B_0 = 5;$$
$$Y = 100,\ P = 100,\ M = 0.3,\ E = 0.48,\ r = 0.04.$$

We have selected relatively low values for the first two parameters, whereas the third one is rather great. This means that it is assumed that believers have intensive feelings about the importance of spreading their ideology and are prepared to sacrifice consumption for this purpose. Also, we have assumed that ε as well as E are rather small. This means that the resistance to be converted is low and that economies of scale in winning believers are present. Variable κ has been introduced as a random variable around a root value of 1.4. This implies that we assume that the innovation and growth of the new ideology takes place amidst a feeling of an underlying crisis, since $1.4 > 1$. But the occurrence of a real crisis depends on many factors not controllable by either believers or government. This is the reason for using a random variation. The value of ω has been taken as 1.8, implying a rather well-organized group of believers. Table 11.1 describes the developments following from these assumptions:

It follows that the number of believers rises with increasing speed, given the parameter values, whereas their individual consumption is constant. The probability to win secular power is very low in the beginning. It increases with the percentage

Table 11.1 Simulated evolution of number of believers, their consumption and the probability to gain secular power

Period	Percentage of believers in population	Consumption of individual believer	Probability of gaining secular power
1	5	0.153	0.019
2	5.787	0.153	0.083
3	6.698	0.153	0.159
4	7.752	0.153	0.113
5	8.973	0.153	0.058
6	10.385	0.153	0.092
7	12.02	0.153	0.241
8	13.911	0.153	0.025
9	16.101	0.153	0.24
10	18.636	0.153	0.093
11	21.569	0.153	0.35
12	24.964	0.153	0.38
13	28.894	0.153	0.321
14	33.442	0.153	0.334
15	38.706	0.153	0.578
16	44.799	0.153	1.072

of believers in the population, but with strong random fluctuation. From Period 11, with believers now comprising more than 20% of the population, it is above 0.32 in Period 15 it increases to more than one half and rises to more than one in Period 16. Since the probability can, however, not be greater than one, this means that the ideological movement secures secular power at the latest in that period, though only about 44.8% of the population has been converted until then.

With different parameter values, the number of believers may not increase or even decline. But what happens if the ideological movement does not vanish as in the former case, but only stagnates and consequently has no chance to win secular power? It seems that there are two possibilities. First, the movement turns to guerilla warfare and terrorism in the hope that with these methods it may finally secure secular power. Or the ideology is adapted in a sense that it does no longer ask for reaching secular power to apply it for the aims of removing in-convertibles, to win new believers and to pursue the course of imperialistic expansion implied by its values. In this case, the ideological movement will try to isolate the believers from outside influences and may even support the demands for toleration and constitutional safeguards to protect itself against pressures from the government.

11.2.4 The Direct Evolution of Mature Ideocracies

We have concluded that the movement of believers will take over the secular power of the state in time, if the conditions stated above are fulfilled. Afterwards they can apply this power to better accomplish their aims. They are especially able to apply force to convert resisting non-believers or to force into emigration, to suppress or to obliterate in-convertibles who are by definition an embodiment of the forces of evil and pose a threat to believers and their supreme values, which are thought to be absolutely true. Consequently, in executing the demands of the supreme values a totalitarian regime is established.

But a different turn of events may occur, even if the conditions are fulfilled for a growth of the number of believers sufficient to finally grasp secular power. Assume that the believers have the option at time t to emigrate during period t to a sufficiently large territory, which is not or only scarcely settled before. Then, if the costs of such an emigration, of establishing a community or state in the new territory and of possibly converting the few original inhabitants are lower than the costs of reaching secular power in the home territory, such action would be preferable to believers. Formally, denote these costs of emigration and community-founding by Ω_t. Then a sufficient condition would be fulfilled if the expected present value of the costs of winning believers during the two-period time horizon were higher than Ω_t:

$$\Omega_t < K_t + (1 - \pi_t)K_{t+1}/(1 + r) \quad (11.2.12)$$

Note that $1 - \pi_t$ denotes the probability of not reaching secular power in period t. Observe also, that the condition is not a necessary condition since secular power may not be gained within the two periods. For the probability to win it amounts only to $\pi_t + (1 - \pi_t)\pi_{t+1}$. We now insert (11.2.2) and (11.2.7) to get the optimal value for the right-hand side of this inequality. It follows that this condition holds if

$$\begin{aligned}\Omega_t < \gamma(1 - M)(Y/P)[(B_t/\{\gamma + \varepsilon(\alpha + \beta)\} \\ + \{(1 - \pi_t)(B_{t+1}/\{\gamma + \varepsilon(\alpha + \beta)^{\gamma}\}/(1 + r)]\end{aligned} \quad (11.2.13)$$

where π_t is given by (11.2.6).

Such settlements established by emigration to new territories and conversion at low costs of the small indigenous population have indeed happened in history. If the supreme values of the ideological groups concerned did not command expansion of the territory settled or the conversion of non-believers and (or) the removal of in-convertibles outside this territory, they had accomplished their ends, since about all inhabitants in the territory were believers and no in-convertibles present. In this case, we will speak of a *mature ideocracy*. A mature ideocracy has accomplished the ends implied by the supreme values, quite in contrast to a totalitarian regime. The latter regime is not saturated like the former. Though both regimes are ideocracies they differ because of this fact. This shows also that a totalitarian regime will vanish when it has reached the aims of the supreme values or when it falters in trying to do so. We will return to this point in Sect. 11.4.

As examples of mature ideocracies which came into being by emigration to scarcely settled territories, consider the Puritans of Massachusetts and the Jesuit settlements of Paraguay. The Puritans admitted, apart from some craftsmen, only believers to their emigration from England. Later, (Protestant) dissenters like Roger Williams and Anne Hutchinson who tried to join them were forced into exile (Morgan 1958, Chaps. IX and X). Thus, from the very beginning, the contents of the supreme values were implemented, since nearly all the population shared or, at least, acquiesced to the tenets of this democratic theocracy.

In the oligarchic theocracy of the Jesuits things were similar, since only Indians converted to Catholicism were admitted as permanent members of the reductions by the immigrated Jesuit fathers. It is true that some exceptions existed for white traders and for gauchos. But the latter lived outside of the settlements and the former were only allowed to stay for a few days (Ezran 1989, pp. 129–133). Moreover, both groups were at least Catholics. Indians who fled the reductions and possibly reverted to paganism or caused unrest, both rare events, were caught and whipped. Women were shaven, rebellious shamans sometimes hanged if no other means helped (pp. 82 and 132). But on the whole, this use of force was rare, since only believers constituted the population. No terror was necessary to reach the supreme values of the creed.

11.3 The Application of Secular Power to Reach the Domestic and Foreign Aims of the Weltanschauung*

After having secured secular power, the conditions for pursuing the ends implied by the belief system of the ideology improve drastically. The leadership can now apply the power of the state to win new converts, to deal with the problem of in-convertibles and to follow an imperialistic policy to spread its ideology to other countries. In the approach applied in Model 2 (presented subsequently) this fact will be reflected in the use of government revenue for proselytizing, removing in-convertibles and applying resources to increase the probability of successful imperialistic expansion. It will also find its expression in a differentiation of tax rates according to whether individuals belong to the group of believers, of non-believers who can be converted or of in-convertibles.

The differentiation of taxes may have different reasons. First, the tax rate set for believers will be determined according to their preferences and restrictions. Connected to this we will exclude the possibility of savings and of voluntary contributions by believers. No important characteristics of the model are lost by doing so, for since believers have now the power to set their own tax rate, this rate can include what they want to give in voluntary contributions or what they want to save. Indeed, since their tax rate is determined according to the preferences of the representative believer, all taxes paid by believers as well as the use of government revenues is voluntary for them. Second, the tax rate for non-believers should be higher than that for believers with the purpose to motivate them to turn to the true creed, but should leave them a disposable income above the minimum of existence. Obviously, such a policy lowers the resistance to conversion. Third, the tax rate for in-convertibles should be the highest. In-convertibles are a nuisance to true believers, apart from the possibility to employ them to increase national product and thus the resources available to reach the ends of believers. But depending on the preferences and restrictions of believers the tax rate might also be set so high, that the remaining disposable income of in-convertibles leads to their removal by starvation. For under certain conditions to be specified the number of them will be reduced, and this can only be done by forced emigration, starvation or by killing them. We have not made explicit these relationships in the model, but only assume the possibility of decreasing the number of in-convertibles and thus of the total population. However, the assumptions of Model 2 imply that only believers (through the representative believer) have an influence on decisions, and that they are not directly concerned about the consumption of non-believers and in-convertibles. As a consequence, and for simplicity, it is postulated that the tax rates applied to them are exogenous, but higher than the rate set for believers.

A further trait of Model 2 is that the influence of decisions on future national product and thus on future available resources has to be taken into account. This is done with the help of a production function.

11.3.1 Presentation of Model 2

We begin by making explicit the influence of the number of in-convertibles, I_{t+1}, and of the probability of reaching the international aims of the creed, π_{t+1}, on the utility of the representative believer:

$$U_t = AC_t^{\alpha}C_{t+1}^{\beta}(B_{t+1}/P_{t+1})^{\gamma}(I_{t+1}/P_{t+1})^{-\delta}\pi_{t+1}^{\phi}. \tag{11.3.1}$$

This implies that an increasing probability to reach the international aims of the ideology raises utility, whereas the proportion of in-convertibles in the population at the beginning of period t + 1 decreases the utility of the believer (δ, with $0<\delta<1$, and ϕ are constants). In (11.2.1) in Sect. 11.2.2 we have neglected these relationships, since believers had no influence on foreign policy and on the number of in-convertibles. We could thus take the respective terms in Sect. 11.2.2 as constants which were incorporated into A. But now the power of the state can be applied to influence these variables, so that π_{t+1} and I_{t+1} are no longer constants.

Note that we can set $\phi = 0$ for an ideology not implying expansionary aims, and $\delta = 0$ if its values do not define in-convertibles. The former relationship holds also if the leadership decides to first limit itself to and perhaps to complete the internal consolidation before pursuing the imperialistic aims. In this case our general model assumes the special form used in Sect. 11.4.1.

P_{t+1} is now no longer a constant, since

$$P_{t+1} = P + I_{t+1} - I. \tag{11.3.2}$$

The production function of the national economy is given by

$$Y_{t+1} = DP^{\eta}G_t^{1-\eta}, \text{ with } 0<\eta<1. \tag{11.3.3}$$

The only consumption good is produced in the amount of Y_{t+1} during period t with the help of employing labor (here represented by the total population P) and the consumption good G, which can be used as a factor of production, too, and is invested by the government during period t. The production ends with the beginning of period t + 1, so that the good produced is then available for consumption, for winning new believers, for removing in-convertibles and for imperialistic policies. G is provided by the government as an input and may be thought of as resources spent on maintaining a legal system, law and order and an infrastructure. Note that we have again dropped subscript t for all variables referring to the beginning of period t, namely P, B, Y and I, since they cannot change or be changed. D is a constant.

The cost function of Sect. 11.2 has to be expanded to take into account that resources are now also needed to reduce the proportion of in-convertibles and to increase the probability of reaching the international aims. We thus get

$$K_t = E(B_{t+1}/B)^{\varepsilon}(I/I_{t+1})^{\xi}(\pi_{t+1}/\pi)^{\psi}. \tag{11.3.4}$$

Again, if the government does not yet want to begin expansion or if a non-expansionary ideology is present, or if no in-convertibles are defined, $\psi = 0, \xi = 0$, respectively.

The number of convertible non-believers at the beginning of period t is defined as

$$N = P - B - I \tag{11.3.5}$$

We assume further, as before, that all individuals get the same gross income Y/P. Since the three groups of the population are taxed differently, this does not lead to a loss of generality. For their disposable incomes are different. The tax rates for believers, non-believers and in-convertibles are denoted by $0 < M_t, H, L < 1$ respectively, of which only the former is a variable, as denoted by the subscript t. Government revenue amounts to

$$T_t = (M_t B + \mathrm{HN} + \mathrm{LI})(Y/P). \tag{11.3.6}$$

Observe that Y has already been produced at the beginning of period t, at the time when the representative believer makes up his optimal plan. It is thus like P, B, I, and N a constant. Y is available for consumption, investment by the government for infrastructure, etc., and for covering the costs implied by (11.3.4) during period t. Note also that the tax rate M_t, which could not be influenced by believers in Sect. 11.2.2, is now a variable, since the believers control the government.

A share $0 \le Z_t \le 1$ of the revenue is planned to be spent on the cost of winning converts, reducing the number of in-convertibles and (or) increasing the probability of reaching the international aims of the ideology. The rest is used for government investment:

$$K_t = Z_t T_t, \tag{11.3.7}$$

$$G_t = (1 - Z_t) T_t. \tag{11.3.8}$$

Consumption of the representative believer in the two periods corresponds to his disposable incomes:

$$C_t = (1 - M_t)(Y/P), \tag{11.3.9}$$

$$C_{t+1} = (1 - M_t)(Y_{t+1}/P_{t+1}). \tag{11.3.10}$$

We have assumed that $M_{t+1} = M_t$.. Since the time horizon is limited to two periods, some more or less artificial assumption has to be made concerning this tax rate, since its optimal calculation would require a three-period time horizon. Moreover, like all variables referring to period t + 1 this rate will be recalculated when period t has elapsed, when the believer reexamines his plan at the beginning of period $t + 1$, that is when his time horizon comprises period $t + 2$.

Finally, we have to add an equation determining the probability to reach the international aims of the creed:

$$\pi_{t+1} = (\omega_{t+1}/\omega^*_{t+1})(Y_{t+1}/Y^*_{t+1})^{\nu}. \tag{11.3.11}$$

Y^* denotes the GDPs of all nations, the subjugation of which or of a part or the whole of whose population is demanded by the totalitarian ideology. Note that we have implicitly assumed that the relative military, political and economic power of the states involved depends on their Gross National Products Y and Y^*. This is certainly a simplification, since sizes of territories and of population also play a role. However, we think that they are not as important as the factors mentioned and that their importance has declined with economic development. Moreover, GDP itself depends on the size of population and of territory, so that they are not fully neglected. Whereas Y refers again to domestic GDP of the totalitarian state, Y^* is possibly composed of several national GDPs. ω, ω^* are parameters describing the efficiency of domestic and foreign organization. They refer to the willingness and capabilities to transform resources contained in Y and Y^* into military, political and ideological means of expansion or defense. They may be increased by the kind of regime, the existence of a monopolistic ideological party, etc. Moreover, the size of ω^* will be critically dependent on whether the nations threatened by expansion take as serious the ideological aims of the totalitarian state and are able to form a cohesive alliance or not.

11.3.2 Presentation and Discussion of the Results of Model 2

From (B.27) and (B.28) of Appendix B, we have

$$I_{t+1}/I = F(P - I)/I, \tag{11.3.12}$$

$$F \equiv [\varepsilon\delta - \gamma\xi]/[\gamma\xi - \varepsilon(\beta + \gamma)] \tag{11.3.13}$$

We are first interested whether the number of in-convertibles is decreased by applying the secular power of the state. According to (11.3.12) and (11.3.13) this is the case, if

$$F(P - I)/I < 1,$$

$$(\varepsilon\delta - \gamma\xi)/[\gamma(\xi - \varepsilon) - \varepsilon\beta] < I/(P - I). \tag{11.3.14}$$

Sufficient but not necessary conditions for the validity of (11.3.14) are given by

$$\begin{aligned} &\xi/\varepsilon > \delta/\gamma, \\ &\text{and} \\ &\gamma/\beta > \varepsilon/(\xi - \varepsilon). \end{aligned} \tag{11.3.15}$$

or if the opposite inequalities hold.

The first set of these conditions is fulfilled if ξ/ε is great enough and if $\gamma \gg \delta, \beta$. The former statement means that the scale factor in the cost function to convert non-believers should be smaller than that for eliminating in-convertibles. This follows since we have $I_{t+1}^{-\xi}$ in Eq. (11.3.4). The second statement implies that the intensity of the valuation of the presence of believers on the part of believers is sufficiently strong compared to the intensity of their valuation of consumption in period $t + 1$ and sufficiently weak in relation to the negative valuation of the percentage of in-convertibles in the population. For the condition implies $-\delta \gg \gamma$. Note also that (11.3.14) is always fulfilled if the number of in-convertibles is rather great compared to the number of believers and non-believers together. The greater this ratio the more urgent it is for believers to reduce the number of in-convertibles.

Interestingly, the change in the number of in-convertibles is not dependent on whether the totalitarian regime follows imperialistic foreign policies or not. For the conditions are not dependent on the values of ϕ, ψ. *This is a remarkable result. It means that the policies pursued against in-convertibles remain the same whether the totalitarian regime spends no, smaller or higher resources on imperialistic foreign policies.*

Let us look next at the consumption of period t. Because of (B.40) we get

$$C_t = \varepsilon(\alpha + \beta)[V/(BS)](Y/P), \tag{11.3.16}$$

with

$$S \equiv \varepsilon\alpha + \varepsilon\beta(2 - \eta) + \gamma + (1 - \eta)v(\varepsilon\phi - \gamma\psi) \tag{11.3.17}$$

$$V \equiv B + \mathrm{HN} + \mathrm{LI}, \tag{11.3.18}$$

from (B.34) and (B.36). We want first to know whether consumption is lower with than without resources spent on imperialistic policies. V is the same in both cases, but not S, as can be seen from (11.3.17). Thus C_t is smaller because of resources spent on expansion if

$$\begin{aligned} &(1 - \eta)v(\varepsilon\phi - \gamma\psi) > 0, \\ &\text{or} \\ &\varepsilon/\psi > \gamma/\phi. \end{aligned} \tag{11.3.19}$$

In words this means that consumption is lower in the case of imperialistic policies implied by the supreme values of the ideology if the ratio of the scale parameter in the cost function for winning new believers to that of increasing the probability of expansion is greater than the ratio of the intensities of the preferences for the former and the latter. (11.3.19) *will turn out, too, to be a critical condition for other relationships.*

It also follows from (11.3.16) to (11.3.18) that consumption in the first period is planned to be the lower, the greater the utility of the percentage of believers in the nation at the beginning of period $t + 1$ and the smaller the productivity of labor in producing output (*provided that* (11.3.19) *is fulfilled*), as measured by γ, η, respectively. Not surprisingly the intensity of the wish to consume in period t, as measured by α has a positive influence on consumption in period t. There is, however, a positive rather than a negative influence of the intensity of the wish to consume in period $t + 1$, as measured by β, provided that $\gamma + (1 - \eta)v(\varepsilon\phi - \gamma\psi) > \varepsilon\alpha(1 - \eta)$. *Assuming that the critical condition* (11.3.19) *is valid*, this is rather more often fulfilled in the case of resources spent on imperialistic expansion. In the other case of non-expansionary policies, the condition is fulfilled if there is a sufficiently strong influence on utility of the percentage of believers and if the scale factor of the costs to convert new believers is not too great. As had to be expected, the size of gross per capita income as well as of the tax revenue from non-believers and in-convertibles have a positive effect on consumption in the first period.

Let us turn now to the development of the number of believers. From (B.46) and (B.48) we have

$$(B_{t+1}/B)^{\varepsilon} = \gamma(\mathrm{VY}/\mathrm{PES})[F(P - I)/I]^{\xi}(\pi/\pi_{t+1})^{\psi}, \tag{11.3.20}$$

$$(B_{t+1}/B)^{\varepsilon} = (\gamma/E)(\omega^{*}\pi/\omega)^{\psi}(Y^{*}_{t+1}W^{1-\eta}/\mathrm{DP}^{\eta})^{v\psi}(\mathrm{VY}/\mathrm{PS})^{1-(1-\eta)v\psi}[F(P - I)/I]^{\xi}. \tag{11.3.21}$$

and from (B.32)

$$W \equiv (1 - \eta)[\beta\varepsilon + v(\varepsilon\phi - \gamma\psi)]. \tag{11.3.22}$$

Let us first see whether the number of believers will grow more slowly if expansionary aims are present. Let us assume that $\psi > 1$, that is that raising the probability to reach the imperialistic aims leads to more than a proportional increase of costs. Then, *if critical condition* (11.3.19) *is fulfilled, a sufficient*, but not necessary condition that the number of believers will grow less is given if $\pi_{t+1} > \pi_t$ (see (11.3.20)). To make sense of this condition, we turn to the value for the probability of expansion in period $t + 1$. Because of (B.47) we get

$$\pi_{t+1} = (\omega/\omega^{*})\left[\mathrm{DP}^{\eta}(\mathrm{VWY}/\mathrm{PS})^{1-\eta}/Y^{*}_{t+1}\right]^{v}. \tag{11.3.23}$$

It follows that the sufficient condition is fulfilled if

$$\pi\omega^*/\omega < \left[\mathrm{DP}^{\eta}(\mathrm{VWY}/\mathrm{PS})^{1-\eta}/Y^*_{t+1}\right]^{\nu}. \tag{11.3.24}$$

To derive the necessary and sufficient condition we have to analyze (11.3.21) and to take into account (11.3.22), (11.3.17) and (11.3.19). It follows that B_{t+1}/B will be smaller in the case of resources spent on expansion if

$$(\omega^*\pi/\omega)^{\psi}(Y^*_{t+1}/\mathrm{DP}^{\eta})^{\nu\psi}/\left[(S/S^\circ)(\mathrm{VWY}/\mathrm{PS})^{(1-\eta)\nu\psi}\right] < 1, \tag{11.3.25}$$

with

$$S^\circ \equiv \varepsilon\alpha + \varepsilon\beta(2-\eta) + \gamma. \tag{11.3.26}$$

Note that this condition does not tell us whether $B_{t+1} > B$ in the two cases. For this to be true, the right-hand sight of (11.3.21) has to be greater than one. We will study this relationship more closely when we simulate the evolution of the system over time.

Finally, let us look at the probability of a successful expansionary policy in period $t + 1$, that is at (11.3.23). It is the greater, the better the domestic as compared to foreign organization, ω/ω^*; the larger the domestic population, the higher the productivity as expressed by D, the greater the initial Gross Domestic Product Y, and the greater domestic revenues from non-believers as represented by V–B; it is the smaller the greater the foreign Gross Domestic Product of the region which has to be conquered according to the ideology, the smaller the initial number of believers and the greater S; it is again the greater the better relative economic strength is translated into military or foreign policy power and thus into the probability to succeed with expansion, as measured by ν. If we look at S (11.3.17) we see that the probability is the greater the smaller the preferences for consumption in periods t and $t + 1$, the preference for converting new believers at home and the greater the productivity of labor versus that of government provided infrastructure, that is η; and finally the smaller the diseconomies of scale in the cost function for winning new believers, i.e.ε.

Is there any difference in the size of Gross Domestic Product if the totalitarian regime tries to increase the probability of expansion? From (B.49) and $\phi, \psi = 0$ we get

$$Y_{t+1} = \mathrm{DP}^{\eta}[(Y/P)(\mathrm{VW}/S)]^{1-\eta}, \tag{11.3.27}$$

$$W^\circ = \varepsilon\beta(1-\eta). \tag{11.3.28}$$

W° denotes the value of W without expansion. It follows from (B.22), (11.3.27), (11.3.17), (11.3.22), (11.3.26) and (11.3.28) that Gross Domestic Product in period $t + 1$ is greater with imperialistic policies if

$$\frac{\varepsilon\beta(1-\eta)}{\varepsilon\alpha+\varepsilon\beta(2-\eta)+\gamma} < \frac{\varepsilon\beta(1-\eta)+(1-\eta)v(\varepsilon\phi-\gamma\psi)}{\varepsilon\alpha+\varepsilon\beta(2-\eta)+\gamma+(1-\eta)v(\varepsilon\phi-\gamma\psi)},$$

$$(\varepsilon\alpha+\varepsilon\beta+\gamma)v(\varepsilon\phi-\gamma\psi) > 0. \tag{11.3.29}$$

Condition (11.3.29) is fulfilled if again the *critical condition* (11.3.19) *is true*, that is if consumption is smaller. This allows to invest resources, consequently to increase Gross Domestic Product and as a result the probability of successful expansion.

11.4 The Evolution of Totalitarian Regimes

Until now we have restricted our attention to a two-period planning horizon and the results following from the execution of these plans. But with the passage of time, plans are revised at the beginning of each new period and are executed each time according to plans in the period immediately following the planning date. Consequently, we are able to calculate the development of the system for several periods, if parameter values are given. In doing so, we will distinguish between the cases in which either an imperialistic expansion is implied by the supreme values of the ideology or in which this is not the case.

To clarify for which ideologies one or the other case will be present, we differentiate between the following categories of ideologies:

1. *Universal ideologies*. These are ideologies whose substantive aims ask for the conversion of all people on earth (except for in-convertibles).
2. *Universal dominance ideologies*. The supreme values of these ideologies do not demand the conversion of all people, but the dominance over all people on earth by an elite population defined by the creed. An example would be the aim of world domination by the Aryan race.
3. *Expansionary ideologies*. These are ideologies aiming for an expansion of their territory or of the number of their believers or of the means needed to reach their supreme values. They do not, however, strive for universal conversion or dominance. A nationalism trying to bring together into one state all the people speaking the same language, would be an example.
4. *Restrictive ideologies*. These ideologies, once they have reached secular power, do not have any aims left for conversion of foreigners, to dominate foreign countries or to expand.

Universal, universal dominance, and expansionary ideologies are motivated to use not only peaceful conversion, but also the secular power of the state in trying to reach their aims. As a consequence, the leaders will try to harness the population and economic means for this purpose, whether by persuasion, force, or terror. Whether and how much force and terror have to be used domestically depends obviously on the degree of consolidation reached before embarking on imperialistic expansion. Also all means, even terror and undeclared war, are justified against resisting foreign nations by the supreme values.

Things are different for restrictive ideologies. If no expansionary aims have to be followed after grasping secular power, a peaceful, mature ideocracy will be established after converting all people open to conversion and solving the problem of in-convertibles. For example, a nationalistic ideology gaining power over a territory comprising all people speaking the same language, and only those, may turn into such a regime. We will return to such mature ideocracies later. In the following simulations, we analyze first the case of a restrictive ideology. Afterwards, we will be concerned with the cases of universal, universal dominance and expansionary ideologies. We can consider these cases together by taking different values for Y in the respective simulations.

11.4.1 Development of Totalitarian Regimes with Restrictive Ideologies

In this section, we will be concerned only with restrictive totalitarian regimes, so that we have to set $\phi, \psi = 0$. The cases of totalitarian regimes with expansionary, universal and universal dominance ideologies will be analyzed in Sect. 11.4.2. For the numerical simulation, the following parameter and initial values will be used:

$$\mathrm{A} = 2,\ \mathrm{E} = 10,\ \mathrm{D} = 3,\ \mathrm{H} = 0.44,\ \mathrm{L} = 0.6,\ Y_0 = 100,$$
$$P_0 = 100,\ I_0 = 20,\ B_0 = 20;$$

$$\alpha = 0.4,\ \beta = 0.35,\ \gamma = 0.636,\ \delta = 0.95;$$
$$\eta = 0.6,\ \varepsilon = 1.21,\ \xi = 1.815.$$

Table 11.2 Simulated evolution of some variables of a totalitarian State I

Period	*C*	*Y*	*I*	*B*	*N*	*P*	*M*
1	1.547	100	20	20	60	100	−0.547
2	2.051	95.887	10	13.406	66.594	90	−0.925
3	1.186	85.858	10	23.051	56.949	90	−0.244
4	0.809	85.676	10	39.462	40.538	90	0.150
5	0.588	91.148	10	76.775	3.225	90	0.419

With these values, we get the following results (Table 11.2).

Some of these results are quite surprising. First the number of in-convertibles is halved within one period, but then remains at the same level. Outsiders might explain this as a new tolerance on the part of believers, but our model shows that it is only the result of rational selfish utility maximizing, given the constraints of the system. Second, the number of believers decreases in the second compared to the first period, but then rises again to quickly reach nearly its highest possible level of 80 in the fifth period. Third, believers do not pay taxes during periods one to three, but get a transfer. That is, they exploit the other groups. Only in periods four and five they pay increasing taxes. This is clearly a consequence of their own efforts to reduce the number of in-convertibles and to convert non-believers. Also, though their consumption first increases in the second period by assigning themselves transfers from these groups, it strongly falls with the decreasing number of their members. Fifth, Gross Domestic Product falls first during three periods, but rises again in the fifth period.

The results are very sensitive to parameter changes. If we select, e.g., $\gamma = 0.638, \delta = 0.954$ and $E = 9.5$, with all other parameters unchanged, we get the values of Table 11.3.

Here the reduction of the number of believers in the beginning is more pronounced, as is the exploitation of the other groups. As a consequence, consumption of believers is higher in periods two to five. The decrease in the number of non-believers proceeds more slowly, and the number of in-convertibles is now more than halved until the second period, but again stays constant afterwards. In fact, a somewhat higher value of $\delta = 0.957$, that is a somewhat more negative or rather hateful feeling of the representative believer leads to an immediate elimination of all in-convertibles until the second period. On the other hand, for $\delta = 0.9485$ the number of in-convertibles would slightly increase to 21.935, whereas the number of non-believers would fall to zero already until the third period. This result reminds one of a situation like in South Africa under the Apartheid: A mature ideocracy of another type with only believers and in-convertibles is stabilized, where the latter (the blacks in South Africa) are exploited by the believers (the whites, whose ideology convinces them of the inferiority of the blacks). Note that this does not imply that consumption by in-convertibles does not rise in later periods. Also, there is no reason in our model to prevent a democratic system in a mature ideocracy of this type, limited, however, to believers.

Table 11.3 Simulated evolution of some variables of a totalitarian State II

Period	C	Y	I	B	N	P	M
1	1.545	100	20	20	60	100	−0.545
2	2.737	95.842	7.742	9.543	70.457	87.724	−1.506
3	1.490	82.845	7.742	16.453	63.547	87.724	−0.578
4	0.994	80.766	7.742	26.915	53.085	87.724	−0.080
5	0.707	83.639	7.742	47.326	32.674	87.724	0.258

Let us return to the example of Table 4.1. Here the situation seems to have stabilized in Period 5: This is true for the number of in-convertibles, but there are also scarcely any non-believers left. To check this, let us assume, that the number of non-believers has reached zero. This means that with $I = 10$ and $B = 80$ we have $P = 90$. Also, we take $Y = 91.148$ from Period 5 as initial value. B is now a constant, so that we have to change Eqs. (11.3.1)–(11.3.10) as follows:

$$U_t = \mathrm{A}C_t^{\alpha} C_{t+1}^{\beta} (B/P_{t+1})^{\gamma} (I_{t+1}/P_{t+1})^{-\delta}, \tag{11.3.1a}$$

with

$$B_{t+1} = B_t = B = \text{const.}$$

$$K_t = E(I/I_{t+1})^{\xi}, \tag{11.3.4a}$$

since

$$(B_{t+1}/B_t)^{\varepsilon} = 1.$$

$$T_t = (M_t B + \mathrm{LI})(Y/P), \tag{11.3.6a}$$

since $N = 0$. From this Model 2a, we derive the two equations (C.25) and (C.26) (Appendix C) with two unknowns M_t and I_{t+1}:

$$\begin{aligned}&[\beta(1-\eta)\mathrm{EP}(I/I_{t+1})^{\xi}][B(1-M_t)]\\&= [\{\alpha+\beta(2-\eta)\}\mathrm{BM}_t + (\alpha+\beta)\mathrm{LI} - \beta(1-\eta)B][(M_t B + \mathrm{LI})Y - \mathrm{EP}(I/I_{t+1})^{\xi}]\end{aligned} \tag{C.27}$$

$$\begin{aligned}&[(\beta+\gamma)I_{t+1} + \delta(P-I)][(M_t B + \mathrm{LI})Y - \mathrm{EP}(I/I_{t+1})^{\xi}]\\&= [\xi(P + I_{t+1} - I)][\beta(1-\eta)\mathrm{EP}(I/I_{t+1})^{\xi}].\end{aligned} \tag{C.28}$$

We compute the solution for these two equations numerically for a few periods to study the further evolution of the system for the parameter values of the example of Table 4.1.

Table 11.4 Simulated further evolution of some variables of a totalitarian State I

Period	C	Y	I	P	B	M	K	T
5	0.669	91.148	10	90	80	0.43	32.305	40.915
6	0.707	105.605	5.241	85.241	80	0.449	38.186	48.397
7	1.233	109.432	2.505	82.505	80		10	49.637
8			0	80	80		10	

It is especially of interest whether the number of in-convertibles will remain stable or whether it will now be further reduced, since the additional costs necessary to win new believers have now vanished. The following results are calculated.

The $I = 0$ in the last line of Table 11.4 has not been obtained by simulation, but has been inserted, since otherwise I would take a negative value, which is out of the feasible range. As can be seen, the situation of Table 3.1 is not stabilized. The resources not needed for conversion any longer, are now spent on eliminating in-convertibles and to increase consumption of believers. Consequently, the number of in-convertibles is further reduced to zero by forced emigration or annihilation. Moreover, for Period 8 we have inserted, not calculated $K = E = 10$, for the costs thus expended should be just sufficient to keep the number of believers' stable. Gross Domestic Product increases during Periods 6 and 7, and is partly used for higher consumption and partly for higher taxes to allow an even higher product to be produced during the next period. Obviously, a mature ideocracy without non-believers and no in-convertibles has been reached in Period 8, provided that the supreme values of the ideology do not ask for expansionary policies.

What will be the stationary state of this mature ideocracy? To calculate the respective values, we have to change Eqs. (11.3.1a), (11.3.4a), and (11.3.6a) as follows:

$$U_t = AC_t^{\alpha}C_{t+1}^{\beta}(B/P_{t+1})^{\gamma}, \tag{11.3.1b}$$

with

$$B_{t+1} = B_t = P_t = P_{t+1} = const.$$

$$K_t = E, \tag{11.3.4b}$$

since

$$(B_{t+1}/B_t)^{\varepsilon} = 1.$$

$$T_t = (M_tB)(Y/P), \tag{11.3.6b}$$

for I is now equal to zero. Note that though B cannot grow, since there are no non-believers left, it could still fall, turning believers into non-believers (heretics). But we know that this will not be the case, given the parameter values leading to Table 11.1. Thus we treat B as a constant. But this implies that K has to be equal to E, to keep B constant. Since P could only change because of a change of I, it is now also a constant, since $I = 0$.

Solving this Model 2b results in the following equation (Appendix D):

$$\beta(1-\eta)\mathrm{EP}(1-M_t) = [\{\{\alpha+\beta(2-\eta)\}M_t = \beta(1-\eta)](M_t\mathrm{BY}-\mathrm{EP}). \tag{D.23}$$

Table 11.5 Simulated values of the stationary mature Ideocracy I

Period	C	Y	I	P	B	M	K	T
8	1.073	109.432	0	80	80	0.234	10	25.607
9	1.079	112.099	0	80	80	0.232	10	26.007
10	1.08	112.349	0	80	80	0.232	10	26.065

This equation is computed for the parameter values of the first example and the initial values $P = B = 80$, $I = 0$ and $Y = 109.432$ (from Table 11.4). By using (D.23) and the other relevant equations of Model 2b, we get the values presented in Table 11.5.

The values for Y, C, M, and T clearly converge to the optimal value. Tax revenue is strongly reduced compared to Table 11.4, since no costs have to be incurred for removing in-convertibles. The mature ideocracy enters a stationary state of the economy. This is not surprising since we have assumed a stationary population and technology and also stable tastes of the representative believer.

11.4.2 Evolution of Imperialistic Totalitarian Regimes

Let us now use simulation to sketch the possible evolution of imperialistic totalitarian regimes, that is, of regimes with expansionary, universal, or universal dominance ideologies. We do so by using the same parameter and initial values as for Table 11.1 in Sect. 11.4.1. This will allow us to compare the development of the system with and without imperialistic expansion. The respective values are as follows:

$$A = 2, E = 10, D = 3, H = 0.44, L = 0.6, Y_0 = 100,$$
$$P_0 = 100, I_0 = 20, B_0 = 20;$$

$$\alpha = 0.4,\ \beta = 0.35,\ \gamma = 0.636,\ \delta = 0.95;$$
$$\eta = 0.6,\ \varepsilon = 1.21,\ \xi = 1.815.$$

We have to add values for the parameters and initial values which were zero or not applicable in Sect. 11.4.1:

$$\omega = 1.25,\ \omega^* = 1,\ \phi = 0.5,\ \psi = 1.3,\ v = 0.2,\ \pi_0 = 0.1,\ Y^* = 850.$$

We have selected a greater value for the first than for the second parameter because an ideologically based regime has a more unified following, can pursue a more coherent foreign and military policy and will presumably have a better organization than its foreign opponents. Further, it has been assumed that the first parameter is influenced by random shocks, so that it fluctuates around 1.25. Since

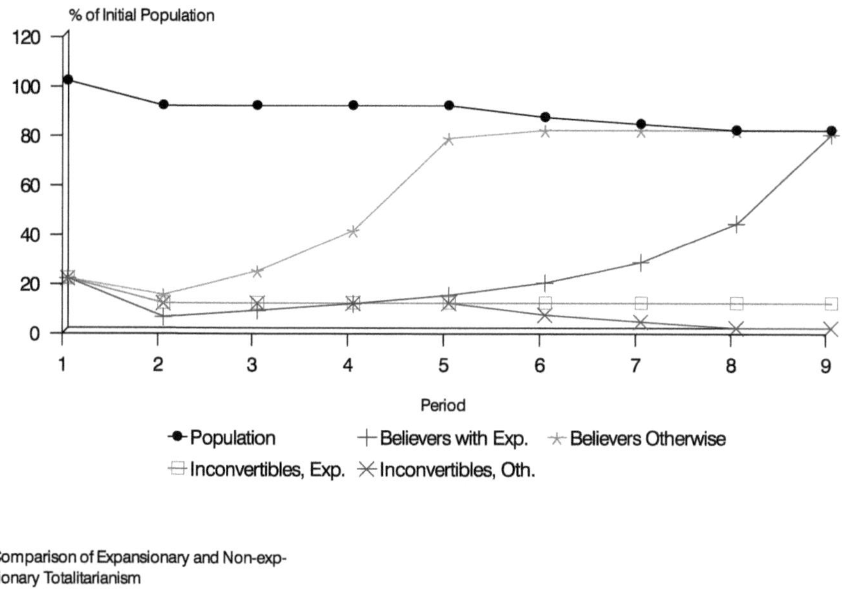

Fig. 11.1 Development of expansionary totalitarian regime: believers and in-convertibles

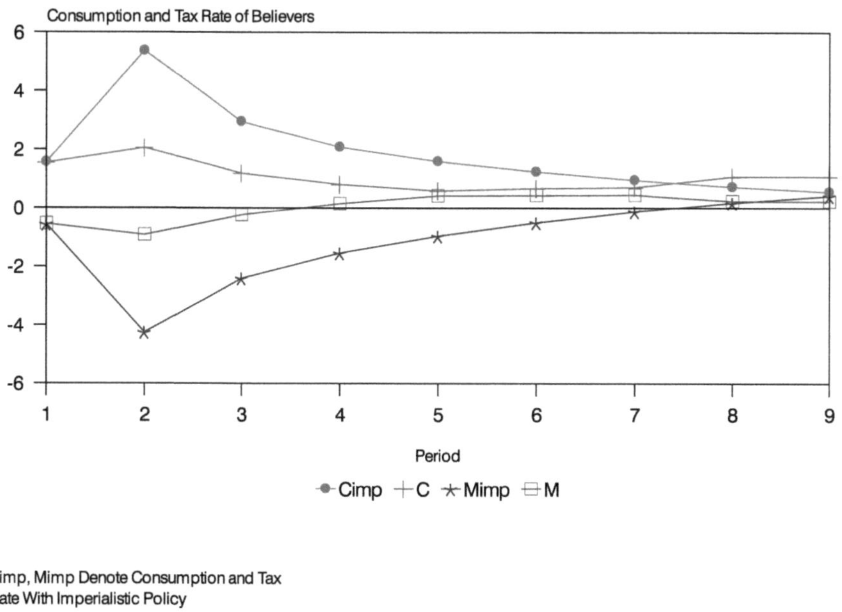

Fig. 11.2 Consumption and tax of believers with and without imperialistic policy

Y^* had to be taken also for a rather expansionary ideology as much greater than $Y_0, \pi_0 = 0.1$ had to be set at a rather small value.

Let us look first at the results for some of the domestic variables (Table 11.1), and then compare them with the values without imperialistic expansion (Figs. 11.1 and 11.2). Finally, in Sect. 11.4.3, we will analyze how the probability of a successful imperialistic policy of the totalitarian regime depends on the economic power of its foreign opponents.

We observe that the number of in-convertibles is halved within one period and then remains stable. But the number of believers is also strongly reduced during this time and grows afterwards until it nearly reaches its maximum of 80% of the initial population, given that the total number of the population diminishes to 90% because of the removal of in-convertibles. Consumption C of the remaining individual believers is very high, but diminishes continuously from the second period. Their high consumption is financed by transfers from non-believers and in-convertibles. For with Domestic Product Y falling until the fifth period, believers enjoy a negative tax rate M, that is transfers, until period seven. The high individual consumption is also only possible because the number of believers is smaller than in the first period during periods two to six. Only after the seventh period have believers to pay taxes, a consequence of their success in reducing the number of in-convertibles and non-believers. Total tax revenue T and expenditures K spent on removing in-convertibles, converting non-believers and on increasing the probability to succeed with the foreign aims of the ideology are decreasing with Y until period four, but rise steadily afterwards. They surpass the level of the first period during the ninth period.

Let us now compare these result with those obtained for the case that the ideology does not ask for further expansion, which implies $\phi, \psi = 0$ in the model.

As can be seen from Fig. 11.1 the number of in-convertibles is eventually reduced to zero after the fifth period in the case in which no expansionary aims are pursued, but not in the other case. This reduction sets in after the number of believers has reached its maximum of 80%. Also, in the expansionary case, the number of believers decreases more strongly and reaches its maximum more slowly

Table 11.6 Simulated evolution of imperialistic totalitarian regime

Period	C	Y	I	B	N	M	T	K
1	1.563	100	20	20	60	−0.563	27.136	21.911
2	5.369	92.118	10	4.46	75.54	−4.245	20.782	16.781
3	2.944	77.723	10	7.095	72.905	−2.408	18.127	14.636
4	2.079	73.587	10	9.835	70.165	−1.542	17.745	14.328
5	1.591	72.964	10	13.264	66.736	−0.936	18.318	14.791
6	1.237	73.897	10	18.28	61.72	−0.506	19.624	15.845
7	0.953	75.961	10	26.584	53.416	−0.129	21.996	17.761
8	0.725	79.508	10	42.317	37.683	0.179	26.639	21.51
9	0.554	85.839	10	78.393	1.607	0.419	37.714	30.452

(compare Tables 11.2, 11.4 and 11.5 with 11.6). Note that we have sketched the development of the total population only for the non-expansionary case.

The development of individual consumption and of the tax rate for believers are compared in Fig. 11.2. Interestingly, individual consumption of believers is higher and their tax rates are lower (transfers are higher) for nearly all periods in the case with expansionary aims. This is related to the stronger reduction of the number of believers (and the corresponding increase of the number of non-believers) in the beginning of this case. The situation is reversed only in the last two periods, in which the expenditures for the expansionary policy have to be borne by believers since the number of non-believers is rapidly falling. Also, since in the non-expansionary case in-convertibles have now been (nearly) obliterated, the costs for their removal have no longer to be born.

The reader should be warned, however, that the results are dependent on parameter and initial values. With different values different "historical" developments are possible, as shown in Sect. 11.4.2.

11.4.3 The Transformation or Demise of Totalitarian Regimes

We have already shown in Sects. 11.2.4 and 11.4.1 that totalitarian regimes may be transformed into mature ideocracies because of their very success in removing in-convertibles and in converting non-believers, if their ideologies do not imply expansionary aims. In this section, we have to discuss what happens to totalitarian regimes whose ideology commands expansion. To do so, we have first to look at the development of the probability to reach their imperialistic aims. The probability obviously depends on the size of Y*, given the development of Y in Table 11.2. For, as has been argued before, it is the relative economic strength which can be transformed into foreign policy and military power. Consequently, the probabilities have been calculated for different values of Y*. Also, we have treated ω as a random variable, since the transformation of economic into foreign policy and military power depends partly on factors not controllable by the totalitarian state. The parameters used in the calculation are those given in Sect. 11.4.2. The results are depicted in Fig. 11.3.

As can be seen, the development of probabilities is not much influenced by the random shocks. Further, the probability that the totalitarian state reaches its imperialistic aims is only permanently above 0.5 in the case in which Y^* amounts only to 10% of initial domestic Y. It once surpasses 0.5 in the case in which Y^* is equal to 50% of initial Y. With Y^* equal to 100% of initial Y the probability remains, except for the second period, below 0.45. This cannot just be a consequence of decreasing Y in the first periods, since it is also true for later periods. In the cases in which Y^* is substantially higher than initial Y the probabilities are always below one third, and this in spite of the fact that we have assumed that

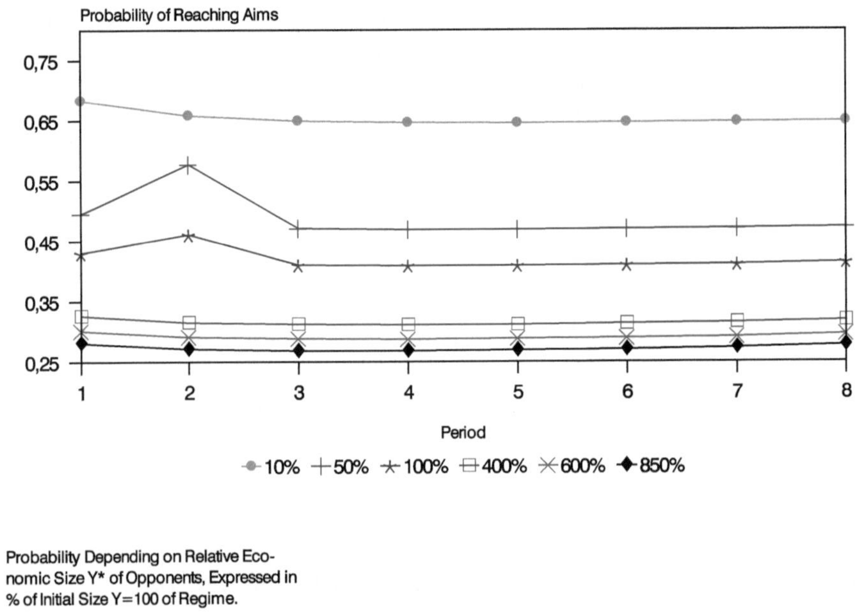

Fig. 11.3 Probability of totalitarian regime to succeed with internationals aims

$\omega > \omega^*$. Though this assumption is reasonable for the beginning, it remains presumably not true with the passage of time. The knowledge of the threat posed by the totalitarian regime will spread and lead to better military preparation, organization and coordination of efforts by the countries threatened. As a consequence, the probability of success should rather fall in time below the values depicted.

What follows from these results? First, imperialistic aims will mostly only be reached, if they are limited in scope. This means that universal or universal dominance ideologies will usually not succeed. This can result in two different outcomes. First, since ideologies mostly imply a somewhat distorted image of reality and an overestimation of the power of the totalitarian regime, war may be waged in spite of a low probability to win and may be lost consequently. Then the totalitarian regime will be removed either by the victorious foreign opponents or by a disenchanted population. Second, if the leadership of the totalitarian regime does not dare to wage war, given the unfavorable odds, it has to reinterpret the ideology, like Stalin did with his "communism in one country", at least until conditions become more favorable. If this is not the case, for instance since the rules implied by the ideology hinder economic development and lead to decreasing relative economic strength, the ideology may in time be changed so much that the regime either turns into a mature ideocracy or into an ordinary authoritarian regime. Similar events could be observed in the former Soviet Union and from 1978 until today in Communist China.

11.5 Conclusions

In the present paper, we have shown how totalitarian regimes can arise or be averted depending on the conditions described by the parameters and the initial values of the system. The main reason for the development of totalitarian regimes is the presence of believers who are convinced that others have to be converted for their own well-being and, possibly, that there exist inconvertible enemies of their creed whose presence is obnoxious to them. The believers are thus prepared to spend resources on winning new converts and to win the secular power of the state. Whether they succeed in this endeavor depends on the costs of converting new believers and on the amount of resources they are prepared to spend for this purpose, given their available incomes and their propensity to consume. Their chances to succeed are greater if a crisis occurs, an event which is mainly outside of their control. Once secular power has been secured, the resources of the state can be used to win more converts, to drive into exile or to kill in-convertibles and to try to reach the imperialistic aims possibly implied by the ideology. If the latter is not the case, the regime may turn into a mature ideocracy after having reached its domestic aims. This would for instance be the case, if all in-convertibles had been removed and all the other population be converted. For in this case no further terror and (or) repressions characteristic of totalitarian regimes are required.

It has been shown also that quite different evolutionary paths of such systems are possible and that totalitarian regimes are transient societies. Either their imperialistic aims are limited and can thus be accomplished with high probability. Then the regime turns into a mature ideocracy after having reached its domestic aims. Or the ideology asks for very ambitious imperialistic aims, for instance the conversion of all people on earth (except for in-convertibles) or the domination of the whole globe by the believers. In such cases it is highly probable that the aims cannot be reached, because either a war is lost and leads to the removal of the totalitarian regime, or the ends have to be adapted to maintain the credibility of the ideology. But then the totalitarian state may again turn into a mature ideocracy, if the ideology has been reinterpreted to remove its unrealistic imperialistic aims. Or the change of the ideology weakens the regime in a way that it loses its proselytizing character altogether, and turns into an ordinary autocratic regime.

The "historical" evolution of totalitarian movements and regimes is strongly dependent on parameter and initial values. If for instance the costs of converting new believers are high and their dislike of non-believers not too pronounced, believers may prefer to spend their disposable incomes rather on consumption than on conversion. But then no totalitarian regime will arise. Also, given the concern for consumption and the wish to reduce the number of in-convertibles and to increase the probability of successful expansion, even a reduction of the number of believers may be happening in the beginning of totalitarian regimes. Similarly, no or not all in-convertibles may be removed as long as other people can still be converted. They all or a part of them may even stay afterwards, so that they can be exploited as workers and tax payers. If, however, their presence is evaluated as very negative by believers and if the costs of removal are not too high, they may be removed at once.

Obviously our formal analysis could not cover all aspects of totalitarianism. To mention just a few examples: First, our models have taken the definition of non-believers and of in-convertibles as given. But these definitions may change in time. Reasons may be heretical developments caused either by innovations of the ideology by "heretics," or because the interpretation of the ideology by the leadership has changed. Moreover, the leaders of the second or later generations may use the instrument of designing opponents as in-convertibles to remove competitors for power. Second, this latter remark shows that the models were not designed in a way that they could describe internal struggles in the group of believers. Third, the leaders of the second or later generations may no longer believe in the ideology and only use it as an instrument to maintain and increase their power. In this case power would have to enter the utility function as an argument and the percentage of believers and of in-convertibles would only remain as a restriction in the calculation of the leadership. There are other relationships which had to be omitted to keep the analysis manageable. But exactly the limited nature of the models enabled us to deduce some important and unexpected results.

Appendix A

From (11.2.1) in Sect. 11.2.1 we get

$$U_t = AC_t^{\alpha} C_{t+1}^{\beta} (B_{t+1}/P_{t+1})^{\gamma} = \max! \tag{A.1}$$

It further follows from (11.2.4) that

$$F_t = 1 - Z_t - M - (P/Y)C_t.$$

By inserting this result into (11.2.5) we obtain

$$C_{t+1} = (2+r)(1 - Z_t - M)Y/P - (1+r)C_t.$$

From (11.2.2) and (11.2.3) we get

$$Z_t = E(B_{t+1}^{\varepsilon}/B^{1+\varepsilon})P/Y.$$

By using the last two equations, we derive the transformation curve

$$C_{t+1} = (2+r)(1-M)Y/P - (2+r)(E/B)(B_{t+1}/B)^{\varepsilon} - (1+r)C_t.$$

From the transformation curve it follows that

$$Q \equiv C_{t+1} - (2+r)(1-M)Y/P + (2+r)(E/B)(B_{t+1}/B)^{\varepsilon} + (1+r)C_t = 0. \tag{A.2}$$

To solve this problem, we use the Lagrange method and form

$$W = U_t - \mu Q \text{ with } \mu > 0. \tag{A.3}$$

To get the necessary conditions for a maximization of this function we derive the partial derivatives and set them equal to zero:

$$\partial W/\partial C_t = \alpha A C_t^{(\alpha-1)} C_{t+1}^{\beta} (B_{t+1}/P)^{\gamma} - \mu(1+r) = 0, \tag{A.4}$$

$$\partial W/\partial C_{t+1} = \beta A C_t^{\alpha} C_{t+1}^{(\beta-1)} (B_{t+1})/P)^{\gamma} - \mu = 0, \tag{A.5}$$

$$\partial W/\partial B_{t+1} = \gamma A C_t^{\alpha} C_{t+1}^{\beta} (B_{t+1}/P)^{(\gamma-1)}/P - \mu\varepsilon(2+r)(E/B)(B_{t+1}/B)^{(\varepsilon-1)}/B = 0, \tag{A.6}$$

$$\partial W/\partial \mu = C_{t+1} - (2+r)(1-M)Y/P + (2+r)(E/B)(B_{t+1}/B)^{\varepsilon} + (1+r)C_t = 0. \tag{A.7}$$

Dividing (A.4) and (A.5) by (A.6) we get

$$\begin{aligned} &(\alpha/\gamma)(B_{t+1}/C_t) = (B^2/\varepsilon E)(B_{t+1}/B)^{1-\varepsilon}(1+r)/(2+r), \\ &C_t = [\alpha\varepsilon(2+r)E](B_{t+1}/B)^{\varepsilon}/[\gamma B(1+r)]. \end{aligned} \tag{A.8}$$

$$\begin{aligned} &(\beta/\gamma)(B_{t+1}/C_{t+1}) = (B^2/E)(B_{t+1}/B)^{1-\varepsilon}/[\varepsilon(2+r)], \\ &C_{t+1} = [\beta\varepsilon(2+r)](B_{t+1}/B)^{\varepsilon}/(\gamma B). \end{aligned} \tag{A.9}$$

It follows from inserting these two equations into (A.7) that

$$\begin{aligned} &(2+r)(E/B)(B_{t+1}/B)^{\varepsilon} = (2+r)(1-M)Y/P - \varepsilon(2+r)E(\alpha+\beta)(B_{t+1}^{\varepsilon}B^{1-\varepsilon})/\gamma, \\ &(B_{t+1}/B)^{\varepsilon} = (1-M)(Y/E)(B/P) - [\varepsilon(\alpha+\beta)B](B_{t+1}/B)^{\varepsilon}/\gamma, \\ &(B_{t+1}/B)^{\varepsilon} = \gamma(1-M)(Y/E)(B/P)/[\gamma+\varepsilon(\alpha+\beta)B]. \end{aligned} \tag{A.10}$$

Inserting (A.10) into (A.8) and (A.9) we get

$$C_t = [(2+r)/(1+r)]\alpha\varepsilon(1-M)(Y/P)/[\gamma+\varepsilon(\alpha+\beta)B], \tag{A.11}$$

$$C_{t+1} = (2+r)\beta\varepsilon(1-M)(Y/P)/[\gamma+\varepsilon(\alpha+\beta)]. \tag{A.12}$$

Appendix B

We substitute Eqs. (11.3.2) into (11.3.1), (11.3.4) and (11.3.10). Next, we transform Eqs. (11.3.1), (11.3.3), (11.3.4) and (11.3.6) to (11.3.11) by taking logarithms. In doing so, small Latin letters are used to denote logarithms. For instance, $a \equiv \ln A, c_t \equiv \ln C_t$. It follows that

$$u_t = a + \alpha c_t + \beta c_{t+1} + \gamma b_{t+1} - \delta \ln I_{t+1} + (\delta - \gamma) \ln(P + I_{t+1} - I) + \phi \ln \pi_{t+1}, \tag{B.1}$$

$$y_{t+1} = d + \eta P + (1 - \eta) g_t, \tag{B.2}$$

$$k_t = e + \varepsilon b_{t+1} - \varepsilon b + \xi \ln I - \xi \ln I_{t+1} + \psi \ln \pi_{t+1} - \psi \ln \pi, \tag{B.3}$$

$$\ln T_t = \ln(M_t B + \mathrm{HN} + \mathrm{LI}) + y - p, \tag{B.4}$$

$$k_t = \ln Z_t + \ln T_t, \tag{B.5}$$

$$g_t = \ln(1 - Z_t) + \ln T_t, \tag{B.6}$$

$$c_t = \ln(1 - M_t) + y - p, \tag{B.7}$$

$$c_{t+1} = \ln(1 - M_t) + y_{t+1} - \ln(P + I_{t+1} - I), \tag{B.8}$$

$$\ln \pi_{t+1} = \ln \omega - \ln \omega^* + \nu y_{t+1} - \nu y^*_{t+1}. \tag{B.9}$$

From (B.3) and (B.5) we derive by using (B.4):

$$\begin{aligned} Q_3 = \ln Z_t + \ln(M_t B + \mathrm{HN} + \mathrm{LI}) + y - p - e - \varepsilon b_{t+1} \\ + \varepsilon b - \xi \ln I + \xi \ln I_{t+1} - \psi \ln \pi_{t+1} + \psi \ln \pi = 0. \end{aligned} \tag{B.10}$$

Moreover, by inserting (11.3.6) into (11.3.8) and this into (11.3.4) it follows that

$$Q_4 \equiv y_{t+1} - d - \eta p - (1 - \eta)[\ln(1 - Z_t) + \ln(M_t B + \mathrm{HN} + \mathrm{LI}) + y - p] = 0. \tag{B.11}$$

Also, from (B.7) and (B.8) we get by using (11.2):

$$Q_1 \equiv c_t - \ln(1 - M_t) - y + p = 0, \tag{B.12}$$

and

$$Q_2 \equiv c_{t+1} - \ln(1 - M_t) - y_{t+1} + \ln(P + I_{t+1} - I) = 0. \tag{B.13}$$

Finally, because of (B.9) we get

$$Q_5 \equiv \ln \pi_{t+1} - \ln \omega + \ln \omega^* - \nu y_{t+1} + \nu y^*_{t+1} = 0. \tag{B.14}$$

We form now the Lagrange function:

$$w \equiv u_t - \sum \mu_j Q_j = \text{max! with } \mu_j > 0. \tag{B.15}$$

To get the necessary conditions for a maximum we derive the partial derivatives and set them equal to zero:

$$\partial w/\partial c_t = \alpha - \mu_1 = 0, \tag{B.16}$$

$$\partial w/\partial c_{t+1} = \beta - \mu_2 = 0, \tag{B.17}$$

$$\partial w/\partial b_{t+1} = \gamma + \mu_3 \varepsilon = 0, \tag{B.18}$$

$$\begin{aligned} \partial w/\partial I_{t+1} = {} & (\delta - \gamma)/(P + I_{t+1} - I) - \delta/I_{t+1} \\ & - \mu_2/(P + I_{t+1} - I) - \mu_3 \xi/I_{t+1} = 0, \end{aligned} \tag{B.19}$$

$$\begin{aligned} \partial w/\partial M_t = {} & -\mu_1/(1 - M_t) - \mu_2/(1 - M_t) \\ & - [\mu_3 B - \mu_4(1 - \eta)B]/(M_t B + \mathrm{HN} + \mathrm{LI}) = 0, \end{aligned} \tag{B.20}$$

$$\partial w/\partial Z_t = -\mu_3/Z_t - \mu_4(1 - \eta)/(1 - Z_t) = 0, \tag{B.21}$$

$$\partial w/\partial y_{t+1} = \mu_2 - \mu_4 + \nu \mu_5 = 0, \tag{B.22}$$

$$\partial w/\partial \pi_{t+1} = (\phi + \psi \mu_3 - \mu_5)/\pi_{t+1} = 0. \tag{B.23}$$

From (B.18) and (B.23) we have

$$\begin{aligned} \mu_5 &= \phi + \psi \mu_3, \\ \mu_5 &= \phi - \gamma \psi/\varepsilon. \end{aligned} \tag{B.24}$$

Inserting (B.16) and (B.24) into (B.22) one gets

$$\mu_4 = \beta + \nu(\phi - \gamma \psi/\varepsilon). \tag{B.25}$$

We use (B.17) and insert the value of μ_3 from (B.18) into (B.19) to get:

$$\begin{aligned}&(\gamma/\varepsilon)\xi - \delta = (-\delta + \gamma + \beta)I_{t+1}/(P + I_{t+1} - I),\\ &[\gamma\xi - \varepsilon(\beta + \gamma)]I_{t+1} = [\varepsilon\delta - \gamma\xi](P - I),\\ &I_{t+1} = F(P - I),\end{aligned} \tag{B.26}$$

with

$$F \equiv [\varepsilon\delta - \gamma\xi]/[\gamma\xi - \varepsilon(\beta + \gamma)]. \tag{B.27}$$

After dividing by I it follows that

$$I_{t+1}/I = F(P - I)/I. \tag{B.28}$$

From (B.21) we derive with the help of (B.18) and (B.25):

$$\begin{aligned}&\mu_4(1 - Z_t) = -\mu_3(1 - Z_t),\\ &Z_t = -\mu_3/[-\mu_3 + \mu_4(1 - \eta)],\\ &Z_t = \gamma/R,\end{aligned} \tag{B.29}$$

$$R \equiv \gamma + (1 - \eta)[\beta\varepsilon + v(\varepsilon\phi - \gamma\psi). \tag{B.30}$$

$$1 - Z_t = (R - \gamma)/R = W/R, \tag{B.31}$$

$$W \equiv (1 - \eta)[\beta\varepsilon + v(\varepsilon\phi - \gamma\psi)]. \tag{B.32}$$

Inserting (B.16)–(B.18) and (B.25) into (B.20) gives

$$\begin{aligned}&(\alpha + \beta)(M_t B + \mathrm{HN} + \mathrm{LI}) = [(\gamma/\varepsilon) + (1 - \eta)\{\beta + v(\phi - \gamma\psi/\varepsilon)\}]B(1 - M_t),\\ &[(\alpha + \beta + (\gamma/\varepsilon) + (1 - \eta)\{\beta + v(\phi - \gamma\psi/\varepsilon)\}]BM_t\\ &= [(\gamma/\varepsilon) + (1 - \eta)\{\beta + v(\phi - \gamma\psi/\varepsilon)\}]B - (\alpha + \beta)(HN + LI),\\ &M_t = [\{\gamma + (1 - \eta)[\varepsilon\beta + v(\varepsilon\phi - \gamma\psi)]\}B\\ &\qquad - \varepsilon(\alpha + \beta)(\mathrm{HN} + \mathrm{LI})]/[\{\varepsilon\alpha + \varepsilon\beta(2 - \eta) + \gamma + (1 - \eta)v(\varepsilon\varphi - \gamma\psi\}B].,\\ &M_t = [RB - \varepsilon(\alpha + \beta)(\mathrm{HN} + \mathrm{LI})]/\mathrm{BS},\end{aligned} \tag{B.33}$$

$$S \equiv \varepsilon\alpha + \varepsilon\beta(2 - \eta) + \gamma + (1 - \eta)v(\varepsilon\phi - \gamma\psi). \tag{B.34}$$

$$1 - M_t = \varepsilon(\alpha + \beta)(B + \mathrm{HN} + \mathrm{LI})]/[\{\varepsilon\alpha + \varepsilon\beta(2 - \eta) + \gamma + (1 - \eta)\nu(\varepsilon\phi - \gamma\psi)\}B], \tag{B.35}$$
$$1 - M_t = \varepsilon(\alpha + \beta)V/\mathrm{BS},$$

$$V \equiv B + \mathrm{HN} + \mathrm{LI}, \tag{B.36}$$

Inserting (B.33) into (11.3.6) and using (B.34), (B.30) and (B.36) we derive:

$$T_t = (Y/P)[RB - \varepsilon(\alpha + \beta)](\mathrm{HN} + \mathrm{LI}) + S(\mathrm{HN} + \mathrm{LI})/S,$$
$$S = \varepsilon(\alpha + \beta) + R, \tag{B.37}$$
$$T_t = (Y/P)(\mathrm{RV}/S).$$

From (11.3.8), (B.31) and (B.37) it follows that

$$G_t = (Y/P)(W/R)[\mathrm{RV}/S)$$
$$G_t = (Y/P)(\mathrm{VW}/S). \tag{B.38}$$

Inserting this result into (11.3.3) we get:

$$Y_{t+1} = \mathrm{DP}^{\eta}[(Y/P)(\mathrm{VW}/S)]^{1-\eta}. \tag{B.39}$$

From (11.3.9) and (B.35) it follows that

$$C_t = \varepsilon(\alpha + \beta)[V/(\mathrm{BS})](Y/P). \tag{B.40}$$

Similarly, we have from (11.3.10), (11.3.2) and (B.35):

$$C_{t+1} = \varepsilon(\alpha + \beta)\mathrm{DP}^{\eta}(\mathrm{WY}/P)^{1-\eta}(V/S)^{2-\eta}/[B(P + I_{t+1} - I)]. \tag{B.41}$$

We derive from (11.3.2) and (B.26) that

$$P_{t+1} = P + I_{t+1} - I = P - I + F(P - I), \tag{B.42}$$

$$P_{t+1} = (1 + F)(P - I). \tag{B.43}$$

Inserting (B.42) into (B.41) we get:

$$C_{t+1} = (\alpha + \beta)\mathrm{VDP}^{\eta}(\mathrm{WVY}/\mathrm{SP})^{1-\eta}/[\mathrm{SB}(1 - F)(P - I)]. \tag{B.44}$$

From (11.3.7) we derive by using (B.29) and (B.37):

$$K_t = (\gamma/R)(Y/P)(\mathrm{RV}/S) = \gamma\mathrm{VY}/\mathrm{PS}. \tag{B.45}$$

Moreover, from (11.3.4) and (B.45) it follows that

$$(B_{t+1}/B)^{\varepsilon} = \gamma(\mathrm{VY}/\mathrm{PES})[F(P-I)/I]^{\xi}(\pi/\pi_{t+1})^{\psi}. \tag{B.46}$$

Inserting (B.39) into (11.11) we obtain

$$\pi_{t+1} = (\omega/\omega^{*})[\mathrm{DP}^{\eta}(\mathrm{VWY}/\mathrm{PS})^{1-\eta}/Y^{*}_{t+1}]^{\nu}. \tag{B.47}$$

From (B.46) and (B.47) it follows that

$$(B_{t+1}/B)^{\varepsilon} = (\gamma/E)(\omega^{*}\pi/\omega)^{\psi}(Y^{*}_{t+1}W^{1-\eta}/\mathrm{DP}^{\eta})^{\nu\psi}(\mathrm{VY}/\mathrm{PS})^{1-(1-\eta)\nu\psi}[F(P-I)/I]^{\xi}. \tag{B.48}$$

Appendix C

We transform Eqs. (11.3.1a), (11.3.3.), (11.3.4a), (11.3.6a) and (11.3.7)–(11.3.10) of Model 2a by taking logarithms:

$$u_t = a + \alpha c_t + \beta c_{t+1} + \gamma b - \delta \ln I_{t+1} + (\delta - \gamma) \ln(P + I_{t+1} - I), \tag{C.1}$$

$$y_{t+1} = d + \eta p + (1-\eta) g_t, \tag{C.2}$$

$$k_t = e + \xi \ln I - \xi \ln I_{t+1}, \tag{C.3}$$

$$\ln T_t = \ln(M_t B + LI) + y - p, \tag{C.4}$$

$$k_t = \ln Z_t + \ln T_t, \tag{C.5}$$

$$g_t = \ln(1 - Z_t) + \ln T_t, \tag{C.6}$$

$$c_t = \ln(1 - M_t) + y - p, \tag{C.7}$$

$$c_{t+1} = \ln(1 - M_t) + y_{t+1} - \ln(P + I_{t+1} - I), \tag{C.8}$$

From (C.3) and (C.5) we derive by using (C.4):

$$Q_3 = \ln Z_t + \ln(M_t B + LI) + y - p - e - \xi \ln I + \xi \ln I_{t+1} = 0. \tag{C.9}$$

Moreover, by inserting (C.4) into (C.6) and this into (C.2) it follows that

$$Q_4 = y_{t+1} - d - \eta p - (1-\eta)[\ln(1 - Z_t) + \ln(M_t B + LI) + y - p] = 0. \tag{C.10}$$

Also, from (C.7) and (C.9) we get by using (11.3.2):

$$Q_1 \equiv c_t - \ln(1 - M_t) - y + p = 0, \tag{C.11}$$

and

$$Q_2 \equiv c_{t+1} - \ln(1 - M_t) - y_{t+1} + \ln(P + I_{t+1} - I) = 0. \tag{C.12}$$

We form now the Lagrange function:

$$w \equiv u_t - \sum \mu_j Q_j = \max! \text{ with } \mu_j > 0. \tag{C.13}$$

To get the necessary conditions for a maximum we derive the partial derivatives and set them equal to zero:

$$\partial w/\partial c_t = \alpha - \mu_1 = 0, \tag{C.14}$$

$$\partial w/\partial c_{t+1} = \beta - \mu_2 = 0, \tag{C.15}$$

$$\begin{aligned}\partial w/\partial I_{t+1} = {} & (\delta - \gamma)/(P + I_{t+1} - I) - \delta/I_{t+1} \\ & - \mu_2/(P + I_{t+1} - I) - \mu_3 \xi / I_{t+1} = 0,\end{aligned} \tag{C.16}$$

$$\partial w/\partial M_t = -\mu_1/(1 - M_t) - \mu_2/(1 - M_t) - [\mu_3 B - \mu_4(1 - \eta)B]/(M_t B + LI) = 0, \tag{C.17}$$

$$\partial w/\partial Z_t = -\mu_3/Z_t - \mu_4(1 - \eta)/(1 - Z_t) = 0, \tag{C.18}$$

$$\partial w/\partial y_{t+1} = \mu_2 - \mu_4 = 0. \tag{C.19}$$

We derive from (C.17) by using (C.14), (C.15) and (C.17).

$$\begin{aligned}&(\alpha + \beta)(M_t B + \mathrm{LI}) = \beta(1 - \eta)B(1 - M_t) - \mu_3 B(1 - M_t), \\ &\mu_3 = [\beta(1 - \eta)B(1 - M_t) - (\alpha + \beta)(M_t B + \mathrm{LI})]/[B(1 - M_t)], \\ &\mu_3 = [\beta(1 - \eta)B - \{\alpha + \beta(2 - \eta)\}BM_t - (\alpha + \beta)\mathrm{LI}]/[B(1 - M_t)]\end{aligned} \tag{C.20}$$

From (C.16) we get by using (C.15)

$$\begin{aligned}&(\delta + \mu_3 \xi)(P + I_{t+1} - I) = (\delta - \gamma - \beta)I_{t+1}, \\ &\mu_3 \xi (P + I_{t+1} - I) = -(\beta + \gamma)I_{t+1} - \delta(P - I) \\ &\mu_3 = -[(\beta + \gamma)I_{t+1} + \delta(P - I)]/[\xi(P + I_{t+1} - I)].\end{aligned} \tag{C.21}$$

Also, it follows from (C.18), (C.19) and (C.15) that

$$\mu_3 = -[\beta(1-\eta)Z_t]/(1-Z_t). \tag{C.22}$$

From (11.3.4), (11.3.7) and (11.3.6) we derive

$$\begin{aligned} &Z_t(M_tB+\mathrm{LI})Y/P = E(I/I_{t+1})^{\xi}, \\ &Z_t = [E(I/I_{t+1})^{\xi}P/[(M_tB+\mathrm{LI})Y]. \end{aligned} \tag{C.23}$$

Inserting (C.23) into (C.22) we get:

$$\mu_3 = -[\beta(1-\eta)\mathrm{EP}(I/I_{t+1})^{\xi}]/[(M_tB+\mathrm{LI})Y - \mathrm{EP}(I/I_{t+1})^{\xi}]. \tag{C.24}$$

Inserting this result into (C.20) and (C.21) it follows that

$$\begin{aligned} [\beta(1-\eta)\mathrm{EP}(I/I_{t+1})^{\xi}][B(1-M_t)] = {} & [\{\alpha+\beta(2-\eta)\}\mathrm{BM}_t \\ & + (\alpha+\beta)\mathrm{LI} - \beta(1-\eta)B][(M_tB+\mathrm{LI})Y - \mathrm{EP}(I/I_{t+1})^{\xi}] \end{aligned} \tag{C.25}$$

$$\begin{aligned} &[(\beta+\gamma)I_{t+1} + \delta(P-I)][(M_tB+\mathrm{LI})Y - \mathrm{EP}(I/I_{t+1})^{\xi}] \\ &= [\xi(P+I_{t+1}-I)][\beta(1-\eta)\mathrm{EP}(I/I_{t+1})^{\xi}]. \end{aligned} \tag{C.26}$$

These are two rather complicated equations with two unknowns, namely M_t and I_{t+1}. The solution is computed numerically for certain parameter values presented in Table 3 of Sect. 3.3.

Appendix D

We transform Eqs. (11.3.1b), (11.3.3.), (11.3.4b), (11.3.6b), and (11.3.7)–(11.3.10) of Model 2b by taking logarithms again:

$$u_t = a + \alpha c_t + \beta c_{t+1} + \gamma b - \gamma p, \tag{D.1}$$

$$y_{t+1} = d + \eta p + (1-\eta)g_t, \tag{D.2}$$

$$k_t = e \tag{D.3}$$

$$\ln T_t = \ln(M_tB) + y - p, \tag{D.4}$$

$$k_t = \ln Z_t + \ln T_t, \tag{D.5}$$

$$g_t = \ln(1 - Z_t) + \ln T_t, \tag{D.6}$$

$$c_t = \ln(1 - M_t) + y - p, \tag{D.7}$$

$$c_{t+1} = \ln(1 - M_t) + y_{t+1} - p, \tag{D.8}$$

From (D.3)–(D.5) we derive

$$Q_3 = \ln Z_t + \ln(M_t B) + y - p - e = 0. \tag{D.9}$$

Moreover, by inserting (D.4) into (D.6) and this into (D.2) it follows that

$$Q_4 = y_{t+1} - d - \eta p - (1 - \eta)[\ln(1 - Z_t) + \ln(M_t B) + y - p] = 0. \tag{D.10}$$

Also, from (D.7) and (D.8) we get

$$Q_1 \equiv c_t - \ln(1 - M_t) - y + p = 0, \tag{D.11}$$

and

$$Q_2 = c_{t+1} - \ln(1 - M_t) - y_{t+1} + p = 0. \tag{D.12}$$

We form now the Lagrange function:

$$w \equiv u_t - \sum \mu_j Q_j = \max! \text{ with } \mu_j > 0. \tag{D.13}$$

To get the necessary conditions for a maximum, we derive the partial derivatives and set them equal to zero:

$$\partial w/\partial c_t = \alpha - \mu_1 = 0, \tag{D.14}$$

$$\partial w/\partial c_{t+1} = \beta - \mu_2 = 0, \tag{D.15}$$

$$\partial w/\partial M_t = -\mu_1/(1 - M_t) - \mu_2/(1 - M_t) - [\mu_3 B - \mu_4(1 - \eta)B]/M_t B = 0, \tag{D.16}$$

$$\partial w/\partial Z_t = -\mu_3/Z_t - \mu_4(1 - \eta)/(1 - Z_t) = 0, \tag{D.17}$$

$$\partial w/\partial y_{t+1} = \mu_2 - \mu_4 = 0. \tag{D.18}$$

We derive from (D.16) by using (D.14), (D.15), and (D.18).

$$\begin{aligned} &(\alpha + \beta)M_t B = \beta(1 - \eta)B(1 - M_t) - \mu_3 B(1 - M_t), \\ &\mu_3 = [\beta(1 - \eta)B(1 - M_t) - (\alpha + \beta)M_t B]/[B(1 - M_t)], \\ &\mu_3 = [\beta(1 - \eta) - \{\alpha + \beta(2 - \eta)\}M_t]/(1 - M_t) \end{aligned} \tag{D.19}$$

It follows from (D.17), (D.18), and (D.15) that

$$\mu_3 = -[\beta(1-\eta)Z_t]/(1-Z_t). \tag{D.20}$$

From (11.3.4b), (11.3.7), and (11.3.6b) we derive

$$\begin{aligned} &Z_t M_t \mathrm{BY}/P = E, \\ &(D.21) Z_t = \mathrm{EP}/(M_t \mathrm{BY}). \end{aligned} \tag{D.21}$$

Inserting (D.21) into (D.20) we get

$$\mu_3 = -[\beta(1-\eta)\mathrm{EP}/(M_t\mathrm{BY} - \mathrm{EP}). \tag{D.22}$$

Finally, it follows from (D.19) and (D.22) that

$$\beta(1-\eta)\mathrm{EP}(1-M_t) = [\{\{\alpha + \beta(2-\eta)\}M_t - \beta(1-\eta)](M_t\mathrm{BY} - \mathrm{EP}). \tag{D.23}$$

References

Arendt H (1968/1951) The origins of totalitarianism. Harcourt, Brace and World, New York

Ballestrem KG (1992) Aporien der Totalitarismus Theorien. Politisches Denken, Jahrbuch 1991. J. B. Metzler, Stuttgart, pp 50–67

Bernholz P (1997) Ideology, sects, state and totalitarianism: a general theory. In: Maier H, Schaefer M (eds) Totalitarismus und politische Religionen. Konzepte des Diktaturvergleichs, vol II. Ferdinand Schoeningh, Paderborn, München, Wien, Zürich, pp 271–298. Also in: *Forum für osteuropäische Ideen- und Zeitgeschichte*, vol 1, no 1, 1997, pp 51–84

Bracher KD (1970) The German dictatorship: the origins, structure, and effects of national socialism. Praeger, New York

Bracher KD (1987) Die totalitäre Erfahrung. Piper, München und Zürich

Drath M (1963) Totalitarismus in der Volksdemokratie. Introduction to Richard Ernst: Macht ohne Mandat. Der Staatsapparat der sowjetischen Besatzungszone Deutschlands. Schriften des Instituts für politische Wissenschaft, vol II. Westdeutscher Verlag, Köln und Opladen

Ezran M (1989) Une colonisation douce: Les missions du Paraguay. Editions L'Harmattan, Paris

Friedrich CJ, Brzezinski ZK (1965/1956) Totalitarian dictatorship and autocracy. Harvard University Press, Cambridge (Mass.)

Linz J (1975) Totalitarian and authoritarian regimes. In: Greenstein FI, Polsby NW (eds) Handbook of political science, vol 3. Macro political Theory. Addison-Wesley, Reading (Mass.) and London

Maier H, Schaefer M (eds) (1997) Totalitarismus und politische Religionen. Konzepte des Diktaturvergleichs, vol II. Ferdinand Schoeningh, Paderborn, München, Wien, Zürich

Morgan ES (1958) The Puritan dilemma. The story of John Winthrop. Harper Collins, New York

Olson M (1993) Dictatorship, democracy and development. Am Polit Sci Rev 87:567–575

Olson M, McGuire M (1998) The economics of autocracy and majority rule: a study of dictatorship. In: Borner S, Paldam M (eds) The political dimension of economic growth. Macmillan, Houndmills, Basinkstoke, London and New York, pp 38–73

Piekalkiewicz J, Penn AW (1995) Politics of ideocracy. State University of New York Press, Albany

Schlangen W (1970) Der Totalitarismus Begriff. In: Aus Politik und Zeitgeschichte. Beilage zur Wochenzeitung Das Parlament, vol 44, pp 3–46

Tullock G (1987) Autocracy. Dordrecht, Martinus Nijhoff

Wintrobe R (1998) The political economy of dictatorship. New York, Cambridge University Press

Wuthe G (1981) Die Lehre von den politischen Systemen. Ein Studienbuch. München

Chapter 12
Summary: Supreme Values, Totalitarian Regimes, and Mature Ideocracies

Totalitarian regimes and mature ideocracies are political regimes basing the legitimacy of their rulers on ideologies with supreme values containing aims lexicographically preferred to all other ends. This means that the believers in these ideologies are requested, if necessary, to sacrifice their own as well as the lives of others to reach these highest aims. As shown in the mathematical formulation of Chap. 11 this does not mean that all believers in the ideology or people only pretending to believe are really prepared to do so. But they have to at least give the impression to be willing. In contrast to mature ideocracies, totalitarian regimes have not yet reached the targets of their ideology and have to thus strive with all means to accomplish what is demanded by their supreme values. This is no longer true for mature ideocracies: They have already reached the aims postulated by their supreme values, and if the whole population is either believing in them or is at least pretending to do so. The only exception may be un-convertibles who are needed as workers for permanently supporting the aims of their rulers.

Ideologies are newly created or revived by charismatic leaders who themselves, or their leading followers, organize an ideological movement with the purpose to win the secular power of a state. After succeeding in this task they have to combine spiritual and secular power to reach the aims embodied in their supreme values, which are believed to be absolutely true. Preconditions for gaining the secular power of a nation are a deep crisis of society and a well-organized movement of believers not shying away from using force if necessary.

The ideological targets require that potential believers who stubbornly resist conversion as well as in-convertibles who are not needed to reach them have to be suppressed, persecuted and if necessary, to be eliminated. Works of art contradicting the creed have to be destroyed, others serving it to be furthered. As a rule, economic development and that of science will be conflicting with the supreme values considered to be absolutely true, so that the regime may suffer in time from a worse development of science and the economy than countries enjoying rule of law, freedom of research and innovation not hindered by specific ideologies.

P. Bernholz, *Totalitarianism, Terrorism and Supreme Values*,
Studies in Public Choice 33, DOI 10.1007/978-3-319-56907-9_12

If the supreme values demand that either all potential believers on earth are converted or that the whole globe has to be dominated, then revolutionary and military conflicts with foreign countries are inescapable. Indeed, totalitarian regimes with such targets have only a chance to succeed if they are one of the Great Powers, and even then, since they will be faced by other Great Powers, their chances to overcome the resistance of them will be rather small. It is thus probable that totalitarian regimes will be either defeated in wars because charismatic leaders are inclined to overestimate their power, that they will reform their ideology in the sense that less expansionary aims are formulated, or that the effort to reach the expansionary aims will be postponed into the future. In the latter case, such regimes may even slowly turn into mature idiocrasies.

In other cases, in which democratic movements loose secular power or have not yet won it they may turn to terrorism. This is especially probable if they see—because of overwhelming military powers of leading adversary nations—no other chances to win or regain the secular power of a state.

The theory presented has recently (until 2016) again been confirmed by the emergence of the Islamic State of Iraq and Syria (ISIS), and by the terrorist attacks of the Taliban in Afghanistan and of Boko Haram in Nigeria striving to (re)gain secular power.

MIX
Papier aus verantwortungsvollen Quellen
Paper from responsible sources
FSC® C105338

If you have any concerns about our products,
you can contact us on
ProductSafety@springernature.com

In case Publisher is established outside the EU,
the EU authorized representative is:
Springer Nature Customer Service Center GmbH
Europaplatz 3, 69115 Heidelberg, Germany

Printed by Libri Plureos GmbH
in Hamburg, Germany